The European Union, Africa, and the Sustainable Development Goals

The European Union, Africa, and the Sustainable Development Goals

From High Ambitions to Weak Implementation

Lars Niklasson

LEXINGTON BOOKS
Lanham • Boulder • New York • London

Published by Lexington Books
An imprint of The Rowman & Littlefield Publishing Group, Inc.
4501 Forbes Boulevard, Suite 200, Lanham, Maryland 20706
www.rowman.com

86-90 Paul Street, London EC2A 4NE

British Library Cataloguing in Publication Information Available

Library of Congress Cataloging-in-Publication Data Available

ISBN 978-1-66695-767-9 (cloth)
ISBN 978-1-66695-768-6 (electronic)

Contents

List of Illustrations

List of Tables

Acknowledgments

A number of people have contributed to this study, for which I am very thankful. Most important is a set of individuals, whom I have offered to remain anonymous, with experience from within the European Union, Sweden, and other member states, in various roles, who have generously taken their time to explain some of these matters to me. Much of the original work was done at the Swedish Institute for European Policy Studies (SIEPS) and has received generous comments at Swedish and international conferences. Exchange with colleagues and guests as SIEPS has also been of importance. Further insights were gained from working in collaboration with the Swedish government commission on the evaluation of development policy, The Expert Group for Aid Studies (EBA). Several people have reviewed the text and have suggested improvements. Any remaining errors are the responsibility of the author.

Other important experiences come from my research on the complex machinery of government in Sweden, including its programs to support internal ("regional") development, in collaboration with EU programs (Cohesion policy). Some of this was done together with the OECD. A further background is my research on the UN Sustainable Development Goals, partly in cooperation with Kenyan diplomat Tobias Ogweno. All of this has added useful background knowledge for this study.

I have benefitted from spending time in Kenya and Benin as guest lecturer, which has given me some knowledge of the African context. Some of these experiences have been digested at international conferences as well as with colleagues and students at Linköping University, Sweden. Sending Swedish students to Africa has been as rewarding as receiving African students in Sweden. Meetings with the political opposition in Georgia and Bosnia, on another mission, added sad insights into the barriers facing political activists in many parts of the world.

Last, but not least, I owe my wife Marie gratitude for putting up with endless discussions and comparisons with her work in transforming health care in Sweden, which is also about radical change in a context of multi-level governance where drivers and barriers need to be identified. I have yet to figure out how to compensate her for allowing me to bring my work along on our vacation the past summer.

Earlier versions of this work have appeared in Niklasson, Lars. 2022. *EU:s biståndspolitik. Hur EU kan bli en starkare aktör i ett globalt system under omvandling.* Rapport nr 1. 2022:1. Stockholm: Swedish Institute for European Policy Studies (SIEPS) and Niklasson, Lars. 2021. *EU:s relation till Afrika: Partnerskap eller hierarki?* Europapolitisk analys 2021:15epa. Stockholm: Swedish Institute for European Policy Studies (SIEPS). The author thanks SIEPS for permission to reuse the material.

Stockholm in November 2023
Lars Niklasson

Chapter 1

The European Union, Africa, and the Sustainable Development Goals

FROM HIGH AMBITIONS TO WEAK IMPLEMENTATION

The European Union (EU) has high ambitions in its external relations, including its relationship with Africa, focusing on achieving the Sustainable Development Goals (SDGs). These goals were adopted by the United Nations in 2015 as a comprehensive set of goals to guide development across the globe until the year 2030. Many of the goals are radical and demanding in relation to the present situation in individual countries where economic and political development is slow. The EU assists African governments and organizations to achieve societal transformation in several dimensions; economic, social, environmental, as well as political, including peacekeeping and "good governance." The challenges in reaching the SDGs imply a need for change in fundamental dimensions such as institutional frameworks, state capacity, and the legitimacy of governments, a task which the EU appears willing to assist with.

However, the ambitions rest on weak foundations and are poorly implemented, as I will show. The policies of the European Union are vague and even partly contradictory. The instruments chosen are ambitious but not focused on the fundamental transformations necessary to assist in making African governments fit for the task of reaching the SDGs. The implementation of the European policies is difficult in the local contexts as well as in the coordination from Brussels.

The European policies in relation to developing countries are criticized for being self-centered (Eurocentric) or even paternalistic, forcing European lifestyles on others. This criticism takes many forms, from criticism of European values to criticism of the strategies applied. One recent theme is that European policies need to be "decentered," meaning that they should be as interested in the perspectives of non-Europeans as in the perspective of the Europeans, to treat others as equals. While the criticism of Eurocentrism may be exaggerated, it nevertheless contains an important message.

My criticism is similar, from a technical (instrumental) perspective, that the EU needs to shift from a focus on intentions to a focus on outcomes, to understand the impact of its policies in Africa. It's not enough to reach agreement in Brussels on how to assist African partners. The policies must be designed to bring about the desired ends and there must be an interest in learning from experience to find out what works. This means to understand the African context, the values and the drivers and barriers for change, which is one aspect of decentering the analysis. This in turn implies a need to link the policy developments to academic research and an academic interest in understanding the causes and effects of social transformation.

Rational learning from policy experience is a technocratic and perhaps unattainable ideal, but nevertheless important, especially when the scope of the desired transition in Africa is large and very challenging. Similar transformation of the European agricultural economies took centuries, as did the development of the rule of law and democracy in Europe. Recent research suggests that developing countries need to find their own paths of modernization, rather than to copy European pathways. This lack of models ready to use, makes the EU ambitions even more difficult.

One implication is that the EU must be interested in learning about pathways of modernization. It must engage with research, state its working assumptions explicitly and be humbler in its strategies and dealings with African actors. It must find ways to talk about problems in Europe and Africa, including counter-productive strategies pursued by individual European or African governments.

A fundamental question is if an organization like the European Union can pursue such a rationalistic policy focused on ends and means in relation to its African partners and allies, as well as in competition with China and other global competitors. The ambitions are difficult even when there is general agreement with the recipients on high-level values such as modernization, economic development, democracy, and the rule of law. This is relevant for European foreign policy in general and development policy in particular.

I will analyze the European policies in three steps, covering their origin, their design and some of the challenges in the context of implementation, including foreign policy aspects. I will primarily apply the methods of policy analysis, investigating intentions, strategies and implementation, which will bring out the gap between what is said and what is done by the EU. Theories and ongoing research will be used to indicate possible interpretations of drivers and barriers in the African context and in the relationship between the EU, Africa, and rivals such as China. The analysis will highlight factors which the EU needs to pay more explicit attention to.

RENEWAL OF THE EUROPEAN RELATIONS WITH AFRICA

African countries have recently become more attractive to Europeans, the United States, China, and other economically developed parts of the world. While much recent focus in Europe has been on the problems implied by migration from Africa, a rising economy and an expanding population make African countries and firms attractive business partners. Africa has great natural resources which many countries and firms in the world want to make use of (Carmody 2016). These are important for economic development as well as for the achievement of the environmental goals set out in global agreements such as the SDGs.

The new perspective which is gaining ground is that Africa could be moving into a more equal partnership with rich countries, in Europe and elsewhere (Langdon, Ritter, and Samy 2018). Optimists hope that Africa will develop much as the countries of Asia did in recent decades and that this would bring mutual benefits to Europe and Africa, as well as the rest of the world. African countries are also important to European foreign and security policy, not least as a possible partner in the global competition with China for influence in the United Nations (EU 2020).

Leaders from the two continents have met through a series of summits by their continental associations, the European Union (EU) and the African Union (AU), respectively. The latest summit of leaders took place in Brussels in February 2022. In preparation for this summit, the European Union launched a revised strategy in 2020, at the early stage of the pandemic. This strategy is interesting as a foundation for increased cooperation but is not without its problems, which I will return to.

While having the ambition to meet as equals, the EU is at the same time providing large amounts of development aid to Africa and other parts of the world. The ambition of such support is to solve immediate problems through humanitarian aid, as well as to support long term development. This is an important background factor, while the relation between the new strategy for Africa and the ongoing support is not very clear. This is despite the common framework for sustainable development among all countries of the world, through the SDGs, also known as "global goals" or "Agenda 2030."

The level of ambition of the SDGs is to achieve fundamental transformations in all parts of the world, which is especially challenging in Africa when it comes to economic, social, and political sustainable development. The environmental challenges can be expected to grow with industrialization. The EU has made a commitment to assist, but the contents of this commitment are vague. There are many European initiatives, for example in peacekeeping, but little in terms of an explicit strategy of how to reach the goals, or even an explicit discussion of the drivers and barriers for modernization in African countries. This is a key weakness in the foundation of the European policies.

The lack of a clearly stated framework of ends and means implies that the European Union may be guided by wishful thinking rather than a thorough analysis of the situation. Shortsighted rhetoric may be more important than long-term transformation. While some silence on problems and solutions in Africa may be out of politeness, it makes development policy very difficult to pursue and the relations with African countries muddled. Hence, the ambitions of the European policies are high, while the implementation is weak. In short, the EU needs to develop its methods of design and intervention—including its interest in and knowledge of the African context—to provide a stronger foundation for its policies and cooperation with African actors.

This situation has several implications. One is about the relationship between Europe and Africa, which has a long history, from colonialism to a possible partnership. It's not clear what kind of relationship this is or what the "partners" aim for. Another implication is for the EU's ambition to become a global leader. If the policies aren't supported by an adequate analysis, the EU might be trying to achieve something it is unable to reach. Hence, there's a need to study policies and actions, to identify strategies as well as the challenges the policies are meant to deal with.

There is a need to scrutinize the design and appropriateness of the policies, to go beyond an analysis of the values and visions of the European Union and their African partners. The ambition of this study is to look underneath the high ambitions of the official policies to understand the foundations and implementation of the policies.

The European Union as a Composite Actor

The European Union is at present the most elaborate continental ("regional") organization in the world, with stronger supranational powers than for example ASEAN (Association of Southeast Asian Nations), Mercosur (El Mercado Común del Sur) or NATO (North Atlantic Treaty Organization; Acharya and Johnston 2007). However, the European policies in relation to Africa are very diverse. Although the EU has legal capacity, it is a complex organization, similar to a federal political system. Global leadership is in many ways a difficult aspiration for the European Union.

The EU was set up as the European Economic Community (EEC) by six countries in the 1950s, mainly as a Free Trade Area. Over time the organization has grown to become a customs union with a common currency (the Euro), a supranational legal system and even some foreign and security policy. It regulates several policy areas related to the common market, including competition policy and environmental policy.

What makes the EU complex is that its 27 member states are still sovereign to pursue their own policies in areas which are not part of the common market, such as welfare policies and foreign policy. In development policy, there are parallel policies by the EU and the member states and therefore a need to coordinate. The treaties of the EU regulate these matters and point out that there should, on the one hand, be respect for national identities and, on the other hand, loyalty with the union by the member states (*Treaty on the European Union,* article 4; EU 2012a).

The political system of the EU is similar to a federal or confederal system, where the member states form the Council, resembling the U.S. Senate. The other part of the bicameral legislature is the Parliament, directly elected by the citizens, similar to the House of Representatives. The executive power is called the Commission, which is appointed jointly by the Parliament and Council in a complex procedure. In addition, there is the European Council, where the heads of state or government meet to exercise long-term leadership, which indicates a further complexity of the executive powers. As I will describe, foreign policy is a mandate of the Council, while other policies are mandates of the Commission and the bicameral legislature, with further arrangements to integrate external action.

EU Development Policy and the SDGs

The European Union has adopted the SDGs as goals for its development policy. It pursues an ambitious development policy, where the EU and its member states together are the world's largest donor, providing more than half of all global development aid. However, the problems with recent operations by the EU, the United States and others in countries such as Afghanistan and Mali illustrate how difficult it is to pursue development policy and how important it is to analyze the theories and assumptions underlying the design of the operations (Pain 2021).

Development aid is based on an ambition to modernize the recipient countries, to raise their living standards. Some critics see this ambition as a form of paternalism, forcing people in poor countries to be more like people in rich countries. Others see development aid as a waste of money due to corruption and other problems in the recipient countries. An ongoing debate in academia and the policy community is about ways to navigate between these extremes to reach the SDGs (Olivié and Pérez 2020). This study will elaborate on these issues, to understand intentions, policies, and outcomes better.

The SDGs are a common framework, a set of 17 goals on issues related to sustainable development, i.e., economic, social, and environmental issues, plus governance issues and global cooperation (Dodds, Donoghue, and Roesch 2017). The goals were adopted by the member states of the United Nations and form the basis for EU Development Policy as well as for national development planning, in Africa and in Europe. The SDGs provide a very demanding agenda of modernization, if taken seriously. The goals indicate that economies must grow to provide funding for social services, while the climate and the environment should be protected (ibid.). There are also demands for democratic governance and the rule of law, which is far from the present situation in many African countries with autocratic leaders, corruption, and other problems (Odusola 2017). I will come back to an implicit temporal relationship among the goals, which makes some of them more fundamental than the other goals (section 2.2).

The SDGs provide a common set of goals for donors and receivers, however a bit vague and not without its problems. The lack of explicit strategies within the SDGs is often seen as an advantage, since it leaves it up to the national governments to work out strategies which fit their specific context. This is at the same time a potential weakness, where the SDGs place a heavy burden on national governments and donors to find workable strategies, based on such elements as the drivers and barriers of change in particular contexts. The development of national strategies is, in other words, highly complex and politically contested. The same goes for external development policies to support these strategies, including recent efforts to stimulate cooperation (Chaturvedi et al. 2021). This furthermore implies a need for analysis and debate, to find out what works and what is acceptable to the people who are affected by the policies. However, such analysis is almost absent from official EU policy documents.

Africa as Context and Actor

While my focus is primarily on the European Union, a contribution is to highlight the situation in African countries, to discuss challenges in the implementation of the SDGs and the European policies, which are based on agreements with the recipient countries' governments and other recipients. The European policies are aimed to produce certain effects in African countries and elsewhere. Hence, the European perceptions of the situation in Africa are key elements of these policies.

As I will show, one of the fundamental problems is that the EU talks about poor countries in Africa and elsewhere but doesn't really show how its set of policies will lead to the achievement of the official goals, the SDGs. The recipient countries are much of a "black box" in the official EU policies. Hence, my intention is to open this black box, to advance the European debate on what it could do to assist Africans and poor people elsewhere, and what some of the fundamental problems with this relationship are. I will make use of ongoing research on European development policy with an ambition to treat the policies as a strategy or a "theory of change" (roadmap), a set of intended causal relations.

According to global agreements, African governments and their citizens should be seen as owners of the efforts to improve their situation. Development aid should be conducted on the recipients' terms. At the same time, there are differences in context which makes this difficult, for example, the lack of democratic support for many African leaders. The continents differ greatly in how their economies and political systems are operating. However, we should acknowledge that there is a great variety of market economies and democracies in Europe too (Schmidt 2002, 2006), and that the variety is even greater in Africa, spanning from rural economies to more advanced sectors, as well as politically from dictatorships to democracies.

Difficult Relations between Europe and Africa

The colonial legacy is a difficult issue in the relationship between the two continents. It is of little comfort that people from other parts of the world were also interfering in Africa or that there were other barriers to Africa's development before, during, and after the colonial period (Thomson 2010). Pre-colonial societies had their problems (Scott 2017), as did the early governments after independence (Lee and Paine 2019). The role of Europeans, then and now, is a contested issue.

The EU says that it wants some form of equal relationship, including support for Africa as well as protection of European interests (EU 2020). The picture is that the EU wants to move away from previous conflicts to future cooperation, though it should be noted that the EU avoids more controversial issues, such as whether it should compensate for damage which Europeans have done to Africans during colonial times or whether it should help Africans deal with the damage caused by autocrats and others during the period of early independence. There is no critical discussion by the EU of existing trade patterns or other global relations in the Africa strategy document (ibid.). Such issues are highly contested and very difficult to deal with, but its absence may nevertheless have a negative impact on the relationship.

The countries of the European Union have a variety of relations with Africa. Some have been colonial powers but have switched, at least officially, to a supportive relationship with the African countries. France has taken an active role through economic and military cooperation with its former colonies, which is highly criticized in France as well as in Africa (Le Monde 2019). Britain, when it was a member of the EU, was often seen as pursuing a more altruistic relationship, along with countries such as Sweden and the Netherlands. The Nordic countries have played a driving role in the support of African development, which for periods also included support for countries in Africa with problematic regimes. However, the altruistic policies in relation to poor countries were often combined with other policies, such as the promotion of exports from Europe.

The countries of Eastern Europe have a very different history, with their own colonial subordination to the Soviet Union within the former economic organization Comecon. Some European states were part of the Soviet Union and its system of economic planning. These countries are now receiving extensive support within the EU to develop economically, while gradually extending their interest in Africa. This indicates some of the complexity on the European side of the EU-Africa relationship.

To add another element of complexity, the EU is to some extent driven forward by its competition with China, the United States, and other countries with an interest in Africa, including Russia, Turkey, India, and Saudi Arabia. This of course adds an element of competition, where Europeans as well as Africans face additional challenges. I will come back to the implications of the tripartite relationship between Europe, Africa, and China, which is the most obvious rival to the EU. A relationship between three parties is potentially very different from a relationship between two parties.

Interestingly, the European strategy includes an element of global cooperation with African states, in international organizations such as the UN (EU 2020). This suggests that Europeans and Africans have common interests, implicitly in relation to China. It furthermore indicates an intention to give African states a better deal, which could possibly turn into a global partnership of common policies. I will touch briefly upon this element of the EU-Africa relationship and the problems involved in developing such a global partnership.

On the African side there is also a great variety of national contexts, even more varied than among the European countries. South Africa is sometimes classified as an emerging superpower, the S in the acronym BRICS (Brazil, Russia, India, China, South Africa). Some African countries score high in terms of democracy and economic development, while others score low

(Langdon, Ritter, and Samy 2018). In addition, there is variation in language, religion, and the degree of national identity. The countries of North Africa are culturally linked to the Arab countries of the Middle East and are very different from the Sub-Saharan countries. The EU deals with the northern African countries through its Neighborhood policy, run by the Directorate General (DG) NEAR, while the rest of Africa is the responsibility of the DG for international partnerships (DG INTPA, formerly DEVCO, Development cooperation), adding to the complexity on the European side.

Some African countries were in the European sphere of influence at the time of the formation of the EU in the decades after World War II. This was also the time when the process of emancipation began for the former colonies. The general process of independence began in India in 1948, while Ghana was first in Africa with independence in 1957. Algeria was effectively a member of the EU as part of France at the time. Discussions were held on closer cooperation with other countries within the concept of "Eurafrique" (Adebajo and Whiteman 2012; Hansen and Jonsson 2014). These developments were resisted by U.S. actions, such as its criticism of the invasion by France and Great Britain to secure the Suez Canal in 1956.

The Two Continental Organizations

The EU aims for strategic agreements with its counterpart, the African Union (AU). On the surface, the European and African unions have great similarities, such as high political ambitions but also that they are questioned in their member states. The differences between the EU and the AU have to do, on the one hand, with the nature of economic cooperation and, on the other hand, with the strength of the organizations. The majority of the EU member states are highly industrialized and can benefit from increased economic integration, while the AU member states are at the beginning of their industrialization process. The benefits of free trade and political cooperation in Africa are, in the short term, more uncertain. Critics point out that trade is low in Africa. Free trade agreements (FTAs) in Africa signal an intention of closer cooperation rather than actual integration. One interpretation is that the regional African trade arrangements are primarily aimed at giving legitimacy to national governments (Herbst 2012).

Another problem with the difference between the continents in the levels of economic development is that it may lead to a hierarchical relationship rather than a more equal relationship. The European side has more potential instruments of dominance and is also aiming to influence the African countries, for example in terms of developing democracy and the rule of law. I will come back to the interpretation of this relationship.

The politically contested nature of the EU and the AU implies that there are problems in forming joint positions among the respective member states and accepting the continental unions as spokespersons of all the member states. It also implies that there may be problems in the implementation of agreements made by the unions. Both elements have impact on how the relationship evolves.

The African Union was created in 2002 to replace the Organization of African Unity (OAU), which was created in 1963. The organization was a driving force behind the countries' liberation processes in the 1960s and 1970s (Karbo and Murithi 2018). All 55 sovereign states in Africa (plus Western Sahara, which is a non-sovereign territory) are members. The new organization has to some extent the EU as a model and receives financial support from the EU. In other words, the EU is something of a big brother to the AU, which can complicate their roles and processes of cooperation. In this analysis I will touch upon the inner workings of the AU, without giving it as much room as the inner workings of the EU. I will come back to a key difference between the EU and the AU in chapter five.

MOTIVES FOR INCREASED COLLABORATION

The above suggests that there are three broad motives for increased collaboration between the EU and the AU. One motive is the potential economic development on both continents and the simultaneous opportunity for environmental gains. Another motive is to solve the security threats in Africa, which threaten stability in Europe too, especially as European countries have great difficulties in dealing with an inflow of refugees. A third motive is to deal with the Chinese expansion in Africa and globally, which may be an overlapping but not identical interest of the two organizations.

Demographics and Economics

It is above all Africa's modernization which offers economic opportunities for Africa and Europe, while the growing population in Africa is both a risk and an opportunity. Combined with a rising standard of living, optimists see an increase in the labor force and production capacity as well as growing markets for consumer goods. Pessimists rather see risks of increased environmental problems when Africa industrializes, as well as the risk of falling living standards and social unrest, unless Africa manages to develop its economy faster than its population grows (Langdon, Ritter, and Samy 2018).

While the rest of the world will have almost no growth in population, Africa will quadruple its population by 2100, as indicated by table 1.1 (UN

2019). Sub-Saharan Africa is projected to grow from about 15 to 35 percent of the world's population by the turn of the next century, from just over one billion inhabitants in 2019 to just under four billion by 2100 (UN 2019). To these figures should be added the population of the countries of North Africa, which the UN counts together with the countries of the Middle East ("Northern Africa and Western Asia"). Almost half of the global population will be African in 2100, before the birth rates level off.

Already, more than 60 percent of Africa's population is under the age of 25, which will lead to strong population growth when today's young inhabitants have children and grandchildren. However, the forecast is sensitive to assumptions about fertility rates, i.e., when the growth trajectory levels off in different continents.

By 2100, five of the ten largest countries are estimated to be African, with a total population of 1.9 billion (table 1.2). The pressure on Nigeria will be great to support a population of over 700 million people. Notable is also that India is projected to outgrow China very soon.

What optimists are embracing is that the strong population growth in Africa is a "demographic surplus," i.e., a chance that a growing working-age population will add to economic development. This assumes that the economy is growing faster than the population. One estimate is that around 18 million new jobs will have to be created each year by 2035 (IMF 2015). More specifically, this means that agricultural productivity must increase and that paid jobs must be created in increasingly advanced sectors. This in turn means that education and health care must expand, as well as housing and infrastructure (Langdon, Ritter, and Samy 2018, 122ff).

A common view is that Africa could develop and integrate into the world economy, as the countries of Asia have done since the 1980s (Henley 2015). The follow-up question is what made the Asian growth possible and how the outside world supported this transformation. I will come back to the

Table 1.1 Estimated population (millions) in the regions of the world. Source: UN 2019.

Region of the world	*2019*	*2030*	*2050*	*2100*
Sub-Saharan Africa	1,066	1,400	2,118	3,775
Northern Africa and Western Asia	517	609	754	924
Central and Southern Asia	1,991	2,227	2,496	2,334
Eastern and South-Eastern Asia	2,335	2,427	2,411	1,967
Latin America and the Caribbean	648	706	762	680
Australia/New Zealand	30	33	38	49
Oceania	12	15	19	26
Europe and Northern America	1,114	1,132	1,136	1,120
Total	7,713	8,548	9,735	10,875

Table 1.2 The ten largest countries in 2100. African countries in italics. Source: UN 2019.

Country	*Estimated population in 2100 (million)*
India	1,450
China	1,065
Nigeria	*733*
USA	433
Pakistan	403
Democratic Republic of Congo	*362*
Indonesia	321
Ethiopia	*294*
Tanzania	*286*
Egypt	*225*

debate on what should be done in Africa to strengthen growth and how others can contribute. Here it is enough to mention that cooperation between the EU and the AU is based, among other things, on the idea that there are mutual advantages in cooperation. Africa needs investment and trade. Europe needs resources and labor as well as natural resources. With economic development, the countries of Africa can invest in welfare. Dependence on humanitarian and other foreign aid can be reduced in favor of nationally funded welfare through taxes (Tadesse Abebe and Maalim 2020, 15).

Security and State Building

Security policy issues imply a more complex perspective on the cooperation between the EU and the AU. The desired cooperation is largely about maintaining law and order in countries with weak governments south of the Sahara (Sahel) and some other parts of Africa (for example Somalia, Libya, the Democratic Republic of Congo). These are countries which find it difficult to get out of their problems on their own to start economic, social, and environmental development.

A common situation is that local warlords see a chance to enrich themselves through armed rebellion (Bates 2008). Religious fanaticism and terrorism add to the situation, though it is a contentious question whether economic circumstances, religion, or ethnicity are the fundamental causes of these problems (Williams 2016). For example, religious fanaticism can be an effect of poverty in a situation which is extremely difficult to change by the individual citizen.

When conflicts arise, for example in relation to terrorist groups, the EU is given a motive to assist with military and civilian operations. The situation may be much more complex, with governments repressing minorities and breaking with national constitutions. For the EU, developing its military capabilities to assist African countries is a major issue. Humanitarian aid is an important contribution in these and other countries with internal conflicts or crises that are difficult to deal with nationally.

The state is weak in many African countries and the order is instead maintained by clans and tribes. In other words, the problems with the weak states are more fundamental than just to kick-start economic development. A vast literature deals with non-functioning governments which enrich themselves, so-called neopatrimonial governance or, in short, "cleptocracies" (Haerpfer et al. 2009). The problem is not unique to Africa but is considered a major obstacle to development there. Peace, the rule of law and democracy are often described as prerequisites for economic development, but research is open about the order and manner in which change can be achieved, which I will come back to.

One version of the problem exists in countries with great natural resources, where governments manage to maintain some kind of peaceful order, but not more. The oil-rich countries of the Gulf of Guinea are sometimes described as "successful failed states" (Soares de Oliveira 2007), since revenues from oil extraction keep them going in spite of fundamental problems. There is also a debate on the role of foreign companies, whether they contribute to the development of such countries and/or settle with corrupt leaders to share the profits with them.

The unrest in Africa is leading to increased migration, by refugees as well as other forms of relocation. For several African countries, it is a great burden to house refugees from neighboring countries in camps. At the same time, governments in Africa want to increase the mobility of the population for economic reasons. Within the regional free trade areas, there is some migration, which can lead to more people finding jobs or being able to start a business. There is also a risk of conflict when there is a high level of migration in poor areas.

For the EU, migration and trafficking to Europe are becoming domestic problems. In the short term, problems arise in dealing with the situation and integrating refugees into the European labor market. There are others who point out that Europe needs more labor and that mobility in many cases benefits Europe. Paul Collier highlights the unfortunate situation for Africa that there are more Sudanese doctors in London than in Sudan (Collier 2018). The conflicts in Europe over migration provide further motivation for the EU to engage in this and to persuade the countries concerned to control their borders.

Competition with China

Cooperation on security policy includes geopolitical aspects of other countries' cooperation with African states. From an African perspective, it is most likely valuable that China, the United States, and other countries want to invest in Africa. For the EU, there is a threat of increasing dictatorships in Africa when China, Russia, and other autocracies are gaining influence over African countries, for example through investments in digital and other infrastructure. Critics also point at tough economic conditions for Chinese aid and increased indebtedness to China among Africa's poor countries.

China has for a long time built up a strong position in Africa and often acts as a counterforce against European interests (Hackenesch 2018). Hence, it is not enough for the EU to be generally benevolent towards African states. The efforts must be made in such a way as to make African leaders want to cooperate with the EU before China, even though China is often an easier partner, especially with its lack of interest in democracy and human rights. This is the "geopolitical" motive behind the EU's new Africa strategy, to face up to competition from China.

The European Union has introduced instruments to be more attractive than China to developing countries. One such instrument is called the "global gateway," to provide financial support. As mentioned above, the EU sees opportunities to cooperate with the AU globally on the regulatory frameworks (EU 2020). Both parties have an interest in maintaining the multilateral order, when countries such as the United States and China hesitate.

EU DEVELOPMENT POLICY IS A KEY POLICY IN EUROPEAN EXTERNAL ACTION

The relationship with Africa, as well as the EU external policies more generally, are interesting cases of the internal complexity of the EU. The shortcomings of the policies and relationships can be understood in relation to the general debates on the design of the European Union.

The Debate on the Nature of the EU

There is a long public and academic debate on the nature of the EU, what it wants to be and what it really is. A collaborative arrangement among national governments, such as the EU (or the AU) can take many forms, from a very loose relationship to something with a strong central core. Over time, the EU has moved from being an intergovernmental organization, where the member states retain strong powers, to becoming a supranational organization, where the legal mandate in many areas have been transferred to the union. This has taken various forms across the policy areas. Foreign policy is mainly intergovernmental while trade policy was transferred in the 1960s from the member states to the union (supranational), though the member states still play a role in the decision making. Development policy is partly national and partly supranational. The mix of formats create further complexities in the EU. Hence, these policies and their interaction make an interesting case of the complexity of the European policies. While they aren't representative of all the EU, they show some of the tensions within the organization.

There is also an ongoing debate on the need for stronger coordination and more supranational policies in relation to other parts of the world, especially in foreign policy. One could theoretically extend this line of argument to development policy, to argue that all policies should be decided in Brussels to streamline European activities. On the other hand, there is already an opposite argument, that coordination has gone too far and that there is a need for greater variety among the EU member states (Delputte and Orbie 2020). This is a classical trade-off in all policy areas, and I will come back to the specific arguments in this area. There is a common debate in federal and other political systems over the balance between centralized decision-making and the appropriate level of independence of the subunits (Fabbrini 2007).

I will mainly focus on development policy since it is highly complex in itself. I will discuss its relations to foreign policy and trade policy, which have become of great importance over the last couple of years. In addition, policies like environmental policy are becoming part of the European external agenda. This illustrates another important characteristic of the EU, that its policies and mandate change over time.

Development Policy Is an Interesting Case

The European Union's development policy is first of all interesting for its very ambitious contents, at least on paper. It is about solving fundamental human problems, helping poor countries develop, so that more people can live in prosperity, with paid work, a good environment, and a functioning democracy. Challenges relate to issues such as ethnic conflicts, repression, corruption, environmental degradation, limited health care, limited education, and so on. The EU wants to contribute to the solution of all these problems through the framework of the SDGs.

Development policy is also remarkable for the vast amount of money which is spent to contribute to solving the mentioned problems. Development policy is in economic terms a major policy area of the EU. It provides a bulk of resources for development in Africa and elsewhere. Hence, this policy is of great importance in the relationship between Europe and Africa, while it is a peculiar kind of cooperation where Europeans support Africans. However, even a relationship based on financial transfers can be complex, with elements of dependence as well as dominance, which I will come back to.

Development policy is particularly interesting since the EU and the member states together are the world's largest donors. What the EU is doing could potentially have an impact on other donors. The total EU spending on development aid is more than 75 billion dollars per year (2020), which is more than half of the total aid in the world (OECD 2021). In 2020, the instruments channeled through the European Commission (the jointly organized EU policy) had a budget of almost 20 billion dollars, funded by the member states in addition to their individual spending on development aid. For the current budget period (2021–2027), the Commission has budgeted almost 80 billion dollars over seven years for this centrally organized policy.

Development policy is part of the EU's overall ambition to influence policies and societies around the world,. The EU wants to be a partner of poor countries and a global leader in issues like peace, human rights, democracy, green transition, and economic growth. It is therefore interesting to analyze the links between development policy, the more general foreign policy, and the related trade policy. It is also interesting to examine whether the whole of the EU (the Commission and the member states) is a cohesive player or whether cohesion is weak.

Commission President Ursula von der Leyen has signaled that the Commission has geopolitical ambitions, which raises questions about the impact of global political perspectives on development aid. The ambition to increase the EU's global influence could lead to measures other than those justified by the EU's ambition to support the development of poor countries and poor individuals. At the same time, a geopolitical ambition could be interpreted as moving from words to deeds in terms of safeguarding values such as democracy and human rights. It remains to be seen what the geopolitical ambition leads to, in addition to a raised level of ambition of the EU.

A particular question on the internal operation of the EU is what influence the small European countries have over development policy, especially since some of the small countries are among the largest donors in the EU family, both per capita and in absolute terms (especially Sweden and the Netherlands). A "pro-small" interpretation is that it is because of countries like Sweden and the Netherlands that the EU development policy has become more altruistic over time. Some Swedes even see the EU a lever for Swedish politics, where Sweden is the brain which controls the large resources that the EU and the other member states have at their disposal. I will discuss alternative explanations of EU policies below.

These concerns point to other issues of internal coordination within the EU. Coherence between the different parts of the EU (Commission,

Parliament, Council, and member states) is an ideal, but in practice there is tension between diverse wills in Brussels as well as in the collaborative action in recipient countries. Such tensions take place between development policy and other policies (much like in national governments) with a risk that other policies, such as agricultural policy, will frustrate the objectives of development policy. Much of the European debate has been about problems with coordination and interaction internally.

In addition, there are fundamental questions about the relationship between donors like the EU and the beneficiaries of development policy, about their motives and interests. Both sides like to emphasize their compatible interests, while they may have mixed motives for engaging in this relationship. For external donors, a particular challenge lies in balancing between respect for the wishes of the recipients and pursuing certain policies in opposition to some leaders, for example the promotion of democracy, human rights and market economy, against corruption and repression by these leaders (Kleinfeld and Nicolaidis 2009). This means that European leaders want to be friends and critics at the same time, while they most likely also want to sell European products and services to the African governments. African leaders' motives generally range from the altruistic to self-enrichment, where relations with other donors may be a strategy to gain independence from European donors.

A milder dilemma is for the EU and other donors to influence the circumstances of the poor countries only to a limited extent, so that the EU does not take over responsibilities and powers. This may be especially pressing in relation to weak governments. There are also normative questions about the relationship the EU should have with the poor countries, whether the relationship is and should be equal between the parties. Critics like to point out that there is an element of paternalism in the relationship between donors and recipients (Barnett 2017). I will come back to the importance of understanding key relationships in development policy.

Lastly, development aid is interesting because it is in a transformational phase. Poverty in the world is decreasing overall, although with some increase during the pandemic, partly because of a new relationship between rich and poor countries, where economies are becoming more intertwined and "globalized." The economic development of recent decades in China and India suggests that development could be possible, but also that many obstacles must be overcome for large-scale transformations to take place in all countries. While the SDGs will not be achieved by 2030 for all countries around the world, there is hope that the eradication of poverty is within reach.

AIMS AND AMBITIONS OF THIS STUDY

The general aim of the study is to analyze EU policies towards Africa, to contribute to the ongoing discussion of what the EU could and should do to assist African governments in reaching the SDGs. There are several relevant European policies and a variety of African national contexts, which makes this a complex inquiry. Development policy and the renewed partnership between the EU and AU are in focus, but I also want to understand the context on both sides, to see if policies are consistent, etc.

An ambition is that this should be helpful to anyone trying to understand and improve the policies, on the European side and among the recipients. The target readership is people who are interested in these issues, including politicians and the general public, as well as students taking an academic interest. This guides the way of writing and the ambition of making explicit some of what is now implicit in the EU documents. At the same time, the ambition is to contribute to the academic analysis of these matters, especially from the perspectives of Policy Analysis and Political Science.

The investigation starts from the view that policies in general, and cooperative arrangements in particular, are riddled with complexities which need to be identified to be addressed. Political organizations like the EU run into problems such as many conflicting wills and limited knowledge of what works. Complex organizations pursue a multitude of policies which are difficult to coordinate. Such obstacles could contribute to shortsightedness, where organizations become preoccupied with internal problems rather than focusing on understanding the recipients and coming up with creative solutions to their problems (below). Neither the European Union nor the African governments it deals with are fully rational. There are some interesting tensions and contradictions on either side.

Hence, there is a need for an instrumental analysis, focusing on the ends and means of EU policies, bringing out overlooked complexities (ambiguities, inconsistencies, contradictions). Such a study needs to go beyond the hidden values, messages, or power relations, which are often in focus in a constructivist analysis. This is much of a traditional evaluation "ex ante" of the policies, based on their design, to see if they will work.

Research Questions

The specific research questions relate to three parts of the policy process from its start to finish, i.e., the origin of the policies, their design and some of their implementation and effects. These parts point at different types of inquiries, which will help us understand the EU as a global actor. They will show how the EU sets out with high ambitions which turn into weak implementation.

1. How did the EU policies develop?
2. Are the policies well designed?
3. Are the policies fit for purpose?

The origin of the policies will mainly be treated as a background (in chapter three), to see how the most relevant policies were developed and how they have become interrelated in the EU. This is a background in relation to the other issues, which makes it relevant to ask which factors drive the development of policies over time. Policy development can be seen as a bargaining process, where timing and learning from experience can be relevant. There is also an international context of norms and agreements which have influence on the EU as well as the recipients, especially in the form of the global framework of the Sustainable Development Goals (SDGs). One of the main points is to show the complexity of these policy ambitions and how they have changed over time.

In academic terms, this touches upon several theoretical frameworks which study bargaining, path dependence and the role of norms. Examples include institutional theory (rational, historical, sociological, and discursive institutionalism) as well as realism, liberalism, and constructivism from International Relations.

The second step is an in-depth scrutiny of the policies themselves (in chapters four and five), to see what they are and how focused they are, if there is vagueness or inconsistencies across relevant policy areas and implementing organizations, including operations by the EU and its member states. It is the instrumental relationship between ends and means which is in focus in the analysis of the design of the policies, together with the question of coherence. Ideally, the goals and the choice of instruments should be consistent, implying that there should also be a competent organization to manage the implementation and to make the recipients in Africa and elsewhere change their behavior to achieve the desired goals. Policies can be symbolic, but they must have a chance of reaching their goals to be trustworthy, i.e., some minimum instrumental rationality.

Academically, this is a form of policy analysis, similar to the reconstruction of "theories of change," which is common in the development aid community (elaborated in chapter two). It implies and leads over to empirical analysis of causal relations among instruments and contexts as well as the process of implementation.

The final step is to investigate the challenges faced in recipient countries and in the relationship between the EU and the African governments (in chapters six and seven), to answer the question of whether the policies are fit for purpose, if they will (can) reach their goals. This is where the decentering comes in, by shifting the attention to the African context. It will be a review of ongoing research in Comparative Politics and International Relations, giving a generalized image of the obstacles facing African countries and the EU in their joint endeavor, including problems related to the relationships involved. The ambition is to make explicit the problems which the EU aims to contribute solutions to, to check for consistency between European policies and the challenges faced by the African recipients. This begins a discussion of what policies would look like if they were "fit for purpose." It is a first step in something that would be a subsequent investigation of how the policies impact on the recipients, which is a very complex question of evaluation.

A grand evaluation of the policies would describe outcomes, processes (including relationships) and side-effects, with an ambition of establishing causal relationships. It would apply comparative methods, quantitatively or qualitatively. The ambition in this context is more limited, to discuss internal consistency and external suitability to the African situation. These issues are very important for the success of the policies, implying that this is a test of whether the policies are designed to reach their goals. This is sometimes referred to as an evaluation *ex ante*, "before the event," without looking at what happens when policies are implemented, which is *ex post*. In general terms, an evaluation *ex post* investigates whether goals are reached and explains the outcomes, while an evaluation *ex ante* is about the design of a policy in relation to the situation, i.e a preliminary inquiry into its fitness for purpose. This is a key element in policy analysis.

This is a contribution to the debate on the SDGs and the EU development policy, since the EU is not very explicit on how it thinks about these matters. It is not a final proposal on what the EU should do in relation to specific situations, but rather the beginning of a discussion of what the EU needs to consider. This might inspire a revised approach to the policies. The analysis will furthermore discuss the inbuilt dualism of the European policies, where the EU at once tries to partner with the African governments, while also working against them, for example through the promotion of more democratic forms of governance. This ambiguity is seldom discussed by the EU itself, though it emphasizes its ambition to be consistent (coherent). Further dilemmas will be identified.

My contribution in relation to other research on EU development policy is to look beyond intentions, to begin analyzing drivers and barriers in the African context, decentering the European policies. I will also contribute to the analysis of the SDGs by breaking them down into their partly contradictory demands on governments around the world. I will connect the research on EU policies to research on African transformation, which is uncommon.

Lastly, I will indicate a theoretical perspective to understand how the EU and African governments are interdependent and need to build trust to make the best use of their collaboration in general and around development funding in particular.

The next chapter will elaborate the analytical framework, i.e., the assumptions, theories and methods, pointing out more specifically what the aim is to do and which perspectives are considered helpful, through an overview of previous research.

Chapter 2

The Analytical Framework and Previous Research

This chapter will introduce the study of policies and politics, as a general background on how to do research on European development policy and other relevant policies. The chapter will also describe the Sustainable Development Goals (SDGs), which provide a general framework for the policies and the strategies, on the European side as well as the African side. This relates to the theme of transformation of African societies, which is one of the intended outcomes of the policies and the SDGs. The chapter will also describe previous research on the relationship between Europe and Africa, as a general context for the investigation. Lastly, I will indicate the research gaps this study is intended to address.

FOCUS ON POLICIES AND POLITICS

This investigation is a case of policy analysis, aiming to understand European policies (development policy, in particular), their origin through politics and their implementation in the African context. This section outlines the broad area of policy research to indicate the kind of aspects which are relevant to discuss in the chapters to follow, with the ambition of showing the high ambitions of the EU and the weak implementation.

Understanding Policies

On the face of it, most national and European policies are rather simple. They are political decisions to reach some goals through some kind of strategy and a set of instruments. However, several complexities make the situation more difficult and more interesting, from a researcher's point of view. Development policy often has clearly stated goals, but these goals tend to be difficult to reach, while the transfer of economic resources from rich to poor countries may have side-effects on the recipients and others, which need to be taken into consideration. Furthermore, the full set of European policies in relation to Africa have conflicting goals and conflicting instruments. Hence, the real world of politics is far from a simple relationship between ends and means.

Policies can in general terms be described as outputs from a political system, often with an ambition to deal with a social problem, ranging from poverty alleviation (welfare policy) to making an organization recognized as an actor in an international context (foreign policy). Policies generally have stated intentions, defined instruments and an organization set up for the implementation to bring about the desired effects. There could be regulatory instruments ("sticks"), incentives ("carrots") and normative messages ("sermons"), often administrated through public agencies. Several policies and instruments are used by European and African governments in their relationship and in the fulfillment of the SDGs. This will be elaborated in the chapters below.

Policy-related research investigates why certain policies were chosen, as well as their operations and impacts (Knill and Tosun 2012). Policies are seldom as simple as they seem. On the contrary, they are often based on compromises or second-best solutions to deal with a certain problem. They interact with other policies and concerns, as well as with contextual factors. Policies often have side-effects, some of which may be unintended. They may not reach their intended goals but could have other impact on the situation on the recipient side as well as in the political context where the decision was originally made. Sometimes this implies a need for cautiousness. At other times it may be necessary to act anyway, especially when dealing with life and death in poor countries.

Stated intentions imply that the policies are instrumental, that there is (or should be) a means-ends relationship at the heart of the policy, identifying mechanisms to change a specific situation. This in turn means that policies are generally based on assumptions about the functioning of societies, what motivates individuals and how they cooperate in society, for example about the role of market coordination and government regulation in the transformation of African agricultural societies into industrial societies. Such assumptions may not be explicitly articulated but could still be important for the functioning of the policies. There is of course a risk that policies relating to the situation in other countries, such as development policy, are based on myths about people in these countries or an exaggerated view of our ability to contribute to solving their problems. In foreign policy, there are also assumptions about the ways other states (governments) function.

Intentions and assumptions can be made explicit as a "theory of change" or a "program theory," a framework of means and ends, indicating how the chosen means are supposed to lead to the desired ends, which is often highly complex (Burns and Worsley 2015). The instrumental (rational, technocratic) approach to policy is concerned with these relationships and how to improve them over time. Goals may be vague or even conflictual, while the means may be based on some kind of wishful thinking. Goals as well as means may be based on values and ideologies. A further question is whether there is a long-term ambition to identify and correct weaknesses over time, to improve the working of the policies.

While being rational on the surface, policies can at the same time be emotional and symbolic. They signal that the authors take a stand on an issue, which could sometimes hide how difficult the problems are to solve. It may be important to show sympathy with some people, even if the instruments applied are not capable of changing the situation (Brunsson 2007). The policies may signal unity and strength, as well as a meaningful purpose of an organization. This situation is sometimes described as a myth or even a cult of rationality.

Looking at the implementation of political decisions, a traditional theme in research is the key role of the implementing organization, in this case the agencies doing development policy, from headquarters to field offices. Public organizations may have their own motives, such as expanding their mandate and increasing their autonomy or their expertise in an area. Professional workers who meet the recipients, so-called street-level bureaucrats (Lipsky 1980), for example in poor countries, may have strong values and opinions, which could come into conflict with official aims and procedures. This could become something of an unexpected deviation, from the decision-makers' perspective. When several organizations are involved, there is a further need for alignment and exchange of information, etc.

Development policies are often implemented through non-governmental organizations (NGOs) or through the bureaucracies of the recipient states. Both add complexities to the implementation. There are examples where the NGOs have an impact on the situation (Wong 2012). Recipient states often work in different ways from the European states. I will come back to the problems of corruption and "neopatrimonialism," where private loyalties take over. States are used by some autocrats as an instrument to maintain power, for example by distributing benefits to friends (Hackenesch 2018).

The chains of political command in the implementation of European policies can become muddled, in part because of the design of the policies in donor countries. The drive for increased efficiency through goals and performance measurements has ironically contributed to distortions in favor of what is easily measurable (Yanguas 2018).

Ideally, there should be some interest in outcomes, providing a feed-back loop to the decisionmakers, to adjust policies over time, to better achieve the desired ends. This is sometimes seen as an overly technocratic view of policies and society, as if it were a heating system, where outcomes are easy to understand (like temperature) and the situation can easily be adjusted by the person in control through available means (like a thermostat). Social problems tend to be more difficult, where the policies themselves can have adverse effects, such as making the target group passive rather than active. A more elaborate understanding of the causal mechanisms can be very useful.

To summarize, policies usually appear to be rational (focused on ends and means) but may have other characteristics in a particular context. They can be studied as means-ends relationships, to learn about intended as well as unintended outcomes. Studying the recipient end of the causal chain ("bottom-up") will add insights about contextual factors, often circumstances which are overlooked in the design of the policies (Lipsky 1980). Hence, the study of policies is more interesting and revealing than it sounds at first.

There are many studies on the complexities of development policy, which I will come back to. Some studies highlight how donors misunderstand the recipients, for example by not taking political factors into account (Carothers and de Gramont 2013). Other studies focus on the difficulties in promoting development and the transformation of societies, for example the weaknesses of central planning (Easterly 2006) and the underestimation of how complex societies and causal relationships are (Ramalingam 2013, Koch 2023). A more elaborated version highlights problems in the relationship between donors and recipients, creating dilemmas for "Samaritans" who want to help (Gibson et al. 2005). I will come back to some of these problems and other problems which are discussed in the literature on development policy and the transformation of African societies.

Explaining Politics

The policies are produced through some form of decision-making, which is often described as the process-stage of a political system. This adds further dimensions to the study of policies, focusing on why certain courses of action (policies) are chosen: who is influential and why? One part of this is to understand the intentions of the actors, their values, goals, and their understanding of society, for example through political ideologies.

More specific questions can be asked about arenas, actors, and agendas. Where are the decisions made? Who is involved? Why did these issues come into focus? The first two questions can often be answered in a formal way, pointing out the design of the political system, the role and mandate of a parliament, etc. The design of a political system like the European Union is important as a regulatory framework of the decision-making process.

The European Union is especially interesting since its "constitution" (treatises) changes over time and its members are sovereign states, which are often reluctant to transfer legislative powers to the European level. Any policy of the EU could be part of a higher-level bargaining on the role and mandate of the EU itself.

The why-question is mainly about motives and bargaining among political parties and other involved actors. Their values, beliefs, and assumptions about the problems and possible solutions are important. The analysis of politics highlights the importance of the assumptions ("ideas") actors have about the situation, for example through their academic training and the organizations where they work. The same goes for the change of these assumptions, for example when new perspectives become dominant in the academic discourse or when certain perspectives come to dominate over other perspectives in the media debate. Politics is not only a struggle over values, but also over worldviews, i.e., assumptions about how society works.

It is furthermore important to note the link to the voters. Politicians generally have a need to show their voters that they are worthy of reelection, that they fulfil promises given in the previous election. Therefore, symbolism as well as clever strategies are important, depending on the context. It is an open question how far politicians are altruists, focusing on the needs of society, and how far they are egotists, focusing on their desire to be reelected. In foreign policy, this connects with the observation that the intended effect is to a large extent to be achieved in other countries, while the voters are domestic. Hence, it is relevant to see how international and domestic motives interrelate in various situations and to what extent policies are symbolic, aimed to attract voters rather than to solve problems in other parts of the world.

There is at the same time a legacy of previous policies, which gives an advantage to new policies which are compatible with existing policies. It is generally easier to build on what is already existing than to make more radical changes in the structure of instruments. This phenomenon is referred to as path dependence, where policies follow in old footsteps (Mahoney and Thelen 2010). Part of this research is to understand how actors sometimes make radical change of the policies in spite of other forces which are barriers to change.

The Literature on Public Policy

The literature on public policy traditionally divides the policy-making process into four (or more) main stages which form a continuous loop (Versluis, van Keulen, and Stephenson 2011). The stylized process begins with a struggle over the political agenda, which could be related to someone's dissatisfaction with existing policies. This stage of the policy process can be very visible but also more hidden. Researchers, media, and lobby groups are important in the struggle over perspectives on the issues at hand. Governments may have various motives for taking up certain issues and not others. Public perceptions of development policy can be affected by other issues and events, which could help or hinder the achievement of the desired outcomes.

The next stage is the decision-making, which is the formal process, after an issue has entered the agenda. This takes place in parliaments and governments at the national level and through the Commission, Council, and Parliament at the European level. Formal bargaining to reach agreement is the key element of this step, which is sensitive to rules of participation as well as more informal aspects such as mechanisms of control and coordination of large organizations. The European policy process is generally less transparent than a national process, due to the secretive nature of the Council.

Decision-making leads to an implementation stage, though in reality these are often interrelated with each other, where public agencies have some influence on the agenda over time and over the choice of instruments, etc. Implementation is carried out by civil servants and other (mainly) non-political staff who need to understand or even make sense of what they are asked to do. The target population should be part of the analysis, since policies normally have an intention of changing their behavior in some way, through the projects and programs run by the implementing organization. Sometimes the target population has influence over the implementing organization, leading to what is called capture.

The general context of a policy is also of great importance, for example if there are other regulations or projects which have an impact on the new project. Ideally, this was taken into consideration when making the decision, but in reality there are often some unforeseen factors which have impact on the implementation of the policies. Such contextual factors could become competing elements in the political arena, with actors pushing for other policies with overlapping or conflicting interests. This is essential to take into account in order to reach the goals of the policies.

Finally, policies have feedback loops, where information on the implementation is used to revise policies. This information can be informal, through media or research. It can also be formal, through a requirement that the implementing organization or other organizations collect evidence about the outcomes. Some such evidence could be facts (often numbers) about key dimensions, indicating if goals are achieved or not. Other evidence can be more elaborate analyses of how the policies work and why certain outcomes are achieved. This is often needed to draw reasonable conclusions on how policies should be adapted over time, i.e., indicating what should be done to a larger or lesser extent in the future. These feedback mechanisms are underdeveloped and not very visible in the EU policies, as I will come to.

Explaining policy outcomes is riddled with complexities, since analysis of causal mechanisms demands more than a snapshot of data. It needs to be done according to some scientific method, to establish what the causal relations are, often including some kind of comparison with a "counterfactual," i.e., similar cases which are unaffected by the policies, to see what happens without the policies (Landman 2003; Hern 2023). This could partly be done through statistical analysis, if there are many cases, or by digging into the history of comparable situations to describe their evolution, if there are fewer cases. In either way, this often leads to a more elaborate understanding of the context and the existence of overlooked mechanisms which have an impact on the desired outcomes.

Theories can provide some initial guidance on what is expected. Economists and others use elaborate frameworks based on simplified assumptions such as individual rationality ("utility-maximization"), which can capture the logic of a certain relationship (chapter seven). Other models are based on the assumption of norm-driven behavior, which is another fundamental human motivation. The presence of two such impulses create further dilemmas and inconsistencies, which are more realistic but also more difficult to explain. These assumptions are controversial yet play an important role in the design and evaluation of policies.

Finally, the feedback loop often becomes politically contested, since it has potential impact on the next round of policymaking. One implication is to separate the task of evaluation from the implementation itself, through independent advice, to increase the potential of critical findings. However, this may lead to less innovativeness and risk-taking on behalf of the implementing organization. There is a large debate on the pros and cons of measuring outcomes, known in development policy as the "effective aid agenda" or in general as "new public management." There is a risk that the attention is focused on what is easy to measure rather than what is important to measure. This could lead to goal-displacement and to shortsightedness (Yanguas 2018). The feedback loop will be of great interest in this study.

However, the stylized image of the policy process makes it sound like an exercise in planning. This should not be taken as an accurate description of how politics works. As indicated, politics can be focused on daily survival, addressing issues as they come ("ad hoc"), rather than with some kind of long-term rationality. It may even be rational to copy what others have done, rather than spending time and effort on designing new policies. There is also a moment of "seizing opportunities," where great leaders see chances of driving through new policies, partly because others are open to see things differently. I will come back to some such examples.

Two Main Perspectives on European Politics

In the general debate on European integration, there are two dominant perspectives on how member states agree on new policies which lead to expansion of the EU's competences (Wiener, Börzel, and Risse 2019). "Intergovernmentalists" argue that integration is driven by the member states themselves, because they sometimes find it rational to devolve powers to Brussels. The second perspective—the "neofunctionalists"—point to the fact that member states are in a situation where those policies and actors which are already supranational (including the Commission and the Court of Justice) make it natural to continue to solve more problems collectively. The latter can be described as path dependence or a kind of self-sustaining process that makes it difficult for member states to resist centralization to Brussels.

The more detailed theories which claim that integration is driven from the bottom up, by decisions by the member states, point to the interests of states in cooperating to achieve benefits such as a larger internal market or a greater role in the world (ibid.). There is also a desire to turn one's own policy into the future EU common policy. More cynical perspectives highlight the "flight from responsibility," that difficult decisions are being moved away from the nation states. The last is less likely in development policy, as national policies are conducted in parallel with European ones.

One version of explanation highlights the process of cooperation in Brussels, where member states develop an understanding of each other's perspectives, which under certain circumstances leads to a new consensus. There is a tension in most negotiating situations between attending to one's own interests and articulating a common interest, finding win-win solutions. Within the EU, negotiators have the dual roles (identities) of being national representatives and European decision-makers at the same time. They are expected to promote and protect national interests, while at the same time finding common ground for joint action. These roles are balanced against each other and can lead to the finding of common "European" interests and new positions if the European identity becomes stronger than the national identity on a particular issue (Checkel 2007).

Interestingly, there are also examples of the leadership of the European foreign policy bureaucracy in the Council bypassing the Brussels decision-making procedures to have a dialogue directly with the foreign ministries of the member states in the hope that doing so will promote a common European perspective. This was a key to the agreement on the 2016 Global Strategy (Morillas 2019). In other words, the national negotiators in Brussels were considered too rigid to reach consensus and were therefore sidestepped.

The perspective known as constructivism highlights underlying ideas and norms, how these influence the actors' perceptions of what is an appropriate policy. The influence can come from within and from the outside. The UN and the OECD have important roles as promoters of new ideas in development policy, as do transnational networks of development agencies (Steingass 2021). This is close to the observation that political entrepreneurs use new ideas to launch new policies (Finnemore and Sikkink 2001).

Another variant is to use popular concepts to reach agreement, such as "the market" in the 90s (Jabko 2006) or "sustainable development" at present. The concept of "sustainable development" has several meanings, which implies that there can be alternative interpretations underneath an agreement (Bernstein 2001). Sometimes concepts are used to justify a course of action, without taking appropriate steps. A concept like "democracy promotion" can be used as a general justification of EU foreign policy, without an explicit strategy to achieve democracy in other countries or to deal with trade-offs in relation to other EU ambitions. Such a vague ambition can be used as a talisman, to justify a course of action, almost like a religious blessing, like saying that we are "the good guys" (Jabko 2006). Such self-promotion is common in development policy.

Sometimes the focus on underlying circumstances leads to a view of political actors as passive and/or irrational. The actors do things that make sense in their context, which is seen as legitimate, without an ambition to reach certain goals, indicating that they merely "muddle through," for example by mimicking what others do or through symbolic moves to attract voters (Brunsson 2007). One would expect this to be common in relation to policies which aim to influence something which is very complex, like economic and political development (ibid.).

Another variant is the perspective mentioned above which sees politics as following established patterns or paths. Early decisions shape politics in certain ways which then become difficult to change. It is easier to make minor adjustments to the existing policy than to completely change it. Even if a policy is adjusted, old political positions can live on and influence its implementation. When political decisions are added to each other, there is a risk that there will be a historical path created in the minds of the actors, meaning that old images of the policy continue while the policies themselves have changed (Streeck and Thelen 2005). This perspective has been applied by Landry Signé to explain why some African governments keep repeating failed strategies of development (Signé 2019).

The paths can be broken by unexpected events which pose challenges to the EU or the African governments. Especially the perspectives which see European integration as a self-sustaining process, contain an element of considering crises as triggers for integration, including in foreign policy. The solution to the challenges faced by the EU is often to move forward and give the Commission an extended mandate to deal with the problems which cannot be solved within the previous competences. Hence, the paths change, but only in one direction within the EU.

These arguments suggest that in understanding the evolution of EU development policy (next chapter), we should look for paths and unforeseen events which lead to adjustments of the paths, but also for more traditional political entrepreneurs who link problems with new solutions. We should furthermore look for links between the European negotiations and the international negotiations under way on these issues. The transformation of international norms or African circumstances can be as important as bargaining power in Brussels.

Explaining EU Development Policy

Recent analyses treat EU development policy as one of several dimensions of the broader foreign policy (Delputte and Orbie 2020), where member states have generally been reluctant to transfer a mandate to Brussels. The history of foreign policy is much about the slow development of joint action in a step-by-step manner. A common perspective sees the politics in this area as a search process or learning process, an experimentation with the tools available, while building trust among the member states (Smith 2004, 2017). The players make the best of the situation while also trying to change the rules of the game so that they can pursue other policies in the future.

It is particularly reasonable to see the emergence of foreign policy in such a way, as an experimentation with the available instruments and subsequent extensions of policy ambitions. Development policy in the EU is different from foreign policy in that it is a more established policy area which has changed direction over time and has become an integrated part of foreign policy, which I will come back to. Changes in development policy appear to be the result of more typical political processes, although there are elements of a search process in development policy too.

One risk of talking about a search process or policy learning is that any change is automatically seen as an improvement. There is a risk that the writing of history will be "teleological," that we start from what today's politics look like and search for factors in history which lead directly to this outcome. The risk, then, is that the rationality of the policy development is overestimated and alternative paths which events could have taken are underestimated. My preferred alternative is to analyze the process as a negotiating game between member states which led to the current situation, with other factors influencing this bargaining in Brussels.

Negotiations between member states in the Council and between proponents of various policy areas within the EU are keys to understanding how the EU is developing over time. The policy choices have often boiled down to a question of bringing issues to the European level or maintaining national policies. However, the question of what is best dealt with jointly in the EU does not have a clear answer but has been at the heart of debates in the EU since its inception. This applies especially to foreign policy, while not as much to trade policy or development policy, which have been part of European policies more or less from the beginning. However, the latter have evolved in form and content. The increased centralization ("Europeanisation") of development policy, which will be discussed below, is an example of a change in the division of roles between the EU and the Member States.

The policy documents indicate an internal debate and constantly adjusted perspectives in development policy. A strong norm in development policy is the need for coordination rather than diversification, which I will come back to (cf. Delputte and Orbie 2020, 155). I will discuss critical views as well as other possible common norms of development policy, such as what works and how to adjust the contents of the policies rather than their coordination.

THE SUSTAINABLE DEVELOPMENT GOALS AS A POLICY FRAME

The relationship between the EU and African governments, including the African Union (AU), is framed in terms of the Sustainable Development Goals, which have been adopted by all member states of the UN as a general framework for their development ambitions. The 17 goals and 169 indicators serve as a common agenda for all governments and international organizations. However, the set of goals is more problematic than is indicated by the individual goals. Specific goals are often relatively clear while the overall message is more complicated.

The goals apply to all countries while the specific needs for change vary across the globe. Rich countries mainly face the challenge of environmental sustainability, while poor countries face challenges in the areas of economic and social sustainability, i.e., industrialization and the building up of systems of social welfare. They generally need to transform their economies to be able to pay for welfare services, while at the same time maintaining environmentally sound policies. This is in a nutshell the fundamental challenge for African governments and their European partners. I will elaborate below on some of the challenges involved and how the European policies take them into account.

Four Themes

The SDGs have four themes. Three of these are part of the concept of sustainable development—economic, social, and environmental sustainability—while the fourth theme deals with the conditions for the implementation of the other objectives. The categories overlap and the goals are intended to be implemented together, but it is easier to describe them in four groups (table 2.1).

The SDGs are the result of international negotiations and follow in the wake of the major international meetings to discuss environmental issues and development issues, including the meetings in Stockholm in 1972 and in Rio in 1992. Between 2000 and 2015, the UN Millennium Development Goals (MDG) had a narrower focus on social issues.

The goals which focus on the environment are vague and refer to the Paris Agreement 2015 and other international agreements. In practice, it is within the framework of the United Nations Framework Convention on Climate Change (UNFCCC) which the global climate work is taking place. The difference with the SDGs is that the latter require that each country deals with all the goals in a consistent manner. In other words, while working towards environmental and climate objectives, they must ensure economic, social, and political development as well. The objectives only specify to a limited extent how to achieve this mixture, leaving much room for governments to work out the specific strategies.

Behind the environmental and climate objectives is an analysis of what needs to be done to limit global warming, summarized for example in the so-called Stern report (Stern 2006). Put shortly, it is a question of reducing the use of fossil fuels, which requires the development of new technologies and the development of government policies to promote these changes. The SDGs

Table 2.1 The UN Sustainable Development Goals grouped into four themes. Source: The author, based on UN 2015.

General area	*Goal*
Environment	No 12: Responsible consumption and production
	No 13: Climate action
	No 14: Life below water
	No 15: Life on land
Social	No 2: End hunger
	No 3: Good health and well-being
	No 4: Quality education
	No 5: Gender equality
	No 6: Clean water and sanitation
	No 7: Affordable and clean energy
	No 11: Sustainable cities and communities
Economy	No 1: No poverty
	No 8: Decent work and economic growth
	No 9: Industry, innovation and infrastructure
	No 10: Reduced inequalities
Governance	No 16: Peace, justice and strong institutions
	No 17: Partnerships for the goals

are cautiously worded on which measures should be prioritized. For example, the goal of reducing subsidies for fossil fuels is put in very weak terms.

The social goals are more clearly stated than the environmental ones. They are about eradicating poverty, hunger, and bad health. In this area, health care and education are two major issues, as well as the expansion of basic infrastructure (water, sewage, electricity, roads, and more). The last three goals (6, 7, and 11) overlap with the environmental group. The social goals have been a major focus in the long-term debate on poverty and development aid. What is new since 1992 is that they are put in context with environmental goals, which creates a tension in the concept of sustainable development (Bernstein 2001).

The third group of goals in the SDGs relate to economic growth, which is intended to supply the financing of the social ambitions. This group of goals is about such things as more efficient agriculture, industrialization, paid employment, economic infrastructure, and about stopping discrimination of poor minorities. The targets apply primarily to poor countries which do not yet have an advanced economy.

There is cause for optimism regarding economic development, since poverty in the world has been halved after 1990, down from two billion to one billion extremely poor people, while the world's population has increased from six to seven billion. This is mainly due to strong economic growth in China and India, where China even claims to have eradicated poverty among its population. This leads to the question why other countries haven't been as successful and, more specifically, if the policies are weaker or the barriers are stronger in other countries.

Globally the need for economic development and higher living standards is very demanding. The UN has advocated the view that the poorest people need some initial help to improve their own situation. For example, investments in roads and electricity would help family farms increase their returns in a first development stage (UN Millennium Project 2005). Trade and foreign investment can be means to expand the economies. These issues have also been part of traditional debates on development policy.

The last two of the SDGs refer to prerequisites for achieving the other goals. Goal number 16 deals with "good governance," including the ambition that national policies should operate according to the principles of the rule of law and democracy, even though the text talks vaguely about "inclusive government" rather than democracy. The World Bank and other aid organizations have advocated the view that corruption must be dealt with to ensure that resources are used effectively.

Goal number 17 on "partnership" deals with international support for poor countries, including investment, knowledge transfer (research and development), and trade. These are resources and opportunities which the rich countries should provide, while poor countries are supposed to fund an increasing share of their welfare through taxes ("domestic revenue mobilization"). In other words, the long-term goal of the UN is to make all countries independent of development aid.

In addition, there is in the SDGs an implicit criticism of the way global governance is organized. It is said that poor countries should have greater influence in international organizations (indicator 6.8).

The Criticism of the Goals

An overarching problem is that the goals are often vaguely formulated. However, most goals are based on previous international agreements, which means that there are more specific contents, but also more histories of compromise which could have an impact on the implementation. Nevertheless, there is a risk that the goals are too vague to really guide the activities by governments and international donors like the EU. There is also the risk that individual goals are taken out of context, forgetting the ambition that they are "a package deal."

Another problem is that there are no sanctions available within the framework of the goals. There may be some sanctions available through international organizations, but group pressure is the only mechanism within the SDGs which will put pressure on the governments to live up to their commitments, by making the commitments public. The goals have some political weight by constituting a global agreement, which gives them a presumption that they will be complied with.

The SDGs have been questioned for focusing only on the formulation of goals as such, while leaving open for various interpretations on how the goals are to be achieved (Kanie and Biermann 2017). On the one hand, the goals provide a very flexible policy but, on the other hand, they leave a large responsibility for the design of policies to individual governments, some of which have low capacity to design and implement reasonable strategies. Traditionally, the debate on development policy has been precisely about which strategies are effective (Williams 2012). This is still a major question of concern for making development policy efficient, implying a strong need to learn from experience.

A problem with focusing on goals rather than strategies is that they run the risk of crowding out the needed discussion on what leads to the achievement of the goals. The SDGs focus mainly on indicators (situations), whereas a more thorough analysis would be about understanding what individual countries are doing and what the outcomes are, to identify causal mechanisms. This would allow for experiences to be transferred and adapted to more countries. Hence, there is a need for a system of learning over time, focusing on what works in different contexts (Niklasson 2019). Some elements of such learning are provided through the UN and through ongoing research, but could be expanded to be useful, by national governments and the EU.

In some cases, the SDGs express elements of strategies (means to achieve the goals), particularly in the areas of economic growth and the financing of welfare services. It is important to acknowledge these elements, i.e., that the group of goals form a context which limit the possible range of interpretations of individual goals. The focus on economic growth is very important in the SDGs. Furthermore, the goals themselves are often uncontroversial, while the choice of means are controversial, among scientists as well as national politicians.

A related criticism of the goals is that the three dimensions of sustainable development are in practice still separated as "silos" rather than integrated. It is up to national governments and the European Union to show that they are able to combine the objectives into a coherent set of policies. I will come to an interpretation of how they are interrelated.

A further criticism is that the consensus at the UN on the goals conceals the existence of ambiguities and alternative options. The goals indicate in several places that economic growth must be combined with attention to the environment, but they don't say much about how this should be achieved. The goals indicate that technological development could contribute to handling this tension in combination with strong national policies. Here the analysis of implementation could provide interesting data on what works.

Another way of expressing the dilemma is that the objectives are about major social transformations which cannot easily be reconciled. Climate change (living fossil-free) is given a lot of room in the general debate, while economic development in poor countries is also a major transformation with consequences for all countries in an economically integrated world. The transformation from agricultural to industrial economies have had major impacts on all societies and will continue to have a major impact on African countries as well as indirectly on the rest of the world. It remains to be seen how the two transformations can be achieved simultaneously.

In conclusion, the SDGs provide a target for national and European policies but is difficult to implement without making a closer analysis of which actions are necessary in particular contexts. There is a need for a qualified discussion of what works in different situations and how trade-offs should be addressed. Otherwise, there is a risk that the SDGs will only be symbolic politics, where issues are taken out of context and chosen because they are popular here and now. The EU needs to show an elaborated interpretation of how the Sustainable Development Goals are to be implemented globally (and in Europe), especially if the ambition is to exercise strategic leadership in the global implementation of the SDGs.

Some Goals are More Fundamental and Should be in Focus for International Support

There are many opinions on the interpretation of the goals. Several interpretations point out that it is important to find synergies and links between the goals which facilitate implementation (see, for example, Kanie and Biermann 2017 or Bennich et al. 2023). The question is how the goals can be translated into national action plans which also take account of local conditions, i.e., the situation and the instruments at the disposal of governments. This is an important issue since political (instrumental) action plans must pass a rationality test, that activities can in fact lead to the fulfillment of the goals.

One interpretation is that the goals form an implicit causal chain, which means that some goals are means to achieve other goals and should be seen in a temporal order, as shown in figure 2.1 (Niklasson 2019). The causal chain inherent in the SDGs is in line with modern research in Political Science and Institutional Economics on economic and social development (chapter six). In short, sustainable development presupposes well-functioning national politics (state capacity), creating the conditions for economic development and for regulations which protect the environment. Economic development creates resources which can be taxed—if citizens have confidence in politics—to finance social welfare. Many specific issues remain to be sorted out, but a key to development is the willingness of the citizens to submit to common rules or, in other words, that the government and the state apparatus are perceived as legitimate.

Good governance (goal 16) is fundamental for this transformation since it is the basis for well-functioning rules, policies, and systems of taxation. Economic objectives placed early in the causal chain, since it is growth which will finance the technological development and expanded welfare (through taxes). There is an assumption in the SDGs (goal 17) that each country will eventually generate its own resources to address its social problems, without this having an impact on the environment. Regulation and politics are important for the construction of welfare programs (education, health, and other)

A well-functioning state: institutions for growth, environment policy and taxes (goals 16-17)

↓

Growth, trade and new technology (within boundaries) create new resources (goals 1, 8-10)

↓

Welfare systems (with limited impact on the environment (goals 2-7, 11)

↓

Prosperity within a healthy environment (goals 12-15)

Figure 2.1. The implicit causal chain of the SDGs. Source: Author.

and for the transition to a fossil-free society and other things which lead to a good environment.

The perceived role of the outside world is mainly to contribute investments and knowledge for technological development (goal 17). This is a technologically optimistic vision, in which all countries will have the opportunity to develop as the countries of Europe did over the last centuries and where new technologies make it possible to reduce environmental degradation at the same time. The SDGs do not mention alternative potential sources of increased living standards in poor countries such as redistribution or standards of "global justice." Rather, they express a liberal view, that the economy creates new resources which can be used to deal with social problems over time, if there is some appropriate political governance. Critics argue that more radical measures are needed to break the dependency of poor countries on the rich countries (Kvangraven 2020).

Behind this pro-growth line of thinking lays, among other things, the observation that two of the three countries where most of the extremely poor individuals live are countries with strong economic development (India and China; UN 2015c). This points to increased national responsibility for poverty reduction as well as to the hope that economic progress in Asia will be followed by progress in the rest of the world. A key to development in Asia was well-functioning states ("developmental states") with much of what is under the label of "good governance." Many poor countries are instead "failed states," dominated by clans and warlords. There are very fundamental social problems which must be addressed in countries such as Afghanistan, Iraq, Libya, and Somalia, which I will come back to.

In this perspective, the political and economic goals are more fundamental than the social and environmental goals, because they lay the foundation for achieving the other goals. Economic resources are necessary for welfare, while state capacity and legitimacy are necessary for efficient policies in all areas. This implies a strategic role by outsiders like the EU to help lay the foundation for efficient national policies rather than taking over responsibility. In chapter six I will focus on the drivers and barriers for the achievement of the political and economic goals.

This doesn't mean that the other goals are less important, only that the first goals are important to the capacity of the African governments to guide the further development of national policies relating to all the SDGs. It may even be that action on the social and environmental goals contribute to making governments legitimate (goal 16), which implies that the causal relations may be even more complex in reality.

It should be added that there are other perceptions of all these issues, in research as well as in politics. Among other things, this concerns the basic assumption of the SDGs, that growth and poverty reduction can be combined with the ambitions to improve the climate and the environment. The view of good governance has also been called into question, by arguments that at least part of such good governance is the result of growth, rather than a prerequisite for growth. The observation is that some dictatorships have managed to launch a national development process and that pressures for democracy will follow (Kelsall 2013). A related position is that "good *enough* governance" is a more appropriate standard for economic development (Grindle 2004). This will be further discussed in chapter six.

An implication of this overview is that the SDGs need to be discussed as a package deal, so that conflicting goals as well as synergies can be considered. The goals are more complex and more advanced than they are portrayed, even when the EU refers to them (below). At the global level, the goals are calling for a more developed multilateral order. For the EU, most of the specific contents are related to what is already being done in relation to poor countries (chapter four).

Another implication is that a greater focus must be placed on solving fundamental problems in national governance, since these problems limit the impact of other efforts. Corruption, dictatorship, and clan-based societies should be opposed with greater force. However, this clashes with the norm that all states are sovereign (Sørensen 2011). Through the UN, some restrictions on national sovereignty have been introduced (Alter 2014, Acharya 2018, cf. Wittor 2016). More could be done.

PERSPECTIVES ON ECONOMIC AND POLITICAL TRANSFORMATION IN AFRICA

The SDGs describe a future situation which demands large-scale transformation of societies, especially in poor countries, like in Africa. To take the SDGs seriously means to devise policies to develop economies, social welfare, and good governance, while maintaining a low impact on the environment. This was traditionally described as a policy of modernization, a term used as shorthand for industrialization and related transformations. Several alternative perspectives have been critical of such modernization.

Normative Criticism of Development and Modernization

In the academic literature, there is a diverse set of objections to the modernization project, of which the SDGs are part. Critics such as Arturo Escobar see development as a hidden exercise of power by the rich countries (Escobar 1995). One type of criticism is that western help is "paternalistic," that

Europeans take control, although the purpose is to help (Barnett 2017, cf. Eriksson Baaz 2005). One variant of the criticism is that we should strive to be "postcolonial," by which is often meant to respect the will of the recipients, not to maintain the European ("colonial") perspective. These issues arise especially in the discussion of conditional aid and in the balance between the wishes and interests of the recipients and the EU.

Against this criticism, there is an opposite perspective, that the rich countries should only cooperate with democracies, so as not to support dictatorships (Dercon 2022). This contrasts with the idea of post-colonialism, which risks ending up supporting autocratic rulers, if the point is that Europeans should always do what African leaders want, regardless of content. Cooperation with autocrats violates European (and African) values and risks delaying development in poor countries, critics say. Is it reasonable to treat autocrats as worthy of equal respect? Balancing these outcomes is a core issue in development policy. The dilemma is to determine when and how it is appropriate to cooperate with dictators (Krasner 2020). There is, however, no such discussion in the development policy documents by the EU.

Another type of criticism against modernization is that, although development and modernization may be something the poor want, the consequences for the environment are negative. There is literature which celebrates traditional lifestyles and sees poor countries as good examples for the rich world (Smythe 2015). Against this view one could argue that it isn't possible to support the growing population in Africa or to expand their welfare systems (health care, education, etc.) without industrialization and expanding the economies (Langdon, Ritter, and Samy 2018). I assume in the following that the developing countries support the SDGs (which they have agreed to) and that there is therefore agreement with the EU on the direction, but perhaps not on the division of roles or the specific strategies.

One further basis for criticism is that developing countries become dependent on the rich countries, even if they develop economically. A common criticism from what is known as the dependency school is that poor countries are kept in subordinate roles, sometimes expressed as a contradiction between the center of the economy in the "north" and its periphery in the "south" (Selwyn 2014). More specifically, this means that subcontractors in poor countries continue to play a subordinate role to multinationals based in rich countries. Such objections need to be taken seriously but lead too far in this context. There is research on when and how subcontractors in peripheral regions (including the European periphery) can develop their business to become more independent (Cooke and Morgan 1998). One such debate concerns China and its economic success, whether China has broken away from dependency and thus falsified the theory (Kvangraven 2020).

Another common criticism is that the international community pursues an economically liberal policy, inspired by economic theories. More precisely, the criticism is that the economic interventions produce negative side-effects and that the exercise of power is overlooked, which is highlighted by sociological perspectives (Poku and Whitman 2018). The debate over what was called the Washington Consensus was about the strengths and weaknesses of economically inspired policies, where several leading economists were also critical of at least some aspects (Serra and Stiglitz 2008, Rodrik 2011). It is easy to agree that it isn't enough to base policies on abstract theories, since an element of adaptation to the local circumstances as well as some learning from experience are necessary. At the same time, some theoretical guidance is most likely necessary to guide policy development.

Sarah Delputte and Jan Orbie see a need to include issues relating to north-south relations in the debate on EU development policy. In an article they point to the absence of alternative perspectives (Delputte and Orbie 2020b). A more general observation is that there are few specific value-based arguments in the official documents of the European Union, except for the fundamental European values stated in the treatises. The adoption of the SDGs as a policy frame seems to be mainly an expression of an instrumental ("technocratic") approach rather than a value-based and political statement.

The African Context

If the EU takes the SDGs seriously, there should be a genuine effort to understand the African context, to elaborate how external action can support outcomes in line with the SDGs. Policies must, in other words, be based on a reasonable understanding of its target population. They must be decentered away from the European intentions, over to the outcomes in the African context. As I will show, the EU is very vague in its understanding of the African context and its drivers and barriers for development. To remedy this, I discuss the foundations of the policies, to begin a discussion of the policies' fitness for purpose, their appropriateness. To put it more forcefully, there tends to be over-ambition on the European side, as well as under-engagement in the specific details (below).

Research on the situation in developing countries is conducted in several academic disciplines. My focus is mainly on research into how authoritarian states are changing and how democracy is emerging, which are central issues in Comparative Politics and in Institutional Economics. Much of the research is on a general level of abstraction, but parts of it are about the impact of development policy on the evolution of the recipient countries. One example is Thomas Carothers, who analyzes the impact of various forms of democracy support on authoritarian states (Carothers 1999; cf. Niño-Zarazúa et al.

2020). Over the past decade, a group of German researchers have focused on EU democracy support to answer the question of when (under what circumstances) EU action will have an impact in different countries.

I will go through some of this research in chapter six, to indicate what economists and political scientists do research on. This will be used to outline issues which the EU is—or should be—engaged in if it is serious about achieving the SDGs in Africa.

General Perspectives on EU-Africa Relations

For this analysis, the general perspectives on EU-Africa relations can be divided into three main categories. One is the instrumental perspective of ends and means, which is the main perspective here. This is challenged by two value-based and partly contradictory perspectives, the post-colonial criticism of Eurocentrism and the focus on power and influence, coming from International Relations. The latter two perspectives have some relevance to this inquiry, especially in their soft versions.

The instrumental perspective is focused on the ends and means of policies in the form of stated goals, strategies, and instruments of implementation. The perspective is concerned with consistency and lessons to be learned from the implementation of the policies, contributing to a discussion of what works in various contexts. It is of great relevance to practitioners but is also conducted academically through what is called Area Studies or Comparative Politics, which asks questions about causal factors related to political and economic development (Landman 2003). Key topics relate to governance arrangements, like processes of statebuilding and the development of democracy.

There is now a revival of interest in this perspective in the academic community, to question ends and means, partly due to the failed interventions in countries like Afghanistan, Iraq, and Mali. Critics blame the simplistic design of policies, where "one size fits all," for the frequent failure of foreign interventions in poor countries, asking for more elaborate and tailor-made policies. Another line of argument is critical of specific issues, like the collaboration with dictators. This study contributes an overview of some of these fundamental challenges for European policies.

The more critical post-colonial perspective makes a general normative claim, that policy and research must free themselves from an implicit bias in favor of European perspectives. One version asks for decentering by giving room for the perspectives of the developing countries (Fisher-Onar and Nicolaïdis 2021; Orbie 2021; Keukeleire and Lecocq 2018). This is highly relevant to the design of efficient strategies and in line with the argument that the EU must be more interested in the outcomes of its policies and therefore the contexts where the policies are applied. From a policy evaluation perspective, it is easy to agree with this version of post-colonialism, that it is the recipient countries which should be in focus, rather than the European intentions. The latter are mainly relevant when we study the selection of policies in Brussels, not their outcomes.

A stronger version of post-colonialism claims that a colonial mindset is still alive in hidden prejudices and assumptions by Europeans, in the form of so-called "othering," where non-Europeans are implicitly seen as inferior. This is sometimes referred to as a form of critical constructivism, in contrast to more pragmatic liberal constructivism (Rumelili 2021, 198). The criticism has some relevance, though it would be a mistake to think that all European policies lack foundation and are based only on stereotypes. The critical constructivism sees "othering" as logically implicit in talking about Europe (ibid.), while it is more reasonable to see this as an empirical and open question about European perspectives and assumptions.

It is common in the post-colonial perspective to argue that academic research must look for original African values and social arrangements as they were before colonization (Fisher-Onar and Nicolaïdis 2021, 298). This is relevant in order to understand and explain the situation in African countries, for example the mix of institutional legacies. However, the strong version contains something of a contradiction when it claims that European norms have no particular value, while all pre-colonial norms are valuable. The general "postmodern," "poststructuralist," or "post-development" perspectives see European norms as coincidental and without justification (Devetak 2013; Köllner 2023), while the post-colonial perspective seems to say the opposite about pre-colonial norms, that they are valuable because they developed historically in those contexts (Fisher-Onar and Nicolaïdis 2021).

In addition to post-colonialism, there is the criticism from what is called realism in International Relations, that these issues are best understood in terms of power and influence, while value-based perspectives and policies should be avoided. According to this perspective, the EU is too focused on its values, while it is easier to pursue European policies if Europeans accept that China, Russia, Saudi Arabia, and the United States compete with the EU on the global stage. The EU should also acknowledge that African countries are not like European countries and most likely have other expectations of these relationships (Hyde-Price 2022). The implication is to acknowledge that actors (governments) have interests, which is the foundation of rationalistic analysis, by realists and others. I will use game theory to illustrate some of the dilemmas for development policy, in a rationalistic version as well as more complex versions which acknowledge that norms are also important as drivers of behavior, beyond realism (chapter seven).

Some versions of realism in IR argue that superpowers have the right to pursue their interests, even by controlling other countries as buffer zones, for example defending the Russian invasion of Ukraine. In such a case it is the realists who are making normative claims, which go against the global norms of national sovereignty. It illustrates that there are normative issues beyond the instrumental perspective applied here and that realists also make normative claims.

The starting point in this investigation is rather that there is strong support for traditional liberal values such as the rule of law and democracy in developing countries (below) and that it makes sense to promote these values, which I will come back to. The SDGs endorse liberal values which form a common base for all governments, whether they live by them or not. This means that the ends of the European policies are to a large extent shared between Europeans and Africans, while the means to achieve them are more contested. There is a difficult question of how to support these values. A common position is that developing countries may need to find hybrid forms and pathways, including non-democratic elements, as the European countries did before.

This implies that traditional values are of great relevance in this context, while liberal ("European") values must also be allowed to be promoted by Africans and Europeans in the African context. This is a minimal liberal position, allowing the development of perspectives which have had great importance in other contexts for political and economic transformations, without assuming that Africans will come to all the same conclusions as Europeans. Hybrid models are most likely necessary, but they must allow for the promotion of the SDGs, including freedom of speech and autonomous political and intermediary organizations (Hackenesch, Leininger, and Mross 2020). It is important that there are individuals, organizations and movements which promote democratic ideals, for example at African universities, in the legal systems, in politics and in the business community, which I will discuss below.

A stronger version of liberalism is implicit in the concept of "Normative Power Europe," which was used as shorthand for the European belief that its policies in relation to developing countries were justified by reference to the values of the European Union which, to a large extent, are based on liberal values (chapter four). To avoid being an example of colonialism or paternalism there must be some external justification for the promotion of these values in countries outside of Europe. In this analysis, the justification of certain values and actions is in the agreement on the SDGs among the governments of the world. There are other perspectives on the European values, as indicated, but it is beyond this analysis to discuss further kinds of justification.

The concept of "Normative Power Europe" was also used as an empirical hypothesis of what European influence in the world is based on, namely its values. However, it is generally held that the concept has failed as a theory of European influence, because others haven't recognized the EU as a superior moral power, while the EU itself hasn't applied the concept consistently (Tiilikainen 2014). Still, the EU has had some success in promoting norms in environmental policy and other areas. The EU is also more of an economic power than a military power (Webber 2016).

I will only discuss parts of the general issue of what European influence is based on, where my analysis will provide some observations. Chapter seven will look specifically at relational issues which can provide an analysis of the logic of the relationship between the EU and the African governments. Chapters three to five will show problems on the European side. Chapter six will show problems on the African side which the policies need to consider.

Research on the Specific Relations

Moving from the general to the specific EU-Africa relations, the EU's cooperation with Africa has gone through several phases and is therefore difficult to summarize briefly. One of the possible problems is precisely the diversity of initiatives and overlapping arrangements, where the EU has revised its policies several times. A critical topic is how the relationship between the parties has changed over time, officially from a situation of European dominance to more of an equal partnership, but in reality to something more complex. An example is trade relations, which look bilateral and to mutual advantage, even generous to poor countries, but is criticized for giving an advantage to the European side (Carbone 2013).

Since the 1960s, EU cooperation with poor countries has revolved around trade agreements with the so-called ACP countries, which are former colonies in Africa, the Caribbean, and the Pacific. The agreements have undergone several phases, named after the places where the agreements were signed (Yaoundé, Lomé, Cotonou, and, most recently, Samoa). I will come back to how the contents have changed over time.

Of equal interest is the overlapping set of partnership agreements and the complexity this adds. A recent question has been whether the trade agreements should be divided into three separate agreements, one for each continent. The EU-Africa strategy is an example of working with a geographic focus rather than by policy area, like trade. However, just before the summit with the African Union in early 2022, the EU came to another general agreement with the countries of the ACP-areas, in effect working with two parallel sets of agreements with the African countries. As I will describe below, there are more agreements on trade with groups of African countries.

Cooperation with Africa as a continent began formally in 2000 with an EU-AU summit in Cairo (Egypt). The EU drew up a strategy, i.e., a basis for an agreement, in 2005. The strategy was called EAS, the European African Strategy. Subsequently, the two organizations decided on a common strategy in 2007, the Joint Africa-EU Strategy, JAES. This strategy was very similar to the strategy under discussion now (chapter five). There were partnerships to address issues in eight different areas, though these were later reduced to five partnerships with issues which were basically the same as the ones being discussed now.

One way to analyze the European strategies is to compare them to American strategies. Lola Raich has compared the JAES with the corresponding U.S. strategy, USAFRICOM (Raich 2016). She reviewed all the eight JAES partnerships and showed that they are to some extent instruments for different entities within the EU. More surprising was that she found that the EU strategy was more homogeneous and responsive to African views than its American counterpart, even though the United States is in theory a more homogeneous player (a sovereign nation) than the EU, which is a conglomerate of national governments (ibid.).

In the research on EU and Africa, it is common to point out conflicts within the EU as an explanation for contradictory European behavior. Gorm Rye Olsen (2007) analyzed such tensions between foreign policy and development policy in the 2005 EU Africa Strategy, which is a theme I will come back to. A later collection of articles by Stefan Gänzle, Sven Grimm, and Davina Makhan (2012) go further to analyze tensions between EU policies and in relation to the ambition to develop a stronger foreign policy after the Treaty of Lisbon, concluded in 2007.

Similar themes were discussed in an anthology published by Maurizio Carbone (2013). In this collection of articles, Fredrik Söderbaum (2013) examined the EU's actions in Africa and the tension between three of its policy areas (Directorates-General), to discuss the concept of actorness, which is about internal consistency. In the same anthology, Richard G Whitman and Toni Haastrup (2013) wrote about the emergence of a "strategic culture" within the EU in relation to Africa.

The researchers point to a common pattern of ambiguities and internal tensions, which I will show is also to be seen in the latest strategy paper. This ambiguity was furthermore described in the more loosely collected anthology published by Adekeye Adebajo and Kaye Whiteman (2012), which analyzes the relationship between the EU and Africa in many articles. It was also discussed in a thematic issue of the *South African Journal of International Affairs* (2018), which analyzed the relationship between the EU and Africa as a whole.

The interest in EU-Africa relations has increased over the last couple of years, resulting in several monographs, edited volumes, and special issues of academic journals. A major contribution is the *Routledge Handbook on EU-Africa Relations* (Haastrup, Mah, and Duggan 2021), with its broad outlook. Of interest is also a special issue on the increasing conflicts in European development policy (*Journal of Common Market Studies*). I will use specific articles from these and other collections in the following. Noteworthy is also the book by Sebastian Steingass (2021), where he shows the importance of transnational networks for policy development in this area.

One of few publications analyzing the African Union, the other party to the agreement with the EU, is an anthology by Tony Karbo and Tim Murithi (2018). Individual articles in the previously mentioned anthologies discuss the AU. In Carbone's anthology, Ian Taylor (2013) and Mary Farrell (2013) review the role of the AU, with Taylor especially critical of many African leaders who primarily want to enrich themselves. Later research analyzes in more depth how the AU works. For example, role perceptions of AU staff are studied in a conference paper by Jarle Trondal, Stefan Gänzle, and Thomas Tieku (2020).

Finally, it should be mentioned that there are several analyses of specific areas of policies pursued and instruments applied to support Africa's development. Research has long been conducted on economic and political development, both on internal factors and the role of external aid, which I will come back to. Some of this has been touched upon above, but the diversity of theories and the wide variety of local conditions make it difficult to design instruments which work in all contexts. Rather, it seems to imply a learning approach to policy, comparing differentiated action, in order to learn lessons about when and how the interventions work. This is a key observation on the nature of development policies.

One example of a such a comparative approach is Simone Beetz's study of democracy support for Rwanda (2015), in which she compares the efforts and outcomes of the actions of the EU and the UN (UNDP). Interestingly, the two organizations do very different things to reach the same goal in this country. Such a comparison highlights the importance of the strategy and the instruments applied. Another example is Helena Skagerlind's (2019) comparison of strategies in two African countries to achieve some of the SDGs. She compares one issue in two contexts, which is a way to elaborate on the role of contextual factors. This shows the relevance of the comparative (qualitative) method to identify causal mechanisms, which are necessary for policy conclusions to be drawn.

A very relevant analysis is provided by Erin Accampo Hern in *Explaining Successes in Africa: Things Don't Always Fall Apart* (2023), where she applies the comparative method to five cases of African policy. For example, she tests the theories on good governance by separate comparisons of similar and different national African contexts, applying the two standard logics of identifying causal relationships. This illustrates the level of analysis the EU needs to be engaged in, which I will return to in chapter five.

European Development Policy and Other Policies

Development policy has been a key policy area in the relation between Europe and Africa. Researchers such as Maurizio Carbone and Jan Orbie have been following EU development policy for a long time. They highlight ambiguities and contradictions, including internal conflicts between development policy and other policy areas. There are broad similarities with traditional evaluation research, which seeks to analyze objectives and implementation through questions about the design of programs and projects and how they affect the beneficiaries (Howlett and Ramesh 1995). This is the tradition I'm following.

I will scrutinize EU development policy, but it is also relevant to discuss how this policy relates to other policies and ambitions by the EU. There are several other policies which are important to the relationship between Europe and Africa. The new European Africa strategy relates to several of these (chapter five). In the next chapter I will discuss foreign policy and trade policy, where trade policy has been of key importance in the relationship for a long time. Foreign policy has a shorter history in the EU but is now a key element of an integrated set of external policies, where security and migration are included too. I will comment on their contents as well as their transformation over time. The relations between the policies and between their respective policy communities are important questions to return to.

The focus on a set of policies opens a line of analysis which cuts the issues differently. While the main line of conflict is here between Europeans and Africans, there are internal conflicts over policy and, more interestingly, some possible agreements among wider policy communities. An observation from within the EU is that people involved in the same policy area but in different geographical contexts can agree over some things and may even see themselves in competition with other policy communities and networks (Haas 1992). A possibility is that people in trade policy have more in agreement with each other than with people in other policy areas in the same government office. This illustrates a rivalry of identities, where a European identity and loyalty comes into conflict with, say, a trade policy identity. Such vagueness in roles may be of relevance in the implementation of policies.

The Role of Interests and Norms

Lastly, the study of formal policies and relationships must be complemented by an interest in the more informal aspects of the EU-Africa relationship, including wider motives and the role of norms. The relationship between the EU and the African countries takes place through several policies with different specific relations, ranging from cooperation to dominance by the EU, which I will come back to.

The relations have a formal dimension where they can be studied "at face value," identifying ends and means, what the parties want and how they bargain over this. The focus on bargaining can highlight competing interests and mutual interests, as well as the risks involved in trying to reach collaborative outcomes. Bargaining can be complex, with internal bargaining going on within the EU and the AU at the same time as the two organizations try to reach agreements.

Development policy is a peculiar kind of bargaining, where the donor is at least partly focused on helping the recipient. Such "help" can include various forms of influence and the promotion of certain values. It is important to avoid assuming that the relationship is only based on altruism. This indicates that there is also an informal relation where the two parties have expectations on each other. The relationship between donors and recipients is not only about money and power, but also about norms.

The complexity of the relationship implies that it can be studied with economic as well as sociological perspectives. Economic perspectives are primarily focused on material interests, bargaining and payoffs, for example in terms of rational "games," while sociological perspectives are about more subtle forms of influence, through norms and a desire to be like the other, imitating ("mimicking") other behavior. I will discuss in chapter seven how these dimensions form a core of the relationship.

Both perspectives are common in International Relations, where relations between states can be studied either in terms of interests and power-relations or in terms of the roles, expectations, and legitimacy of the relationship between states. While simplistic versions of the two are incompatible, it is reasonable to think of the two as separate dimensions of a relationship and to try to understand how they are interrelated and why either of them dominates the relation.

One example of the role of norms is when the EU's influence over other countries is analyzed as a process of "Europeanisation," which can take place in several ways, through coercion, norms, socialization, and mimicry (Schimmelfennig 2018). To some extent, norms can also be seen as a background factor, as something which shapes the interests over which bargaining takes place. One of the contributions of a constructivist perspective is to ask how the actors' positions were formed, before bargaining takes place. I will come back to these issues in chapter seven.

RESEARCH GAPS ON THE EUROPEAN POLICIES

There are three research gaps which motivate this investigation, related to the three research questions introduced in the previous chapter. One is about understanding the intentions of the European Union, which is an important dimension of the bargaining over policies in Brussels. There are several studies of how the policies were formed, indicating certain (official) motives, while the strategic thinking on how to reach the European goals remains vague. The EU is almost silent on how it aims to produce the desired outcomes. As I will come to, the intentions are quite vague, and the policies lack an explicit argument about the African context and how the European policies can make a difference. The policies are also vague on how much responsibility the EU is taking on and how much remains with the African governments. These matters have only to a limited extent been explored by other researchers.

The second important research gap is related to the outcomes of the EU policies. Not only are the intentions vague, but the EU is also vague about the effects of its policies and how they can be improved over time. In other words, the official documents stay at the level of intentions, not commenting on achievements or lessons learned. New ambitions are added to the older ones in a matter resembling symbolic politics rather than a serious attempt to solve problems in Africa and elsewhere. This is also not very often commented on by other researchers. It is common to point at various problems within the EU, but not the lack of official discussion of these matters by the EU. There is a more general debate on how and why the EU is weak in learning from experience, which I will touch upon.

There are some advanced evaluations commissioned by the EU, but they are too few and too isolated to make up a "system of learning," which is something some of the member states aim for nationally. Especially the northern European countries have an ambition to state goals explicitly and to analyze the contribution of policies with an ambition to improve the policies over time and in a public manner through "spending reviews" or various forms of evaluation.

Thirdly, there is a gap in the academic literature on how large-scale transformations, such as indicated by the SDGs, can be achieved. There is literature on sustainable development as a major transformation, with a focus mainly on the environmental dimension (Grin, Rotmans, and Schot 2010). There is also literature on sustainable development in Africa, which mainly deals with specific cases rather than the general analysis of the challenges (House-Soremekun and Falola 2011; Hanson, Kararach, and Shaw 2012; and Mutasa and Paterson 2015).

The academic literature discusses many minor issues, but they seldom add up to a grand strategy on this large-scale transformation, though there are examples of "roadmapping," especially in relation to the environmental goals. Bearing in mind that this is a very complex issue, I'm aiming to begin closing the gap, by showing how the grand themes of Economics and Political Science can be connected to the aims of development policy.

There was once an interest in grand theories like modernization theory and dependency theory, with their focus on the bigger picture of development. Even with a rather straight-forward analytical framework of drivers and barriers, there are many factors which are relevant to development assistance. These can be found in the African context as well as in the relationship between Europeans and Africans (chapters six and seven).

The lack of research on these complex issues is to some extent similar to the lack of a general discussion of the SDGs, though there are many works on how to stop global warming, which is an important part of the SDGs. The other dimensions of sustainable development—social and economic development—are not always researched in the same context. This is a problem in so far as all dimensions require large transformations and point in partly opposite directions. One of the interesting aspects of the SDGs is that they aim to achieve a very complex set of goals simultaneously, indicating a need for elaboration of possible strategies.

The three research gaps relate to the overall theme "from high ambitions to weak implementation." If the European ambition is interpreted as influencing large-scale transformation in Africa, it is indeed very high. The lack of a public discussion of ends and means, intentions and outcomes, suggests that the implementation is problematic.

Hence, questions need to be asked about the design of the policies, as well as their consistency and appropriateness: can the policies work as intended? Can they be carried out in a cooperative relationship? Europeans and Africans want to be more than just a pair of donors and recipients, stuck in a hierarchical relationship. The spirit of EU policy and the SDGs is rather that the weaker parties should become stronger and independent. The relationship ought to become more of a partnership with mutual gains.

To fill these research gaps, it is reasonable to scrutinize the design of the policies and how the policies are implemented. The link between challenges on the recipient side and the design and execution of policies must be investigated. The policies need to be taken seriously, assuming that they are intended to be fulfilled, while side-effects and hidden motives are considered. Even if this can't be the final word on these matters, the observations are intended to be helpful in the further development of policies.

Methods and Material

I will do several kinds of analyses which add up to an investigation of intentions, implementation, and fitness for purpose. I will explain the development of policies as well as scrutinize what is done in practice. This leads to an investigation of the African context, to start a discussion of fitness for purpose. A final element is to add a theoretical perspective on the relationships involved, to show how the situation can be understood on a higher level of abstraction. I will review large amounts of research on these issues.

The study is about understanding and problematizing the design and the results of the policy. The ambition is to understand the factors which influence policy, to substantiate conclusions on how the policies can be improved. I will touch on relations between development policy and other policies, in particular trade and foreign policy.

The area of development policy is an interesting case because the common European policy has become more like the northern European policies (below), in particular by shifting the focus from the former colonies to supporting poor countries in general and by both the EU and its member states embracing the SDGs.

The European development policy is furthermore of interest because it has focused on the coordination of instruments managed by different elements of the EU (policy areas and member states). The policy is conducted "for" recipients, but with an unclear picture of how their problems can be solved. The EU texts are more about intentions than the results achieved. My ambition is to say more about the strategies, to contribute to ongoing discussions over strategy, that is, a more detailed discussion of options for action. It should be noted that the EU also tries to influence global policy on these issues.

What is unique about this study is that I bring together analysis of intentions and outcomes. I see partly different explanations for EU policy than the previous research has done. I also see more problems with the implementation of the policies and a need to decenter the policies.

This is mainly a review of existing research, complemented by a selection of interviews with people who have insights into the European decision-making processes. Several of the interviewees want to remain anonymous and therefore I do not provide any names. Among those interviewed are researchers and officials, active in Stockholm and Brussels, as well as in other member states and recipient countries. As far as existing research is concerned, the selection has been made according to the snowball method, that is, by looking in ever wider circles, starting with current research on EU development policy and its strengths and weaknesses.

Limitations

One limitation in the following is that the focus is on policymaking in Brussels. For reasons of time, I have chosen not to study the behavior of the member states (see Karlsson and Tallberg 2021). I will only briefly touch upon the role of the so-called EU Delegations, in which the member states work together to achieve common objectives. Among other things, I touch on the ongoing discussion on the room for maneuver the delegations have in relation to the European External Action Service (EEAS).

I have not been able to study the EU's country strategies and have therefore not been able to assess the specific strategies of individual recipient countries. Nor have I studied the European debate on aid policy, in the European Parliament or in other contexts, even if it would contribute to a deeper understanding of the evolution of the policy.

A geographical demarcation is that I primarily discuss the countries of sub-Saharan Africa because the poverty problem is greatest there. This means that I am downplaying the problems that exist in other poor areas, for example in Asia and in the countries south and east of the EU, including Ukraine, which are dealt with within the part of development policy known as the European Neighborhood Policy (ENP). The political aspects of the relationship with the EU are probably stronger in the neighborhood than in countries further afield, due to its proximity to countries such as Russia, Iran, and China.

Another limitation is to downplay the theoretical perspectives to make the text more accessible to the interested public. The beginning of this chapter elaborated the contents of policy analysis, as a general framework for my investigation. The following chapters (three to five) will elaborate the European policies, to identify the contents as well as problems inherent in the policies. As previously mentioned, this will touch upon explanations of the design of the policies as well as factors which have an impact on the implementation. The last two chapters will elaborate on the situation in Africa and the relationship between the EU and the African governments. Both contain empirical observations as well as theoretical perspectives (on development and relationships, respectively).

Outline

To answer the main questions, I will first describe how EU policy has changed over time and what role northern European countries have played in relation to other factors affecting politics (chapter three). This is intended as an introduction to the issues and to contextual factors which have an impact on policy development. While my focus is on development policy, this is closely linked to trade policy and foreign policy. These three policy areas have been influenced by internal factors as well as external influences of various kinds.

I then discuss the current state of politics, the way in which development policy is designed and how it is implemented (chapter four). This includes objectives, strategies, and funding, but also coordination between policy areas (horizontally) and with member states (vertically). The description is the beginning of an analysis of intentions, outputs (programs), and outcomes (impact on Africa). It is important to get a realistic picture of how the policy is conducted.

The analysis of development policy is followed by an analysis of the new strategy for Africa (chapter five). This strategy is wider and doesn't even refer to the goals of development policy. While it is obvious that the strategy and development policy are related, they illustrate some of the complexities within the EU, such as many wills and the need to simplify messages to reach agreement.

I will also discuss EU policy in relation to the challenges it faces (chapters six and seven). Since development policy is based on an ambition to help others, it is essential to identify challenges and factors which can help to address these challenges. This involves highlighting the situation in the recipient countries, what they want as well as what they may need help with. To respond to the latter, I raise several factors which affect development. This also provides a basis for reasoning about how the EU and China compete for influence in poor countries.

Chapter six will introduce a rough "theory of change" (roadmap) for achieving the SDGs in Sub-Saharan Africa. The ambition is to create a focusing device for donors and recipients to make priorities and to set in place a system of learning to revise the "theory." Chapter seven will apply game theory to important relationships, which is intended to provide a grounding of some structural dilemmas.

As indicated previously, this is not a full-scale evaluation of the policies, but rather a more limited discussion of how EU policy relates to the factors (drivers and barriers) highlighted in research on Africa and developing countries more generally. It will address the appropriateness of policy, i.e., its fitness for purpose, based on previous research. Some examples of impact, intended as well as unintended, will be discussed. In the final chapter I will draw conclusions and give some suggestions on what the EU could do to improve the situation if it wants to be taken seriously.

Chapter 3

The Evolution of the European Policies

The SDGs form a framework for the relationship between the EU and the African governments through the European development policy. This is an EU policy area with high ambitions which is intertwined with other externally oriented policies, which has not always been the case. On the contrary, the history of the evolution of development policy is a story of how ambitions have gradually increased and how development aid has become part of foreign policy. What is remarkable is also how the EU and the member states have been intertwined to become—on paper at least—a more unified player, now known as "Team Europe." I will focus on foreign policy, trade policy, and development policy in this chapter, to elaborate the details of development policy in the next chapter and comment on a broader range of policies in relation to the Africa strategy in chapter five. The chapter provides the main answer to my first research question, how the policies developed.

The evolution of European policies can be divided into three phases according to their legal foundations, the treatises agreed by the member states. The first period is from the founding of the EU in 1957 until the entry into force of the Maastricht Treaty in 1993, when the EU instituted its formal foreign policy. The second is the period of the Maastricht Treaty (1993–2009) while the third is the period after the Treaty of Lisbon entered into force in 2009, since further legal capacity was given to the EU. I ignore the Treaty of Amsterdam (1997) and the Treaty of Nice (2003), because they mainly dealt with other issues. In the externally oriented areas, minor additions and adjustments were made to the wording of the texts. The Treaty of Nice added the wording on reducing and eradicating poverty and creating sustainable development, which is a cornerstone of EU policy.

If one wants to understand the political processes behind the revisions of the treaties, it is the decades just before the respective treaty which come into focus. Events in the 1980s led to the agreements at Maastricht in 1991, while events in the 1990s and around the turn of the millennium led to the new agreements at Lisbon in 2007. Similarly, events in the present create tensions in the organization which may lead to new treaty revisions. Over the last two decades there have been intensive adjustments of policies, for which it is difficult to give a comprehensive explanation.

Among causal factors, the role of small and self-proclaimed altruistic European states is worthy of highlighting. The role of countries like Sweden and the Netherlands must be sought in relation to other factors which influenced developments up to the Treaty of Lisbon and the developments that are currently under way. To identify possible explanations, an overview of what happened will be given, as well as an overview of common types of explanations, based on theoretical perspectives.

Something should also be said about international (global) policies during this time. All relevant policy areas are subject to international cooperation, which is partly complementary or even a substitute to the European policies. They are also relevant as international regulation through horizontal regulatory frameworks. In this context, it is important to touch upon the relations between the EU, the member states and international organizations like the Organization of Economic Coordination and Development (OECD), the United Nations (UN) and its various sub-bodies, as well as the World Trade Organization (WTO).

FOREIGN POLICY

It is reasonable to start with the evolution of foreign policy, since it has been a very big issue for the member states and has also been the subject of extensive research. Furthermore, it is reasonable to see foreign policy as a framework for development policy, even if the two policies have been created at different times and have separate legal mandates.

Michael E Smith (2004) describes how, back in the 1970s, the member states saw a need to coordinate to avoid conflicts on the international stage, even though cooperation within the then European Economic Community (EEC) was mainly about the internal market. Gradually, foreign policy cooperation developed to be quite extensive in the 1980s, but outside the then EEC. One interpretation is that there were some politicians, but not all, who wanted to see a stronger European mandate and stronger global regulation of the economy. For example, French President Francois Mitterrand had a vision that globalization required European and international regulation of the economy (Abdelal 2007).

The big question for the EU and the member states at the Maastricht Summit in 1991 was whether to establish a Common Foreign and Security

Policy (CFSP) and what form and mandate it should be given. The solution was to create it as its own "pillar," its own legal area, outside the common EEC legislation, where trade and development policy was placed. The Maastricht decision created a hybrid, in which foreign policy became an intergovernmental policy area alongside the more supranational policies. The implication was that the member states agreed to meet at the EU but reserved the right to conduct their own foreign policy and to veto proposals for joint action. The enhanced organization was referred to as the European Union, to indicate a variety of "pillars."

The design chosen was something of a least common denominator which all the member states could agree on. The unfortunate consequence was that the set of externally oriented policies were divided into several categories. The Commission's responsibility for development aid and trade policy remained, while foreign policy became a responsibility of the Council. The individual member states retained the right to conduct their own foreign policy (and development policy) on the issues that had not been agreed to transfer to the EU. The situation has evolved over time, but the fundamental problem of shared responsibility between several parties and legal mandates remains.

Further initiatives have been taken to make policy more effective through the Treaty of Lisbon. In addition, a number of concrete joint efforts have been made, creating a repertoire of capabilities and competences at the European level. Cooperation on security policy, including military cooperation, has furthermore emerged in the context of foreign policy. At the present, foreign policy is intertwined with other external policies, despite differences in decision-making procedures, which I will describe below.

The simplest explanation for the decision on the establishment of foreign policy in 1991 is that the outside world changed in a way that required joint action. The member states which were hesitant changed their minds on European cooperation. This was largely because the Cold War between the United States and the Soviet Union ended with the fall of the Berlin Wall in 1989 and the subsequent dissolution of the Soviet Union. This led, among other things, to the independence of the countries of Central and Eastern Europe, as well as several states that were formerly part of the Soviet Union, including the three Baltic states. A common view is that this made the member states see the need for a common but limited foreign policy to act together with greater vigor (Smith 2004, 178).

Alternative explanations point to foreign policy as an important area of manifesting unity and creating an image of the EU as a cohesive and ambitious organization, although in some ways the reality is different (Bickerton 2011). This perspective argues that the member states don't have clear objectives that precede the policymaking, but rather create the foreign policy to support a new self-image of the EU and, in turn, new objectives for the member states. In other words, the function of foreign policy is to promote integration rather than dealing with existing challenges (ibid.).

With the end of the Cold War, the EU became attractive to neutral states such as Sweden, Finland, and Austria. Sweden joined through the so-called EEA Agreement, signed in 1992 and entered into force in 1994, and joined the EU formally in 1995. For the EU, this led to an adjustment of the balancing points in the Council, including its development policy, from a focus on the former colonies to a focus on poor countries in general.

After 1993

The Maastricht treaty opened the door to a common foreign policy, but its content remained an unwritten card. This was the beginning of a period which can be described as a search process in foreign policy, which also partly concerned trade and aid policy. Most interesting in this context is that the EU built up its capacity to carry out international operations (Smith 2017). The post of High Representative for Foreign and Security Policy and President of the Council on Foreign Affairs (HR, for short) was relatively weak, but skilled individuals such as the Spaniard Javier Solana made ambitious attempts to unite the member states.

The post-Maastricht debate was very much about whether the EU was and should be a different type of superpower than, for example, the United States, a "normative" power. It was pointed out that the EU had influence over other states by virtue of its values and economic power rather than any military capability. There was also a debate on a capacity-expectations gap, that the EU was unable to live up to the expectations that had been created (Hill 1993). The self-image has changed over time, so that the Commission is now talking about the EU being a geopolitical player (Youngs 2020).

There were some major European and global events which were driving the further development of a common European foreign policy. One was the wars in former Yugoslavia, beginning in the mid-90s, directly on the borders of the EU, when the EU was unable to agree on a course of action. A major global event were the attacks in the United States on September 11, 2001, and the subsequent war on terrorism. It symbolizes a new kind of threat, but also the difficult issue of how to deal with it. From a European perspective, it was partly disturbing to see the United States take action outside the UN and other global organizations. In other words, it was not only a major challenge for the United States, but also for the international legal order.

Within the EU there was a deep division over the ensuing war in Iraq, with some governments taking part on the American side and others distancing themselves from the war. This contributed to an intensive political search process in the years after the turn of the millennium, which also included new solutions through development policy for the poor countries that were seen as the bases for the terrorist attacks.

Important were also international policy reversals which pointed towards the possibility of a more expansive foreign and security policy with coercive measures against those who do not comply with international rules. An agreement was reached between a group of states (without the United States) in 2002 to establish an International Criminal Court (ICC) to convict war criminals. This is interesting as an extension of the international legal order and a marker of fundamental values (Alter 2014). In addition, the EU was a driving force in other areas where the United States kept a low profile, for example in the creation of the Kyoto Protocol on the climate (Webber 2016). This pointed towards a stronger global role for the EU, partly distancing itself from the United States.

Another important change was that the UN was given a mandate in 2005 by its member states to intervene in certain types of civil war, when national governments cannot live up to their so-called responsibility to protect the civilian population (R2P in the international jargon; Acharya 2018). Such a mandate changes the way it is acceptable to interfere in the internal affairs of other countries, by a minor but important limitation of the sovereignty of nations.

After 2009

The subsequent Treaty of Lisbon in 2007–2009 was mainly created for internal reasons of the European Union, namely that the proposal for an EU Constitution was voted down in several national referenda. Some of what the member states had agreed to was returned here in the form of a traditional EU treaty revision. It was also an opportunity to revise foreign policy.

In 2007, the question was how to make foreign policy work more effectively, without making it too strong and without restricting the individual foreign policies of the member states. The solution was to have a joint head of the externally oriented sections of the Commission (trade and development aid) and the Foreign Affairs Council. The post of High Representative and President of the Council on Foreign Affairs (HR) was merged with the position of Vice-President for externally oriented policies (VP) of the Commission, creating a new post as "HRVP." The European External Action Service (EEAS) was given the role of coordinating the new set of policies. The EEAS was created through transfers of staff from the Council, the Commission, and the member states, indicating some of the difficulties in creating a common culture and strategy. The background was that foreign policy is intergovernmental and based on another legal mandate than trade and development policy (the *Treaty on the European Union* and the *Treaty on the Functioning of the European Union,* respectively), which gradually had become supranational. This implies different roles for the EU institutions and the member states, creating a need to find more creative instruments for coordination. Trade and Development policy follow the dominant model, where the Commission takes initiative and implements policies, much like a national government. The Council and Parliament act like two chambers of a joint legislature, like the U.S. Congress. With foreign policy, the Commission and Parliament have very restricted roles, since it is all in the hands of the member states and the Council leadership, the HRVP and the president of the European Council.

In short, foreign policy has continued to evolve through a search process (Smith 2017), but also through some new ambition and talk of geopolitics in recent years. The 2003 Security Strategy (EU 2003) was followed by a Global Strategy in 2016 (EU 2016), as an instrument to create a common vision for the whole set of externally oriented policies. These are comprehensive strategies alongside all the specific strategies developed by the EU for policy areas, thematic areas, and geographical areas. The situation is described as development policy having been dragged into the political divisions over foreign policy, with the effect that development policy has become more "politicized" (Hackenesch, Bergmann, & Orbie 2021).

An important recent event was the piecemeal withdrawal of the United States from the international stage, which became particularly evident in President Trump's rhetoric and in the withdrawal from Afghanistan under President Biden. The American reversal, combined with China's growing global role, has contributed to the focus on geopolitical perspectives in the public debate and in the Commission's rhetoric (Youngs 2020).

The question of what a common foreign policy (including development and trade policy) should look like is hardly resolved yet. There are new situations where supporters of increased integration can say that a more coordinated and integrated external policy would be a good thing, for example to eradicate poverty more effectively and to achieve the SDGs. Opponents could continue saying that the common foreign policy is too complex or that the member states cannot give up the right to conduct their own foreign policy. This is a tug-of-war between unified action and national action, which is recognizable from many other areas of the European Union and from more general debates on federal political systems, i.e., how to strike a balance of power between the center of the political system and its semi-autonomous sub-units.

TRADE POLICY

Trade policy has overlapping ambitions with foreign and development policy which provides a background to why development policy has become important to the EU. Trade and development policy entered the EU much earlier than foreign policy, as elements of the single market (Woolcock 2012). Trade policy was created as a result of the EU becoming a customs union in the early 1960s, since a customs union by definition has a common trade policy. The individual member states have to give up their trade policies to the common policy, which is a difference from foreign policy as well as development policy, where the member states have their own policies alongside the common one.

Trade policy includes what was originally the main development policy instrument, an agreement with the former colonies on access to the EU's internal market. This was later developed in several dimensions. An important part was the expansion of the group of former colonies when Britain, Portugal, and Spain joined the EU. Since then, there has been a focus on the ACP countries: Africa, the Caribbean, and the Pacific.

The ACP-agreement has become a set format of the policy, but the content of the agreement has changed over the now four generations of agreements. The first was concluded in Yaoundé (Cameroon) in 1963, the second in Lomé (Togo) in 1975, the third in Cotonou (Benin) in 2000 and the last in 2021, though the enactment has been stalled. The agreement has changed over time, for example to include elements of conditionality, which makes the relationship between Europeans and Africans more conflictual and also more vague, to combine elements of altruism with elements of hierarchy.

The early agreements gave the ACP countries access to the European market for certain goods, while other countries—sometimes poorer—did not receive the corresponding favors. This was criticized internally in the 1990s and also by Sweden and other new member states, which wanted to include all developing countries in the EU's development policy. The special treatment also violated the primacy of poverty reduction which dominated the international debate in the 1990s. It was furthermore criticized after the turn of the millennium by the WTO for violating its principle of equal treatment of all countries.

The way out was to offer all the poorest countries free access to the European market, for all goods except arms, "Everything But Arms" (EBA) 2001 (Stevens 2013). The Cotonou Agreement eventually led to specific trade agreements with several countries, including with regional groupings in Africa, the Economic Partnership Agreements (EPA) from 2007 onwards (ibid.). The process has been slow and has faced criticism from African countries, including the fact that the EU brought the countries together in groups other than the existing regional divisions (trade areas) in Africa. This has led to further problems, for example that countries which have trade agreements with a particular country automatically receive a trade agreement with the other countries with which that country has agreements. In this way, the diversity of overlapping free trade agreements can become an obstacle for making new agreements.

The special relationship with the ACP countries is now regarded by some as an anomaly, since the EU has in the meantime concluded agreements with regional organizations in Africa, Latin America, and other continents. The neighborhood policy, with its local partnerships, can also be seen as an overlapping circle of cooperation (North Africa, parts of the Middle East, the Balkans, and parts of the former Soviet Union).

In addition to the trade agreements with other countries, the EU has had a high ambition to influence global trade policy within the World Trade Organization (WTO). The creation of the WTO in 1995 built on the previous agreements within the General Agreement on Tariffs and Trade (GATT) but was nevertheless an important change in the global regulatory framework and thus the conditions for the EU's action. The WTO is—or has been—a common arena, regulator and conflict-solver in the field of trade. The WTO has been important for the emergence of global markets and global companies with subcontractors in poor countries.

EU trade commissioners have often had a high political profile. Pascal Lamy, who was Commissioner from 1999 to 2004, was an aide to former Commission President Jaques Delors and later became head of the WTO. He was succeeded as Commissioner by Peter Mandelson in 2004–2008, who was a high-profile associate of Tony Blair, after a brief interlude in 2004 by Danuta Hübner.

To economists, trade agreements are important steps in kick-starting economic development, both in Europe and in developing countries. It is about creating larger markets, but also about strengthening competition between existing companies. One of the ideas is that trade can lead to specialization which also drives efficiency. To critics, trade agreements are instead instruments to restrict the freedom of action of governments and to force them to conduct liberal policies. The simplest trade theories ignore circumstances which may be important for the outcome (Rodrik 2011, chapter 3).

For the EU's political strategies, it is equally interesting with the failure of the so-called Doha Round 2001–2008 to reach an agreement in the WTO on new rules with a development profile. The EU and other rich countries felt they were pursuing demands that would be beneficial to poor countries ("Singapore issues"), while India and other emerging "new economies" saw it differently (Hopewell 2016). In practice, this has closed the possibility of using the WTO as an arena for new global rules.

One effect of the stalling of multilateral trade policy is that the EU, like the United States, is reaching bilateral agreements with other countries and groups of countries. Trade agreements with African states, among others, have become more important for the EU's ambitions to contribute to global regulatory frameworks and to reach the SDGs.

DEVELOPMENT POLICY

Development policy is a policy area of the EU with high global ambitions. The EU has been a strong player within the UN, through its individual member states as well as jointly. In the beginning, however, the ambitions were more modest. The background to the EU's development policy is shared with trade policy, which in the early years was mainly about nurturing relations with the former colonies, through access to the EU's internal market and through some development aid from a common fund, the European Development Fund. This fund was outside the common budget and was an intergovernmental structure. Similar solutions existed in other areas (e.g. foreign policy and research policy), where cooperation began in an intergovernmental mode and was later brought into the common legal order.

The beginning of development policy was much related to events in the former colonies. In the 1950s, a process of liberation began, in which the former colonies became independent with large development needs, economically as well as politically. At the same time countries such as Sweden (then outside the EU) supported liberation movements in these countries. The latter was in a way a seed for an alternative policy of development aid, working with more instruments, with a larger number of poor countries and with a focus on values, such as support for democracy and market economy.

Interestingly, there was an early need for development aid and democracy support in Europe too. Portugal and Spain had been dictatorships since the interwar period (1926–1974 and 1939–1975, respectively), while Greece was a dictatorship for a few years in modern times (1967–1974). It was natural to offer these countries membership to help stabilize the young democracies. The same attitude later led to the countries of Central and Eastern Europe being offered membership. During the 1990s, the focus of development policy was very much on relations with the countries of Eastern Europe, their development needs and possible membership of the EU. The countries of Eastern and Central Europe, which joined in 2004 and 2007, were in practice former colonies of the then Soviet Union. These countries are among those that still provide low volumes of development aid (Karlsson & Tallberg 2021).

Membership of the EU is the strongest form of development aid that the EU can offer, both in terms of access to the EU's internal market and in the support traditionally given to the applicant countries. This now applies to the Balkan countries and some countries further to the east, while all of the neighborhood policy can be seen as an offer of development aid and some economic integration with the EU.

After 1993

The Maastricht Treaty opened up the possibility of pursuing a more general development policy for all poor countries. The EU was given a stronger mandate for development policy, while increasing the need to coordinate with other policies, as stated in the new treaty. In other words, it was already identified as a problem that policy areas and member states could clash with each other. Coordination must also be carried out with the recipient country governments and with international organizations (Latek 2015). These overlapping expectations are a key dimension of EU development policy and a major obstacle, which I will come back to.

In the international debate of the 1990s, the battle raged over the "Washington consensus," especially the demands by rich countries and the International Monetary Fund (IMF) for structural reforms in poor countries. The background was a critique that the original development policy, which mainly financed strategic modernization projects, did not lead to economic development (Williams 2012). The weak economic policies of the governments of many poor countries appeared to be a major part of the problem, while critics warned that poor people would suffer from a tougher policy towards these governments.

At the end of the 1990s, a new international consensus emerged somewhat surprisingly, including a Millennium Declaration within the UN, focusing on poverty reduction rather than economic reform. A process of events led to the renewal of global development policy in the 1990s, which ended with the UN being given a greater role as a source of common policies. I have previously mentioned the creation of the UN Millennium Development Goals (MDGs), which were followed by the Sustainable Development Goals (SDGs, "Agenda 2030"), which provide a broad and common agenda for development efforts and with references to the UN climate agreement. The European countries contributed in various ways to the emergence of the new policy.

This process of a new policy consensus is interesting for its content and for how it happened. Sakiko Fukuda-Parr and David Hulme (2011) describe an unintended outcome of a process in which the problem of poverty took center stage, while a focus on policy goals became popular among governments and international organizations. Through Secretary General Kofi Annan, the UN took the opportunity to step forward with a Millennium Declaration, which was then put into practice through a set of goals, based on previous work by the OECD. Several circumstances coincided and turned into a global policy shift (ibid.), while there was some continuity with the "Washington consensus." Poverty reduction in the SDGs has similarities with the priority of economic growth in the "Washington consensus."

Maurizio Carbone points out that EU development policy evolved towards the focus on poverty reduction in the 1990s, but subsequently took a new direction. In the 1990s, development policy was a relatively autonomous policy area in the EU. It had its own agenda and was the main instrument for exchange with poor countries, partly because trade policy had not had much impact (Carbone 2013, 483). Put simply, the EU development policy became more similar to the more altruistic policies of Sweden and other small states, compared to how it was designed in the past, with a focus on former colonies. The Council statement on Development Policy in 2000 introduced a focus on poverty reduction (EU 2000, Haglund Morrisey 2016:, 266).

Politically, the years around the turn of the millennium were unusual. It is the only period in which the member states and the EU have had a majority on the left. Romano Prodi was President of the Commission from 1999 to 2004 while in large member states such as Germany and Great Britain the "Neue Mitte" (New Center) dominated with Gerhard Schröder and Tony Blair, respectively. Development policy was an area of interest to the new majority.

What was new after the turn of the millennium was that the EU began to see development policy as part of something broader, where instruments from other policy areas were becoming more important. This was about the wider foreign policy taking on a larger role, as a general context (Delputte & Orbie 2020). Maurizio Carbone dates the reversal to about 2002 and points to explanations that I will return to (Carbone 2013). Delputte and Orbie (2020) show that the coordination ambition of the EU shifted in this way at this time. In the following years, various ways of integrating interventions within what is known as the "security/humanitarian/development nexus" were initiated.

According to Carbone, the new contents of the policies appeared in two key documents. One is the European Security Strategy (ESS) of 2003 (EU 2003), which states that security is a prerequisite for development, and the other is the 2006 Global Europe trade strategy (EU 2006), which showed that trade agreements have a higher priority than other external relations (ibid., 484). Carbone points out that the 2007 Treaty of Lisbon was aimed at facilitating the integration of the relevant policy areas (ibid.).

This new view includes elements such as promoting better coordination and efficiency globally and at the same time increasing the member states' financial commitments. The new positions were manifested at the UN Conference on Development Finance in Monterey in 2002 and internally through a settlement on coordination and division of labor between member states, including through the Code of Conduct on Division of Labor 2007 (EU 2007, Carbone 2013, 487). This indicates that there was a link between reforms within the EU and reforms at the global level, which it is interesting to seek an explanation to.

Streamlining the focus on the poorest countries meant, among other things, that development aid to 20 middle-income countries was phased out, based on the fact that the countries' overall level of development was at a certain level. Critics have pointed out that most of the world's poor people live in middle-income countries and thus fall outside the target area of EU action (Carbone 2013, 488).

In 2005, two important documents were decided upon. One was the "European Consensus on Development" (ECD), with the main message that the EU and the member states adopted the MDGs as a foundation for its policies. The consensus manifested an agreement to reach the spending target of 0.7 percent of Gross National Income (GNI) by 2015 and a focus on the poorest countries. The consensus document also focused on efficiency through evaluations and indicators, as well as increased interaction between the EU centrally and the member states, including common programming (chapter 4). Critics, however, argue that the consensus document expressed more of wishful thinking than an accurate description of the situation. The collaboration within the EU was described at the time as "ice-thin" (Hettne, Söderbaum, & Stålgren 2008, 37).

In the same year, the EU launched the central concept of "Policy Coherence for Development" (PCD), which sends a message aimed at other policies and towards the member states, that they should be coordinated with development policy. The PCD focuses on internal relations, in contrast to a focus on substantive objectives, as in the ECD the same year. PCD was described as a means of achieving the Millennium Goals, but PCD can also be seen as an alternative agenda to the UN goals (Carbone 2013, 489). Furthermore, coordination in the implementation phase was more about coordination in relation to foreign policy than other policies coordinating in relation to development policy (ibid.). In practice, development policy was subordinated to foreign policy.

The background to this change was a debate both internationally and within the EU about the fragmentation of development policy. Among other things, it was claimed that some countries received a lot of support while others received too little, referred to as "darlings" and "orphans, respectively. This was linked to a more general debate on political governance, in which critics argued that the demands for results and measurements of efforts led donors to do more of simple interventions, where they can show good outcomes. This contributes to choosing countries where it is possible to invest a lot, rather than those countries that are least attractive to investors, but which may have the greatest need. This is one of the fundamental dilemmas which makes development policy difficult to pursue.

The risk involved in a focus on outcomes is a theme of the general debate on "New Public Management," which also points to the risks of setting goals for policies, rather than focusing on strategies and means (Yanguas 2018). In short, there is a tension between the general need to coordinate efforts and to do so specifically through common objectives, which have side-effects. This is a governance dilemma for development policy as well as for other policy areas.

In 2005, the first Africa Strategy was launched, which formed the basis of an agreement with the African Union (AU) in 2007. This is interesting because it opened the way for a more cooperative approach and because it focused on the whole of Africa, despite the fact that there was an overlapping trade agreement with the ACP countries in the so-called Cotonou Agreement in 2000 and an overlapping partnership with the countries of North Africa, through the neighborhood policy.

The continued policy shift took shape through a long series of agreements within the EU, before and after the Treaty of Lisbon, with links to international policy, in which the EU has been a driving force. In 2006, a package of measures on joint programming (by the Commission and the member states) was issued, followed in 2007 by a Code of Conduct on the Division of Labor in Development Policy, which focused on three sectors per country and a maximum of five donors per sector. This was followed in 2008 by a Fast Track Initiative on Division of Labor and in 2009 by an "Operational Framework on Aid Effectiveness."

After 2009

The Treaty of Lisbon, which entered into force in 2009, provided increased opportunities to coordinate development policy with foreign policy through its construction of the High Representative/Vice President (HRVP) and the European External Action Service (EEAS). The 2011 policy document "Agenda for change" continued the theme of streamlining and focusing (EU 2011). According to Sarah Delputte and Jan Orbie, it also showed a change in the EU's ambitions, to wanting to become a major foreign policy power (Delputte & Orbie 2020, 146). This was an issue that recurred in 2013 with the launch of a "comprehensive strategy for external conflicts and crises" (EU 2013).

During the 2014–2020 financial period, the new division of roles between the Directorate-General for development cooperation (DG DEVCO, now DG INTPA), the EEAS, and the EU Delegations in the recipient countries was carried out. There were major problems in implementing the new way of working. It was also a turbulent time, with a migration crisis in Europe and an accompanying need to make agreements with neighboring countries on direct action but also longer-term measures, such as building the capacity of African states to deal with security threats.

In 2017, a revision of the European Consensus on Development was carried out, which I will describe in more detail in the next chapter. Here, development policy was linked to the UN Sustainable Development Goals and to the EU global strategy (EU 2017). In theory, the SDGs involve major policy adjustments, from the old roles of donors and recipients, towards a more balanced relationship in which poor countries (and especially those with relatively high incomes) take greater financial responsibility, while the outside world increasingly sees poor countries as objects of private and public investment; complemented by technology transfer and research collaboration (UN 2015, Niklasson 2019).

In parallel, cooperation with the African Union was revised, focusing on certain areas. A new Africa strategy with partially overlapping content was launched in 2020 by the new Commission, albeit with some conflicting principles, demonstrating the difficulties for the EU (member states and DGs) to agree (chapter five). Another possible sign of difficulties in agreeing is that the analysis within the strategy is completely general, without adapting to the situation in the different recipient countries.

Two important changes recently implemented are the introduction of a combined budget instrument (Neighborhood, Development and International Cooperation Instrument, NDICI) which increases the room for wider and more flexible action. Critics warn that it could lead to an erosion of the original intentions of the development aid budget, such as a focus on the poor. Another change was the new title of the Commissioner and in the name of the Directorate-General for development cooperation (DEVCO). From now on, the area of responsibility is called "International Partnerships" (INTPA), which signals a shift in perspective from hierarchy to partnership, partly influenced by the new perspective of the SDGs.

The pandemic has had some impact on EU policies, not least by putting its finger on things like the vulnerability of poor countries and the weakness of international instruments. A recent article argues that the challenge of the pandemic was a moment of crisis which the Commission tried to use to push for further integration of the development policies pursued by the member states (Burni et al. 2022).

Among recent events, there are signs that internal roles within the EU are changing, which can have long-term consequences. Media reported that there was no chair for Commission President Ursula von der Leyen during her visit to Turkey's leader Erdogan in April 2021 and that the President of the European Council, Charles Michel, felt entitled to the single chair that was offered the two EU leaders. It is also interesting that the High Representative (HRVP) Josep Borrell was not even on the trip. This seems to indicate that

Charles Michel, as chair of the European Council, the body of national leaders, thinks he is the most senior representative of EU foreign policy, which would be a new interpretation of this role.

A final reflection is that, although the actors in development aid policy are obviously driven by an interest in the general situation in poor countries, there has been very little explicit interest in the specific situation in individual countries and the complexities of the challenges they face. In the public documents of the EU, the dominant perspective has been general and with little room to problematize obstacles and solutions. The EU has aimed to develop specific country strategies which are intended to provide a more adapted analysis of the individual situations, which I will come back to.

It is noteworthy that some issues which are important in the research on developing countries have been almost entirely missing from the documents on EU development policy, such as the problem of high corruption and the social structure of clans/tribes and personal loyalties, as opposed to European-like state-based systems of law. At best, this is so obvious that there is no need to comment on it. At worst, it is evidence that the internal debate of the EU hasn't been able to focus on the problems of the recipients, because they have been overshadowed by the internal problem of finding agreement among Europeans.

POSSIBLE EXPLANATIONS FOR THE EVOLUTION OF THE POLICIES

The description of the policy evolution indicates that there were major transformations in the EU as well as the global context over the past three decades and that these changes are related. The adoption of common European policies is of course a major change while the global order has changed in contradictory ways, in the form of increased cooperation through the MDGs/SDGs as well as increasing conflict in the global trade system.

Focusing on the European situation after the Maastricht Treaty (1993), there are three major changes which are the most important to explain. In chronological order, the first was the shift of focus from the former colonies to poor countries in general, which took place in the 1990s. Then came a shift at the beginning of the new millennium, in which externally oriented policies were to be more coordinated with each other, first with a focus on development policy and later with a focus on foreign policy, described as foreign policy taking over from the previous coordination of (only) development policy. Finally, we can see ongoing changes at present, in which the Commission is seeking a more equal relationship with the African Union through its new Africa strategy (chapter five), while there is a discussion about a more geopolitical role of the EU, for instance by filling the gap when the United States chooses a more restricted global role.

I will discuss possible explanations, starting with the role of the small northern European states in the decision-making, with a more altruistic profile than the European average (below). This is not only of interest to the northern countries, but to understand the European dynamics more generally. Development policy seems, at least to some actors, to be an example of small country influence in the EU. Other factors can be seen as additional explanations since they do not contradict the hypothesis that small countries have had influence, but rather add that other things have also been important.

The explanations below are based on general perspectives on how change within the EU can be analyzed. The neofunctionalist perspective can point to a need for ever more developed policies and mandates at the center of the EU, while the intergovernmentalist perspective can point to specific situations where the member states have an interest in joint action (chapter two). I will especially focus on member states, political leaders, and others who have an interest in reforming the European as well as the global policies. These perspectives can be combined with an interest in how norms and perceptions of the situation change, as constructivists would focus on.

These explanations are looking backwards to find explanations in previous times. In chapter five I will discuss the case of the ongoing Africa strategy, where the situation is riddled with complexities and where the relevant question is where these complexities will lead. In other words, it is at the beginning of a policy process where causal factors are more open and indeterminate.

The Small Northern Countries

The northern European countries are often described as more altruistic in development policy than the rest of the EU, with Sweden and the Netherlands as leading altruist countries. One question, however, is how big a difference there actually is between the member states. To stay with the example of Sweden, the country is also a strong player in other policy areas with overlapping and partly contradictory ambitions, such as trade policy, where the altruism is more obviously blended with the interests of a small export-oriented country.

Swedish researcher Anne Haglund Morrissey (2016) makes an ambitious comparison of Swedish and European development policies, where she shows that Sweden was ahead of the EU in taking new positions at several times. Such a temporal order is necessary for Sweden to be likely to have had influence, but it's not sufficient. Other circumstances may have been important, as Anne Haglund Morrisey points out (ibid.). One is that there is a group of countries that have similar positions, sometimes called "Nordic Plus," since they are the Nordic countries as well as the Netherlands, Belgium, Ireland, and, in the past, the United Kingdom.

The main example of Sweden being ahead of the EU is the Swedish Policy for Global Development (Swedish government 2003) with its focus on policy coordination, which was presented before the European Policy Coherence for Development (Haglund Morrissey 2016, 259). However, the debate within the European Union is older than that and was first manifested in the Maastricht Treaty, which was agreed in 1991. Policy coordination was most likely an issue even before, as it is an eternal problem in all organizations with many policy areas. It should also be mentioned that the Swedish policy hardly lived up to the expectations in the early years, because the instruments for coordination in the Government Offices were very weak (Statskontoret 2014).

The focus on the recipient countries was part of the Swedish policy, which came before the corresponding principles of the EU and the OECD, including the Paris Declaration in 2005. Anne Haglund Morrissey regards the documents "European Consensus on Development" (EU 2005) and "Agenda for Change" (EU 2011) as examples of changes in the EU in line with Sweden's positions, through their focus on "soft values" (Haglund Morrissey 2016, 266f). On the other hand, she sees the big issue of a focus on poverty reduction as an example of something that came later to Sweden than to the global debate.

Anne Haglund Morrissey dates Sweden's focus on poverty to the mentioned policy, which came after the UN Millennium Declaration. The two cases indicate opposite patterns of influence. However, it is reasonable to see the focus on the poor as a Swedish and Nordic profile for a longer time, perhaps even since the 1960s, which indicates a small-country influence on the EU and that Sweden's membership in 1995 contributed to a reversal of the EU's position, from support to the former colonies into general support for poor people and poor countries.

Ole Elgström (a Swede) and Sarah Delputte (2016) give a partly similar picture of Sweden and the Nordic group having influence, with the above policy as an example of Swedish and Nordic influence on the EU. Most of their article examines whether the Nordic countries have become more like the other member states and, if so, what this is due to. Despite their question, they see elements of the EU as well as the international order moving in the Nordic direction, rather than the Nordic countries being "Europeanized" (ibid.). Gorm Rye Olsen sees convergence rather than "Nordicization" of the EU (Olsen 2015). All in all, the changing positions indicate some success for small-state development policy.

However, it is too strong to conclude that Sweden alone has had great influence over the major issues. The idea of coordination is older than the Swedish policy, but Sweden may have contributed to a continued interest in this. The focus on poverty reduction was both a Swedish and an international issue. Sweden may have contributed to the new policies, but can hardly have pushed it forward on its own.

Another problem for the analysis of Sweden's role is that there are more important changes to explain. The focus on poverty reduction seems to be the most important change in the "Swedish" direction of EU policy. This contrasts with the second policy reversal, when foreign policy began to dominate over development policy. As I mentioned, Carbone points to a change shortly after the turn of the millennium, in which development policy became part of the overall foreign policy. His analysis is consistent with the view that Sweden was influential in the 1990s and continuously so. However, he doesn't mention Sweden's role, but points to other explanations.

The causal relationships are not easy to sort out, but the picture of the role of Sweden differs depending on what the focus is on, the changes in the 1990s or the ones a decade later. The latter policy change seems to rather have something to do with the influence of the UK.

The Role of the United Kingdom

Maurizio Carbone provides the most elaborate explanation for the changes in EU development policy. He highlights the importance of the UK for the reversal around 2002 and does so through a chain of circumstantial evidence, which is convincing but not necessarily the last word on the matter. Carbone points out that several member states were dissatisfied around the new millennium that EU development policy was bureaucratic and did not prioritize the poorest countries. There was talk of renationalizing contributions to the European Development Fund (which was outside the EU budget). The British Minister for Development, Clare Short, was particularly critical, writing in May 2000 that the EU was the worst aid organization in the world (Carbone 2013, 486). Eleven years later, a British evaluation pointed out the opposite, that the European Development Fund was very good, even in comparison with the most ambitious international aid organizations (ibid.).

Assuming that both statements were fair at the time they were made, the explanation for the reversal may be that the EU was moving in the direction Britain wanted. The inference that this change was largely to the credit of the British is based on the high profile of the development minister Clare Short and the backing by Prime Minister Tony Blair, who had great influence in the EU during this time with a center-left majority in the EU.

Another indication that there was in fact a major policy reversal is that the EU more clearly pushed the call for international coordination, including at the UN Conference on Development Finance in Monterey in 2002. At the same time, the member states increased their funding for development aid. It is not difficult to imagine a European agreement to demand more effective global policies in exchange for a greater financial contribution. Hence, external action was linked to the similar reversal internally. The new course of policy can thus be regarded as a political change which was pushed forward at the highest level. It was more than a search process within given frameworks. Rather, it was a change of policy path, in which European policies changed and at the same time became an instrument for influencing global politics.

In this analysis, it is Tony Blair who is the political entrepreneur who saw a new path by dealing with several problems at the same time. In part it is about his views being popular at the time, but also about the controversy surrounding the Iraqi War. Blair was the European leader who most clearly cooperated with the United States and was criticized at home for doing so. It was a difficult situation, and it is reasonable to think that the public criticism of Blair increased his personal interest in showing results in development policy, for example at the G7 Summit at Gleneagles (Payne 2006). For the other member states, the motive may have been to strengthen the global role of the EU.

A recent analysis adds further complexities to the role of national politicians, by pointing at transnational networks where politicians and civil servants meet their counterparties from other countries, European as well as global (Steingass 2021). The point is that concepts and ideas develop through informal consultations before they enter the formal decision-making, implying that the influence by peers is a cause behind the more official causes of the new policies. However, in this case it seems that the consensus emerged after the policies were revised by Tony Blair and other political leaders.

The Relationship between Internal Policy Areas

The focus on informal networks has been applied to the internal rivalry over policy developments, nationally as well as internationally. The EU policies are influenced not only by competition among the member states, but also by competition across the policy areas and among the institutions in Brussels. A common situation in Brussels, as well as in national governments, is that individual ministries (Directorates-General in the EU) propose alternative means to deal with specific situations, based on their areas of responsibility and competing academic perspectives, which is why the communities of civil servants and politicians by policy area are referred to as "epistemic communities" (Haas 1992). The communities form alliances for influence with likeminded groups (ministries) at various levels and sometimes with other groups to pursue common interests or to block other alliances (ibid.).

I have described development policy as part of the ongoing collaboration across many policy areas under the leadership of the HRVP and EEAS. In the next chapter I will give some examples of tensions which indicate that there are at least partly rival ambitions (e.g. Sicurelli 2010). I will also touch briefly upon the situation in the recipient countries where the member states have to collaborate among themselves and with the institutions in Brussels, indicating a matrix of tensions and possible alliances. The European competition over policy furthermore includes policy areas with opposing interests, for example in agricultural policy or economic policy.

This internal competition is reinforced in Brussels by the fact that some policy areas, such as trade and development, are handled within the Commission, while other areas, like foreign policy, are managed by the Council, and all of them through the "European foreign service," the EEAS. In addition, the European Parliament has influence over some of the decisions, such as the budget and trade agreements. Party political perspectives have some relevance, both within the Parliament and across the other institutions of the EU, although the latter is rarely mentioned in the analysis of how the EU works. This ongoing competition over policy is important as a background to the coordination of the flow of decisions in Brussels. Forming alliances across member states, institutions, and policy areas (DGs) are likely more important in the smaller ongoing adjustments than in the major shifts of policy direction.

It is interesting that one of the important shifts has been to make development policy part of the overall foreign policy. This is a reasonable change, from a general perspective of policy efficiency, based on the observation that the development policy objectives are difficult to achieve without the broad set of instruments available in the EU (next chapter). At the same time, development policy faces difficult trade-offs, such as whom to cooperate with and how. These difficult issues require more of a holistic approach to find answers. Hence, the need for integration may explain why member states want to place greater responsibility with the EEAS.

In short, there is rivalry as well as a need to collaborate across policy areas. However, other lines of conflict seem to be of greater importance to the major shifts in EU policies than these turf-wars, for example different views on the global role of the EU.

The EU's "Great Power Ambitions"

The relationship between development policy and foreign policy has been dominated by the latter since the turn of the millennium. It is also interesting to note where trade policy stands. It has a strong role internally but has not succeeded in speeding up multilateral cooperation within the WTO. This points to a strategic problem for the EU, to work out how best to act in the international community. An interesting detail can be found in the Africa

Strategy, where the EU wants increased cooperation with the AU within the United Nations (EU 2020).

The most important difference across perspectives now is between those who want to make Europe stronger on its own (the "realists" in IR) and those who want to cooperate more with others ("liberal internationalists"; Youngs 2020). What is appropriate for the EU to do may differ depending on how you see the situation, from specific policy areas, member states, or political groups.

The Commission is talking about geopolitics while other factors point towards such an ambition. Maurizio Carbone claimed already in 2011 that the new interest in Africa was not based on events in Africa nor competition with China (Carbone 2011, 217). Carbone rather believes that the EU has great power ambitions and that it sees Africa as an appropriate area to develop its ambitions. This could also explain why foreign policy has taken a lead in the internal coordination of policies.

The ambition to influence global politics has become more important to the EU. One view is that the EU is using its development policy as such an instrument to influence global policies. Maurizio Carbone believes that the European Consensus (ECD) and the Policy Coherence for Development (PCD) 2005 were not only aimed at developing European policies, but also at increasing the visibility and the legitimacy of the EU. He furthermore believes that the slow implementation in Europe of the proposals in these policy documents shows that the international aspect was important (Carbone 2013, 487).

The EU had an ambition to differentiate itself from other international organizations, for example by offering partnerships instead of (or alongside) demands on recipients, and by adhering to multilateralism when the United States preferred unilateral action (Carbone 2013, 493). However, the EU has not fully complied with this and has not succeeded in creating coalitions for multilateral action with the US or China (ibid.).

The EU's increased ambitions could become a problem for countries such as Sweden and the "Nordic Plus," which are important actors also at the global political level. There is some faith in Sweden and other northern states among the world's poor countries, which probably means that these countries are helping make the EU more attractive. On a general level, it can be noted that there are risks as well as opportunities for Sweden in being part of the EU. From a Swedish perspective, it can be an advantage to influence the EU in its global role, especially if the EU takes positions like those of Sweden.

Rivalry with National Development Policies

When the EU takes a stronger role, one would expect some complaint from national development agencies, especially if they lose some of their autonomy. Maurizio Carbone mentions such opposition from the national development organizations, which he claims were opposed to the Commission's stronger role as coordinator of European operations (Carbone 2013, 487).

It has been stressed in other contexts, that it is important for new policies in the EU that national organizations choose to support EU proposals. For example, it is considered that the liberalization of the telephone markets was facilitated by the actions of the national monopolistic telephone companies, which saw opportunities rather than constraints in a European liberalized market for telephony (McCann 2010). One can hypothesize a similar situation in development policy, if national agencies think they will gain influence over a wider set of policies rather than only losing control over national policies.

One explanation for the lack of a critical public debate might be that national agencies are influenced through their European cooperation to adjust their policies and values. Such "Europeanization" of national politics and agencies have been noted. Gordon Cumming discusses differences across the member states in the extent to which they are influenced by the EU, especially the French resistance to such influence (Cumming 2015). Niels Keijzer identifies a difference over time in the strategy by the Commission, from complementing to copying the policies of the member states, indicating the complex relations between Brussels and the member states (Keijzer 2021).

In the current debate, there is no sign that national development organizations have fundamentally divergent views from those pursued by the EU. Other works discuss differences in norms and practices across national agencies for development aid (Dietrich 2021). The external criticism comes primarily from interest groups such as Concord, which brings together civil society organizations as independent providers of aid projects, from think tanks which evaluate policies and discuss future strategies, as well as from researchers and opinionmakers (chapter five).

It is interesting to note that there seems to be an attitude within the Swedish development policy community of the other kind mentioned, that Sweden can gain from international cooperation, that European cooperation becomes a leverage for Swedish interests, which can be implemented with a European budget and—if the EU is a lever at the global level—perhaps also with a global budget. Other national organizations may have similar views.

External Norms and Changes

The influence between the EU and the global political system goes both ways. It has been important for the EU to influence global policy and, as global policy has changed, it has also been important for the EU to revise its internal policies. The decision on the UN Millennium Development Goals (MDGs) around the turn of the millennium affected the "European Consensus" in 2005. The same was true of the discussion on the SDGs around 2015, which was followed by a "New European Consensus" in 2017. In constructivist parlance, the latter cases are examples of the global construction of European policies (Hollis 2014), i.e., the EU following international norms.

Another perspective is to see the EU involved in bargaining on several levels, where the international bargaining is dependent on European bargaining, which in turn is dependent on national bargaining. The linking of issues goes in all directions to find a set of acceptable outcomes. Maurizio Carbone explains the bargaining between the EU and the ACP countries (now the Organization of African, Caribbean, and Pacific States, OACPS) as a double two-level game, where each party of the international bargaining needs to agree internally too (Carbone 2022).

The EU has been widely described as a "norm-taker" rather than a "norm-maker" and, in development policy, as a "payer" rather than a "player." The new international doctrines have influenced the EU to adopt a new approach to the issues, based on the new international norms. The MDGs constituted a new architecture for development policy (Carbone 2013, 484), while the SDGs have a more developed set of goals which can be read as a liberal strategy to promote democracy, rule of law, and market economy (above). The OECD DAC and the WTO are also important international standard-setters. As has been shown above, the EU played an important role in the international context after the turn of the millennium.

I have also mentioned specific events on the international stage, such as the end of the Cold War in 1989–1991, the terrorist attacks in the United States in 2001, and the withdrawal of the United States from Afghanistan in 2021. These have influenced the debate on what role the EU should play and how Europe can become a stronger player. As I have touched on before, it is the interpretation of events which is of interest to political reforms, since it is the political interpretation which makes the events (the "crises") triggers for various measures by spurring a willingness to do new things. The desire to change will generally be stronger if the old policy is perceived to be a failure. This could lead to new political majorities which can decide on new policies and this is also why constructivists are interested in what drives these changing perceptions.

Changes in the Recipient Countries

For development policy, it is interesting if the recipient countries are undergoing transformations which change the context for the policies, especially if they are becoming richer and thus less dependent on development aid and more able to cooperate in new ways. This is one way to explain the new EU Africa strategy, which talks about partnership and investment. Changes in some African countries and an upcoming population increase, combined with access to natural resources, provide a new situation which is a reason for the EU to renew its relationship with Africa. It is then possible to seek solutions which benefit the EU as well as Africa, in economic development as well as in environmental policy. I mentioned this as an underlying perception in the SDGs as well.

However, material ("structural") changes are not a sufficient explanation. As noted, it is rather the perceptions of the situation in Africa which explain policy change since real life changes can be interpreted differently. One such important background is whether the actors see opportunities for mutual gains or if they think that one party's gain is automatically the other one's loss, which I will come back to in chapter seven.

The SDGs and the new EU Africa strategy can be interpreted as examples of learning at a high level of decision-making. I will return to the issue of what changes are taking place in developing countries. There is a lot that changes, at least in some of the poor countries, but it is unclear what role the EU and other external actors have in this. In addition, developing countries have strengthened their political profile and have stronger views on what the EU and other donors should do (Carbone 2013, 485). A more equal relationship means, by definition, that the EU cannot dictate which agreements to make.

SUMMARY AND REFLECTIONS

The description of the evolution of development policy and the two related policy areas (trade and foreign policy) gives a picture of the circumstances under which the policies have evolved. I pointed out a few shifts that are particularly important to seek explanations to. The final section discussed such explanations within the EU and beyond. In short, they are about negotiated policy change as well as new perspectives on the ends and means of policy.

At least two shifts have taken place in development policy, which can be partly explained by events outside the EU. The focus on poverty reduction was the first shift and it emerged in international politics in the 1990s. Factors within the EU have influenced the EU's adoption of these principles. Internal policy changes can be understood as an increasingly strong consensus among the member states on what is called a Nordic perspective on development policy, especially as the Nordic perspective also had an international impact through the UN Millennium Goals. This is, however, not the same as saying that the Nordic countries have been the most influential.

The desire to better coordinate external policies after the turn of the millennium, which was the second shift, is based, among other things, on a changed view, in which the various policies are seen as complementary instruments. In part, this may stem from the focus on poverty reduction, if one adds the observation that poverty has many causes, including armed conflict. This became clear during the migration crisis after 2015. Part of this perspective is the perception that the EU needs more capacity to act internationally. This view could be based on a development policy perspective as well as on a foreign policy perspective.

Greater coordination internally by the EU presupposes a greater willingness by the member states to act within the framework of the EU. The question then becomes who has driven this perspective within the EU. In the present, it is France under President Macron which is pushing for such positions, but at the turn of the millennium it was rather Britain under Prime Minister Blair. For altruistic small states like Sweden, there is a dilemma, whether European cooperation constitutes a strengthening ("leverage") for the altruistic perspective or whether it creates conflicts that reduce efficiency and/or change the national development policy profile.

The ongoing third shift with a greater global role for the EU could be justified by the ambition of development policy to solve fundamental problems, especially in combination with the withdrawal of the United States from its global role. The EU has already embarked on a major political path and there is much to be said for filling the gap that arises if the United States continues to withdraw from international situations.

It remains to be seen whether this leads to rethinking the fundamental principles of what the world order should look like and how the EU should act to promote peaceful development. Traditionally, the EU has been a strong supporter of the multilateral order with its regulations and organizations. This order is now under pressure and possible alternative courses must be sought by the EU and other defenders of the multilateral order.

In the academic debate, it has been argued that new major powers such as China must be allowed to share responsibility for the basic rules of the game in the UN, WTO, and other organizations (Hale, Held, & Young 2013). Others see a greater need to hold China back. This is of course a question of its own, but the issue can at least partly be addressed through the lens of EU development policy (chapter seven).

Chapter 4

EU Development Policy and the SDGs

This chapter describes the components of EU development policy, as the main policy related to the SDGs, from the overall objectives to the chosen activities and their implementation. This touches upon questions of coordination between the Commission and the member states, as well as between development policy and the other policies which constitute the EU's external action. I will problematize and point out ambiguities. Together with the next chapter, this chapter provides the main answer to my second research question, whether the EU policies are well designed.

The ambition is to give a realistic picture of how the policy is designed and how it is conducted in practice, as part of the EU's decision-making machinery. It is particularly interesting to highlight ambiguities which may lead to divergence from the objectives in the practical implementation of the policies, which I will discuss further in later chapters.

THE EU'S OBJECTIVES

The EU objectives are stated on two levels, in the treaties which define the mandate of the EU and in the policy documents which are agreed under the treaties.

Treaty-Based Objectives

Since 2009, the Lisbon Treaty (formally The Treaty on the Functioning of the European Union, TFEU; EU 2012b) regulates EU development aid. This treaty is the latest agreement between the member states on the EU's mandate. Article 208 states that "the main objective of union policy in this area shall be poverty reduction and, in the long term, eradication."

The concept of poverty reduction signals an interest in vulnerable individuals rather than states, while the concept of eradication indicates a high level of ambition. It is also ambitious in terms of coverage, since poverty is often interpreted multidimensionally, as a description of economic, social, political, and other problems (Sen 1999). This is clearly an ambitious goal, wide as well as deep, implying a need for strategic thinking to help people in other countries support themselves in several ways.

A world without poverty implies a process of major change to the world as we know it, possibly with global economic and political integration as in the EU at present. It will have great consequences for all parts of the world, much like the globalization of Southeast Asia had on Europe and North America.

It can be assumed that the goal is more than a façade. It is meant to be achieved, although the details are left unspecified. It is meant to guide policy development within the EU, although there are other policy goals it must be weighed against. This context of multiple goals and vagueness will be elaborated in the following.

The same article of the TFEU states that the policy must be conducted within the framework of the principles and objectives of the Union's external action, as well as the objectives set by the UN and other international organizations. In other words, development policy is part of a larger whole, which to some extent is decided by the international community. Several other EU policies have international dimensions and may affect relations with poor countries (Barbé, Costa, and Kissack 2016).

An important principle mentioned in the Treaty (the same article) is that other policies in the EU should consider the objectives of development cooperation. It is also stated that the policies of the Union and the member states should complement and reinforce each other. This highlights the need to coordinate policies internally, which in turn implies a risk that development policy will have to yield to other considerations. In addition, there is the need to coordinate with other donors, as a result of international agreements, such as the so-called Paris Declaration 2005 (Latek 2015). All in all, this manifests the so-called principle of Policy Coherence for Development (PCD), discussed in the previous chapter.

The TFEU furthermore contains rules for cooperation with other countries (Articles 212–13) and rules for humanitarian aid (Article 214), as a specific form of development aid, with no other ambition than to alleviate urgent distress. This indicates the distinction between the two types of aid, with and without a long-term objective such as poverty reduction.

The TFEU refers to the more general principles contained in the initial provisions of the Maastricht Treaty (formally Treaty on the European Union, TEU; EU 2012a), originally of 1993, but revised later. It sets out the values of the Union (Article 2) and its objectives (Article 3), as well as broader objectives in line with the UN Sustainable Development Goals. These are set out in Article 3 and in the subsequent articles laying down general rules for the union's external action (Articles 21 to 22):

> In its relations with the wider world, the Union shall uphold and promote its values and interests and contribute to the protection of its citizens. It shall contribute to peace, security, the sustainable development of the Earth, solidarity and mutual respect among peoples, free and fair trade, eradication of poverty and the protection of human rights, in particular the rights of the child, as well as to the strict observance and the development of international law, including respect for the principles of the United Nations Charter (Article 3:5).

The list provides a broad set of objectives for the EU's external action, with an affirmation of values as well as interests. The objectives set out by the treaties raise questions about the relationship between the policy areas, whether development policy is part of the general external policy or whether the whole of external policy is development policy. It is unclear how they make up an integrated set of objectives for the EU as a whole. On the one hand, development policy seems to contain the highest (most advanced) objective, to eradicate poverty, but on the other hand, development policy is dependent on instruments from other policy areas (trade, defense, foreign policy).

What is listed in the broader objectives may be conditions for poverty reduction as well as effects of the same (peace, security, trade, human rights). This implies a risk that the strategies become muddled if all policies depend on each other.

A supplementary question is how the responsibility for the various objectives is distributed within the EU. Articles 23–46 (TEU) deal with specific provisions for the common foreign and security policy, while articles 13 to 22 deal with the overall organization of the EU, including development policy. A noteworthy detail is that since 1993, the rules on EU external action have promoted coherence between policy areas (Article 21).

In addition, there are specific rules on measures for the neighborhood, referring to the nearest countries to the south and east of the EU, which form a geographically distinct part of the EU's overall development policy (North Africa, the Middle East, the Balkans and parts of the former Soviet Union): "The Union shall develop a special relationship with neighboring countries, aiming to establish an area of prosperity and good neighborliness founded on the values of the Union and characterized by close and peaceful relations based on cooperation" (Article 8 TEU).

In conclusion, the general principles point to a broad set of objectives which are common to development policy and related policies. They open an important discussion about which instruments should be used in the broad external policy, by whom and in what order. The principle of coherence highlights the risk that separated actions will be counterproductive. The relevance of international regulation is also highlighted.

It should furthermore be noted that there is a more detailed discussion among legal scholars about the interpretation of specific concepts and how the rulings of the Court of Justice of the European Union affect the meaning of the treaty texts (e.g. Broberg and Holdgaard 2014).

Principles of Development Policy: The SDGs

The latest specific principles for EU development policy—within the framework of the treaties—were formulated in 2017 in what is known as the New European Consensus on Development (EU 2017). The title refers to a revision of the original European Consensus on Development of 2005 (EU 2005). These consensus agreements were established between the member states (the Council), Parliament, and the Commission, within the framework of the overarching provisions of the Treaties. The most recent document emphasizes that the purpose of the agreement is to guide all efforts made by the member states and by the EU institutions (EU 2017, 4), which is the point of calling it a European consensus. Whether everyone will let the agreement guide their actions is a different question, to which I will come back.

The theme of the pan-European agreement is to make the SDGs the EU's development policy objectives. Such an approach is easy to understand when all member states and all developing countries have agreed at the UN that these goals should apply to all countries. As described in chapter two, the goals deal with sustainable development (economic, social, environmental) and the development of governance, rather than the more vague concept of poverty reduction, which is the main objective of the EU treatises. The document emphasizes that there are broad similarities with the 2016 EU Global Strategy (EU 2017, 5), which aimed to give external policies a comprehensive approach.

However, the EU document does not restate the goals by the UN, but formulates its own text with similar content, structured according to the five themes used by the UN and others to summarize the content of the goals, by five words starting with the letter P: people, planet, prosperity, peace, and partnership (ibid.). The content of "people" is close to the poverty reduction objective of the EU, which suggests a possible ranking of the five "P's," where the most fundamental are the challenges of people (welfare) and planet (environment), while prosperity (economic growth), peace and partnership (cooperation) are means of achieving the key objectives. I noted in chapter two that there is a causal chain implicit in the SDGs, which now can be expressed in terms of the "five P's" (figure 4.1). I will come back below to a description of the content of the five themes.

There is a great deal of general support for the SDGs among governments, organizations, and academics, but also some criticism from researchers and activists that they avoid controversial issues and that they constitute a mixture of ends and means, which I mentioned in chapter two. The SDGs are vague on issues such as the need to reduce fossil fuel subsidies, the importance of democracy, and the fight against corruption (above).

It is noteworthy that the EU document doesn't indicate what it sees as strengths or weaknesses with the UN goals. The EU accepts the UN document as it stands and even maintains ambiguities from the text by the UN, for example whether it is absolute poverty or relative poverty (inequality) which is to be reversed, suggesting political compromises in the two organizations (EU 2017).

However, the styles of the two texts are different. While the UN text is action-oriented, not least through a detailed structure of targets, the European text is more political and "chatty." It sets out problems to fix, without specifying how this should be done. In addition, reasoning based on values is mixed with reasoning that points at causal relationships (ibid.). In other words, it is not a scientific text aimed at clarifying alternatives or justifying the chosen measures with references to research and proven experience (which was not the ambition).

Nor does the document describe the internal problem of aligning these objectives with those of other policy areas (ibid.). The text thus sets out principles which are valid *prima facie* ("at first sight"), before aligning or compromising them with other principles and objectives of the EU. This means that there is no automatic priority of these policy positions, despite the principle of policy coherence (PCD, above). Hence, the text gives large room for maneuver for the EU.

The text contains various commitments for development policy, several of which had already been made in the past, such as the use of at least 20 percent of development aid for the purpose of "social inclusion and human

Peace and Partnership = A well-functioning state and international support (goals 16-17)

↓

Prosperity = Growth, trade and new technology (goals 1, 8-10)

↓

People = Welfare systems (goals 2-7, 11)

↓

Planet = Prosperity within a healthy environment (goals 12-15)

Figure 4.1. The five themes of the SDGs, grouped as a causal theory, similar to figure 2.1. Source: Author.

development" (EU 2017, 9). The text also contains boxes with important themes, which set out certain priorities. This applies to youth, gender equality, migration, sustainable energy, investment and trade, as well as good governance. One phrase which was important in the debate on incoming refugees in 2017 is that development policy aims to address the root causes of forced migration.

Following the discussion of the five thematic areas, the text goes on to describe how to implement EU development policy, especially in terms of better cooperation with member states, recipient states, and civil society organizations. Particularly interesting is a section describing how the general principles should be differentiated according to the situation in the recipient countries. It states that financial assistance should be focused on the countries where the needs are the greatest and development aid can have the greatest impact (ibid., 45). However, it is not clear whether both conditions must be met or whether it is sufficient that only one is fulfilled. On the other hand, it is said that this applies in particular to the least developed countries and to situations of vulnerability and conflict (ibid.). Later in the text, it says that the EU will also cooperate with middle-income countries, especially in terms of their poor population, and with more advanced developing countries, as they are important globally in achieving the SDGs (ibid., 46). In the latter case, it should be a matter of policy dialogue rather than financial support.

Another chapter concerns the mobilization of resources, in developing countries, within the EU and globally (ibid., 48ff). This includes improving the capacity of developing countries to take actions which can lead to the fulfillment of the SDGs, but also their ability to finance measures through their own taxes. The reasoning points to global agreements on the tax structure of the world, the integration of poor countries into world trade and research cooperation (ibid., 52f). This is in line with the SDGs (goal number 17).

In conclusion, the document provides some clarity to the European policy, by linking it to the SDGs. Although there is scope for different interpretations of the SDGs, they at least provide a common frame of reference for all interested parties, to discuss the choice of measures and to analyze the impact of these measures. It is interesting to note, among other things, that development policy is described as not only supporting development through financial contributions, but also through dialogue. The prioritization of countries with high needs and/or good conditions for development aid is also of interest for the further analysis. Through its subsequent regulations, the Council has reduced some of the ambiguities noted here, including that priority is given to countries most in need (EU 2015, 6).

It is clear in the texts that development policy aims to achieve certain effects. It wants to contribute to transformations in the recipient countries. Sometimes the ambition is purely humanitarian, to alleviate distress, but it is often political, for example by supporting the development of democracy and market economy. In short, the ambitions of this important policy document are very high.

Two questions need to be asked. The first is if the ambitions are as clear as they seem at first. In other words, are there ambiguities in these texts which have an impact on the situation? The other question is what activities the EU is pursuing to reach its objectives. It's not enough that the intentions are good (in line with EU values). A successful development policy must also show reasonable results. Therefore, the choice of strategies and instruments, as well as the design of the implementing organization, are of great importance. This concerns the foundations of the high ambitions.

Additional Goals of the EU

There are further policy documents of relevance in the European Union. The most important in this context is the Africa strategy, which I will discuss in the next chapter. Of importance is also the Action plan on Human Rights and Democracy (EU 2020e), which includes a list of specific ambitions for the EU. It overlaps with the SDGs but is more precise. The headlines are the following: Protecting and empowering individuals; Building resilient, inclusive and democratic societies; Promoting a global system for human rights and democracy; New technologies: harnessing opportunities and addressing challenges; and Delivering by working together.

The first two headlines cover many ambitions, including specific human rights for individuals and rights related to democracy and the rule of law. However, possible rights linked to the economic and environmental dimensions of the SDGs receive only limited attention (ibid., section 1.3). Such inconsistencies between policy documents may have an impact on the implementation of the policies of the EU, where each policy may be treated as a "silo," a stand-alone priority, rather than an opportunity for integration and learning across the policy areas.

One explanation for the inconsistencies is the different backgrounds of the UN policies. The Action Plan, the Council Conclusions, through which it was revised (ibid.), and the annual reports on Human Rights and Democracy in the world (EU 2023a) refer to international legal frameworks such as the Human Rights Based Approach (by the UN, based on its declaration on human rights), which has its own history, separate from the SDGs.

The EU documents link to further guidelines within the EU on gender, disabilities, etc. Additional specific details of regulation can be found in the previously mentioned trade agreements with the ACP countries as well as in the framework for the financial instrument used by the EU, the so-called Neighbourhood, Development and International Cooperation Instrument

(NDICI), which I will return to. The latter framework specifies spending targets for various important themes. This most likely focuses the attention on the selected items, while increasing the risk that the more general policy development is neglected.

A question is then if these specific ambitions of the detailed regulations are integrated (Sabourin and Jones 2023). Another question is if they support or limit the ambition to achieve the SDGs, for example in Africa. Ken Godfrey and Richard Youngs argue that there is overall a conflict of various EU policies which limits the promotion of democracy (Godfrey and Youngs 2019, 13). Interestingly, there is an ambitious EU document which aims to link the Human Rights Approach to Sustainable Development (EU 2021).

It must be noted also that the Action Plan for Human Rights and Democracy has the character of a highly specific to-do list, as exemplified in item 2.1i on corruption (EU 2020e):

> Provide comprehensive assistance to prevent and fight against corruption by supporting public administration reform, effective anti-corruption strategies and legal frameworks, including whistle-blowers and witness protection, specialised bodies, parliaments, independent media and civil society, and developing anti-corruption guidelines. Support the ratification and implementation of the UN Convention against Corruption.

The text is obviously more specific than the New European Consensus on Development (above). On the one hand, this implies a stronger priority of certain courses of action. On the other hand, there is a risk that the actions of the EU lose the broad approach of the SDGs, which is open for treating issues together and in context. The priority is a selection of items, such as "supporting public administration reform," which refers to ongoing activities by governments in recipient countries. It may exclude more critical interventions, for example to support civil society actions related to the reform of public administration or to influence the development of public administration more indirectly, such as through trade (below). I will come back to such alternative courses of action.

Another risk is that the specific items limit the analysis of causal mechanisms since the choice is already made. Hence, the combined effect of having a broad and a detailed policy document would be relevant to investigate, to find out if they limit the EU or create opportunities to rethink strategies. It is clear that the complexity of the EU is increased by this mix of policy ambitions. In this context it is the SDGs which give the EU room to develop their strategies and interventions. It is also the SDGs which imply that some issues are more fundamental in that they lay a foundation for background drivers of development, as explained in chapter two. As stated, I will regard political and economic development (peace, partnership, and prosperity in the figure above) as the most important ambitions of the European support for the achievement of the SDGs.

What Does the EU Really Want?

It is unclear how much of the responsibility the EU assumes for the development of other countries. Although the EU's overarching objective is to eradicate poverty, the EU regulation states that the EU's role is (only) to contribute to the recipient countries themselves implementing the SDGs (EU 2015, 4). The difference is very important, as the level of ambition and division of responsibilities is of great importance for the choice of actions by the EU. If the EU assumes great responsibility to improve the development of countries which are dictatorships, for example, it implies a strong role for foreign and security policy. If, on the other hand, the responsibility is limited, or the level of ambition is not specified at all, then the objectives risk losing their guiding role in EU policy. This has great implications: should cooperation be suspended with dictatorships? Should the EU take a clearer stand for democrats, including the opposition in countries with authoritarian leaders? If so, international conventions set limits, creating dilemmas for democratic countries (Sørensen 2011).

Since the target formulations and the New European Consensus on Development (EU 2017) do not specify the role or responsibilities of the EU, they could be considered *ad hoc* responsibilities, not based on generalized principles, despite the elaborated principles in the treaties. The overall objectives of the policy are therefore not as clear as they give an impression of. Specific activities may have clearly specified objectives, while the EU's overall objectives provide great flexibility but weak guidance. This makes it difficult to analyze achievements or efficiency afterwards. It is also difficult to learn over time, to develop the strategies in the light of experience gained.

As touched upon in the previous chapter, political scientists discuss why the EU has chosen these objectives and principles, whether they are aimed at formalizing something that member states already agree on or creating a stronger Europe. A previously mentioned interpretation is that foreign policy aims to support cohesion among member states (Bickerton 2011). Major steps have been taken to increase cohesion and create stronger "actorness" within the EU. The EU is in a sense a moving target, in the ongoing internal debates on how far the European policies should be integrated. Some vagueness can be excused but may also be a barrier to achieving the objectives.

There is furthermore a discussion that political objectives may have other purposes than what is stated in the texts. With development policy, there may be domestic political motives to attract altruistic voters, especially if a government also supports opposing interests, such as the export of the defense industry. Foreign policy can affect the balance between the left and the right within the same political party. This applies to national policies and may also apply to the European situation. For some countries, historical ties with former colonies and/or vulnerable geographical locations with large flows of migrants are also relevant (Haglund Morrisey 2016, 271).

As mentioned above, some researchers believe that policies articulate goals which cannot be achieved but aim to create a positive image of the policy and the politicians (Brunsson 2007). The latter underlines the need to analyze what the EU is doing in practice to achieve its objectives.

Even without taking self-centered motives into account, the situation is more complicated than the policy documents relevant to development policy indicate. There are, for example, additional ambitions of the European Union, which are official but not clearly formulated in the Treaties. Such an ambition is mentioned in the new Africa strategy (next chapter), where cooperation with African countries is partly about cooperating globally, in particular at the UN (EU 2020). The Africa strategy suggests an alliance aimed at promoting common affairs within international organizations, which is a foreign policy strategy.

African countries are thus beneficiaries of EU action in Africa as well as partners at the global level, which opens up for a discussion of whether the two roles are fully compatible. On the basis of the values and goals expressed in the treaties, it is reasonable to see development aid policy and global cooperation as forms of partnership. However, the Africa strategy contains demands on the African countries to comply with the EU's will in migration and security policy (below). In other words, the general picture of all relations with African countries is more multifaceted (cf. Bengtsson and Elgström 2012).

A conclusion is that coherence is either sacrificed or given a very limited meaning. It is close at hand to consider whether the EU has a meta-strategy which integrates its strategies in different areas, for example whether commitments to others in one context can be rewards for the desired behavior in a different context. The EU Global Strategy (EU 2016) aims to apply to all policy areas but is generally vague.

The Perspective of the Recipients

Before proceeding with the analysis of the EU it is relevant to comment on the perspective of the recipients. It is fair to assume that developing countries and their citizens want to move in the direction set out in the SDGs, especially as several of the goals are carefully formulated to avoid conflict. All governments have agreed to the goals and that is partly why the EU has made the goals their own, in the internal as well as external context. The African Union, which is the main partner organization in Africa, has similar objectives in its strategy, which runs until 2063 (African Union Commission 2015). In addition, the African Union has defended democratic values when individual countries have experienced regime change that violates their own constitutional rules (Hackenesch, Leininger, and Mross 2020, 5).

Opinion polls show that there is strong support for democracy among the population of African countries. The Afrobarometer surveys show that more than two-thirds of Africans prefer democracy to other forms of government and that over 70 percent reject autocracy and one-man rule (Gyimah-Boadi 2019, quoted in Hackenesch, Leininger, and Mross 2020, 6). More than half believe that it is better to have a government that can be held accountable than to have one that is effective (ibid.), which is a key issue in the choice between democracy and autocracy. This is particularly noteworthy in view of the fact that the majority of Africans live in countries which are classified as "electoral autocracies," that is, countries with elections which are rigged and where the political debate is limited in different ways.

Similar results were shown in large surveys already 20 years ago. The analysis of Afrobarometer data showed that support for democracy and the market economy was based on citizens' knowledge, independent thinking, and experience, rather than having to do with cultural values or structural circumstances (Bratton, Mattes, and Gyimah-Boadi 2005, 10). The experience of Africans is more important to their opinions than what they learn in school, but the history of the countries has some significance, especially if there have been more democratic periods with several political parties (ibid.).

The numbers are interesting as a basis for continued democracy support. They show that there is a strong African interest, that it is not the outside world that wants to impose western values on Africans. They are also interesting because external support for democracy has proven to be most effective if the recipients have already achieved a certain minimum amount of democracy (Hackenesch, Leininger, and Mross 2020, 7).

At the same time, it cannot be ruled out that national leaders have other objectives, such as preserving autocratic or religious rule, even if they have signed up to the SDGs. One example is Rwandan leader Paul Kagame, who has made a name for himself for working against corruption and for taking part in coups d'état in his own country and two neighboring countries. Other examples are leaders of strongly religious countries who have also signed up to the SDGs in spite of national regulations which are not fully compatible with the SDGs. It is clear that they do not interpret all the goals in the same way as Europeans do (with variation even in the European interpretations).

Although there is a general consensus, it is natural that the leaders of the recipient countries have their own ideas about cooperation with the EU and other donors. In the discussion on the EU's Africa strategy, there are researchers who have taken upon themselves to formulate positions for the African Union, when the AU has not presented its own position (chapter five). Such contributions to the debate are interesting because they point to possible shortcomings in the EU proposals, for example where actions and impact can be interpreted in different ways. The comments contribute to a comprehensive view of the matters. Interestingly, some of these researchers also express a wish that the EU should help the AU solve fundamental problems, such as holding general elections in African countries and getting African governments to implement what the AU has decided (Tadesse Abebe and Maalim 2020).

A number of international agreements in the twenty-first century have aimed to strengthen the recipient countries in relation to donors. Among other things, it is a question of coordinating the efforts of many donors to make the situation easier to handle for the recipients. The EU has been a promoter of the principle of the recipients' ownership of development aid but does not always live up to it. The problems are partly due to the fact that development aid is governed on the basis of objectives and results, which can lead to excessive measurement of short-term efforts, which in practice leads to fragmentation of efforts (Yanguas 2018). This is a fundamental problem with policies defined in terms of goals, which I will come back to.

In addition, there is criticism that the rich countries of the wealthy North are overtaking the poor countries of the South by advocating global regulation despite proposals for African alternatives. This applies to security policy ("Pax Africana"), economic cooperation, and the possibility of having an African Criminal Court instead of the International Criminal Court (ICC). Rita Kiki Edozie highlights several of these African initiatives and how they can be interpreted (Edozie 2014).

A related question is whether other countries are competing with or even working against the ambitions of EU development policy. While countries such as China, Russia, Iran, and Saudi Arabia have endorsed the SDGs, they have ambitions and values which point in directions other than those of the EU. Research has highlighted the need to analyze the EU's efforts in relation to countries pushing in a different direction (Babayan and Risse 2015). I will come back to the relationship with China.

ORGANIZATION AND DECISION-MAKING

As I have touched upon, the broad policies aimed at poor countries and poor people are organized in several Directorates-General of the Commission, the main executive power of the EU, while the Common foreign and defense policy is dealt with by the Council, where the member states meet. Coordination takes place in Brussels through the European External Action Service (EEAS) and locally in the recipient countries through the EU Delegations (EUD). In addition, there are policies pursued by the Member States on their own, more or less coordinated with the EU policies. In Brussels, Council working groups—where the member states deliberate with each other and with the Commission—are important for the evolution and coordination of new strategies.

The background to the complex organization is that development policy has emerged as part of the economic policy core of the EU, as described in the previous chapter. Like trade policy, development policy has been complementary to the internal market, originally aimed at the former colonies of the member states. Foreign policy has been adopted later and originally without any competences transferred to the Commission. In legal terms, the first are supranational, while the latter is intergovernmental, meaning that the member states decide by consensus on a case-by-case basis.

The task of coordinating the policies falls with the previously mentioned High Representative, who since 2009 is also Vice-President of the Commission (HRVP). The HRVP is often described as "double hatted," since the two roles are very different, with one intergovernmental role (HR) and one supranational role (VP), placing the burden of coordination very much on one person, with the support of the EEAS. The requirement for coherence is partly a response to the context of the complex division of responsibilities between the member states, the Council, and the Commission. The Parliament is involved in deciding on budgets and regulations, etc. Much of the work is conducted in the Council working groups, by representatives of the member states.

The relationship with the member states is complicated since each country has its own development policy, often with agencies and other organizations which have strong positions and long experience of pursuing aid policy in a certain way. This is difficult for the EU to handle, as it is in federal countries where states have their own policy mandates. The general rules for the EU are vague in this respect, stating partly contradictory principles, that there should be respect for the diversity of member states, as well as loyalty to the common EU policy, which creates a general dilemma and a need for a trade-off for the EU (TEU Article 4).

Internal Coherence

EU development policy is managed by three DGs in the Commission, as indicated before. One is responsible for relations with the countries close to Europe, the so-called neighborhood policy (DG NEAR). Another is responsible for humanitarian aid (DG ECHO) while a third is responsible for the rest of development aid (DG INTPA, formerly DG DEVCO). Humanitarian aid is seen as an independent part, focusing on immediate crises and gaining the confidence of the outside world by not being an instrument for achieving other objectives. A common description is that they are "in, but out" i.e., in the policy portfolio, but operating on its own. Between the other two, there is a greater need to coordinate efforts, for example within the framework of the EU Africa Strategy, which relates to North African countries (DG NEAR) as well as to Sub-Saharan countries (DG INTPA).

Development policy has close relations with some other policy areas and DGs. Two were described above. Foreign and security policy is of great importance for long-term relations with other countries and for the management of crises, while trade policy is of great importance for the economic relations with other countries. In addition, there are several other policy areas with some relations or even conflicts with development policy. One is agricultural policy, which is important for developing countries by regulating the access to the EU's internal market. Policy areas with international ambitions include economic policy, research policy, and environmental policy. Some of these are part of the EU strategy towards Africa (next chapter).

The coordination ("coherence") of policies has been a major issue for development policy. The term "nexus" is used to describe the intersection of policy areas such as development aid, security, and migration (Furness and Gänzle 2017). Much of the discussion is about cooperation and synergies, but also about tensions between the ambitions of policy areas.

In the local implementation of EU policies, the so-called joint programming between the member states and the Commission is of great importance. Local action is in principle governed by country strategy papers, which have been developed in dialogue between the policy areas. In practice, the local EU Delegations are of great importance for the implementation of policies. An ongoing struggle concerns how much room they should have to adapt the policy instruments to local conditions. The reports on these country strategies are often negative. For example, researchers who had access to the documents wrote that for the periods 2002–2007 and 2008–2013, actors in the recipient countries were not involved in the design of these country strategy papers (Carbone 2013, 486). Furthermore, the joint programming is difficult to achieve (Carbone 2017).

Ongoing research highlights the general problem of managing complex organizations. Part of this is that the policy areas often have their own perspectives on activities, which has to do with internal cultures and differences in scientific perspectives. Policy areas recruit from different organizations (including borrowed/seconded national experts) and cooperate with different academic disciplines. As mentioned before, the policy areas in fact operate as separate and rivalrous groups, referred to as epistemic communities (Haas 1992). One hypothesis is therefore that it may be easier to cooperate across similar policy units ("silos") at national and international level than with other EU policy units. This means that there may be relevant lines of conflict in the implementation of policies between policy areas, as well as between the institutions, member states, or political parties.

Local Implementation

Planning and local implementation follow the budgetary periods, which means that planning began in 2018 for the long-term budget for 2021–2027. A new Commission took office in the fall of 2019, following elections to the European Parliament in the spring of 2019. The focus of the work is governed, inter alia, by letters of instruction given to each Commissioner by the Commission President Ursula von der Leyen and the mandate given to each Directorate-General.

A major change in the current budget is the merger of several financial instruments into the previously mentioned Neighborhood, Development and International Cooperation Instrument (NDICI). The aim was to create flexibility in the use of money, to adapt the instruments to the specific situation in each local context. A previously mentioned risk is that money for development aid will be used for broader purposes. Most notably, the former independent European Development Fund (EDF) has become incorporated into the budget. The Fund was previously used for the ACP countries, linked to the specific agreements that existed with them, such as the Cotonou Agreement. In the new budget, some earmarking remains, while flexibility has increased. An early assessment of the new budgetary process is that it has a more analytical approach than before, with the aim, among other things, of adapting efforts better to the situation in the recipient countries (Herrero 2018).

It is too early to draw conclusions on the effects of the new instrument, but it is interesting to learn from the experience of earlier ambitions to coordinate efforts. For the previous long-term budget (2014–2020), there are analyses of the implementation of such initiatives. That budget was the first created after the Treaty of Lisbon in 2009 and the establishment of the EEAS. A highly critical analysis of the planning ("programming") was carried out in 2015 (Herrero et al. 2015).

Overall, the ambition was mainly about reaching a consensus on regional and national plans between the EEAS and DG DEVCO (now DG INTPA). The regulations were new and not so easy for the operative staff to interpret. This concerned several of the important principles of development policy, set out in the policy documents (EU 2017). Firstly, the EU should focus on countries with the greatest need, while other policy documents added countries where good results can be achieved, which may be two conflicting norms, as discussed above. Furthermore, the priority should be on democracy and human rights as well as sustainable and inclusive growth, with 20 percent of the funds in social development. It was also stressed that bilateral aid should be limited to three areas (sectors) per country. The need to coordinate efforts was emphasized (Herrero et al. 2015, 8).

Following agreement on the budget with the member states, it was established that 84 percent of the funds should be used for national and regional plans ("NIP and RIP"). The allocation of funds to individual countries should follow quantitative criteria, including performance measures, but left a wide range of policy considerations (ibid., 13ff). This had the adverse effect of making it unclear what the subsequent decisions were based on and whether the EU wanted to reward the recipients for certain behavior (ibid.). Such vagueness in the implementation can easily destroy the intended transparency of the principles set out at the beginning of the process.

The planning process began with the EEAS and DG DEVCO establishing common guidelines for the EU delegations' proposals for country strategies but also giving conflicting information on the supporting documents they wanted to be submitted (ibid., 22). Subsequently, the EU Delegations were expected to carry out analyses and consult their host countries. The planning in 2013 was complicated by the fact that negotiations on the budget took longer time than intended, creating a need for temporary solutions (ibid.). There was some criticism of the division of roles between the EEAS and DG DEVCO, which was new after the Treaty of Lisbon (ibid., 24ff).

The 2015 report shows that the guidelines were followed, but with some unexpected results. The priority areas were broad and it turned out that the more specific priorities were in sustainable agriculture and energy (ibid., 29f). In practice, the focus was not as clear as intended, since the planning followed other guidelines on prioritizing, for example, food safety (ibid., 30). The theme of democracy was difficult to evaluate, partly because the objective of good governance is included in many areas (ibid., 35ff). The principle of limiting country strategies to three areas was broadly followed. However, the preliminary evaluation indicated that the choice of areas was rarely based on a needs analysis or the desire to coordinate with the member states' efforts. Instead, it followed the EU's overarching priorities.

These are severe criticisms, even if one allows for some slack in the implementation phase. They indicate a mismatch between the highly elaborated principles and the muddled implementation, suggesting that the EU needs to find a better balance and to learn more from experience.

The evaluation showed that the learning from experience was weak, since the majority of country strategies did not make use of previous experience or evaluations (ibid., 44f). A criticism was that the country strategies were not anchored in good analyses of the national context (ibid., 49). The reasons for this include the absence of a method of analyzing the development programs and the context of recipient countries, the absence of EU-wide strategy papers for the various countries ("joint framework documents") and the prohibition of hiring external consultants to carry out strategic analysis (Political Economy Analysis, PEA; ibid. 49f, cf Copestake and Williams 2014).

These points are clear limitations of the EU policies, while it can't be ruled out that local representatives of the EU with long experience can find ways to improve the effectiveness in particular situations. The EU ambition is to build a system which has the capacity to select appropriate instruments in each country, rather than to base its choices on personal experience, i.e., non-formal, unarticulated ("tacit") knowledge.

Not only was coordination within the EU ("horizontal") limited, but so was coordination with the recipients and other donors ("vertically"). There was some criticism that the recipient countries were not treated as owners of the operations, despite a requirement that each recipient country appoint a responsible liaison officer ("national authorizing officer," NAO; ibid., 50ff). There was also criticism that it was difficult to coordinate donor efforts, within the EU and with others (ibid., 54ff). Joint programming with the member states was in some cases perceived as very difficult to carry out in addition to other coordination (ibid., 57). The implication is that the EU tries to coordinate in too many directions at the same time, which leads to lack of coordination and a stronger influence by particular individuals in the local context.

The authors of the report were critical of the idea of streamlining by focusing on sectors. They instead pointed to thematic planning, across sectoral boundaries, in countries such as Denmark, Sweden, and Finland (ibid., 67ff).

The report cautiously warned that the new governance and follow-up system would not work, as there was a lack of capacity to carry out proper local analyses that go beyond inputs, outputs, and impacts. According to the authors of the report, this must be anchored in an analysis of the national contexts and so-called theories of change which give a reasonable picture of the complex relationships between interventions and can be improved over time (ibid., 76). This is particularly relevant when development aid is only part of the overall investment in developing countries (ibid.). This is a key observation in the report, which clearly shows that the foundations of the EU ambitions are weak and points to a solution in terms of "theories of change" (chapter six).

Furthermore, the report warned that staff cuts cannot be met only with formal systems for disseminating knowledge among employees (Learning and Knowledge Management Strategy, LKMS; ibid., 66, EU 2014). Rather, priorities are needed to set the level of ambition in EU development policy (ibid., 75).

In conclusion, the description of the implementation is devastating, showing several aspects of "high ambitions and weak implementation." The message is that the official aims and ambitions are not carried out in the local contexts. The reason is that the EU is unable to design a machinery of implementation to carry out its specific decisions. These ambiguities and contradictions are of great interest to the analysis of the EU policies.

It should be said in comment that the problems are to some extent shared with other policies which are complex, at the national level as well as in international cooperation. However, tensions are problematic for a policy aimed to achieve certain effects in other countries, which implies a focus on the means to reach the ends. It is reasonable to ask whether small adjustments in the choice of objectives and means are sufficient, or whether there is reason to reformulate the objectives and/or choose other means of implementation (cf. Delputte and Orbie 2020). The following analysis may contribute to such a discussion.

Three Coordination Projects

Further examples of local implementation problems can be found in relation to three specific pilot activities aimed at coordinating actions between policy areas (DGs). These experiments have in common that they deal with crises and fragile states, which has been done through a Trust Fund for Africa launched in 2015 and through the so-called Sahel Alliance of five African countries in 2017. In addition, in the same year, a special pilot study was carried out on the theme of operationalization of the humanitarian-development nexus. To understand the internal rivalry of policies as well as models of coordination, it is interesting to note that the initiatives have been taken by different bodies in the European system: the Commission, some member states, and the Council, respectively.

An early analysis showed the need for coordination and pointed to the strengths and weaknesses of the three initiatives (Jones and Mazzara 2018). The three experimental activities contributed in different ways to linking actions across several DGs and with member states' efforts, but none of the three lived up to the high expectations of integrated field activities (ibid.). The evaluation identified classical problems in cross-organizational coordination, including difficulties in bringing rules and procedures into practice (even with strong political backing), conflicting requests from member states to be part of the joint actions and at the same time their desire to profile themselves, and a negative side-effect of the new coordination, the bypass of established coordination and anchoring procedures (ibid., 13f). Other effects of the new forms of coordination were that local actors had difficulty in developing ownership, that existing cooperation activities were not involved in the new projects and that communication between Brussels and the field activities was poorly developed (ibid., 14).

The observations indicate that coordination is much easier said than done, to put it politely. They show mixed motives (to be included and to be independent) and counter-finality, that the solutions to the early problems create new problems, suggesting that it is difficult to control coordination from a central perspective. A possible interpretation is that the local actors need to learn over time how to approach the goal of coordination. I will discuss in chapter seven how a focus on relations may help guide some similar situations. What is clear, is that the EU policy documents such as the New European Consensus on Development (EU 2017) overstate the ability of the EU to reach its high ambitions. These documents state intentions without commenting on the large problems of implementation, as if the EU wants to hide the true state of its policy implementation.

Another judgment of coherence was given by Maurizio Carbone, who argued in an earlier analysis of policy coordination that views on the three key policy areas (development, foreign, and trade policy) and their potentially overlapping ambitions have changed over time. On the one hand, the EU opened up trade from poor countries through the principle of free access to the European market for "Everything but arms" but, on the other hand, the EU pursued strong positions of principle and vested interests within the WTO, which has made it more difficult for poor countries to export to the EU (Carbone 2013, 490). In terms of security and development, according to Carbone, the impact seems to go mostly from security to development, while representatives of development policy do not affect security policy as much (ibid.). As regards the overlap with foreign policy, the EU shows both examples of power politics towards Africa and partnerships in global strategies such as MDG (ibid.). This shows ambiguities or even contradictions at a high level of policy coordination, adding difficulties to the picture of local implementation.

Carbone points out that fragmentation within the EU makes it easier for developing countries to influence the EU (Carbone 2013, 493). In other words, internal divisions make the EU a weaker party than it would be as a more cohesive player. The implication is to simplify policies or streamline them further. A focus on relations would bring out the logic of the situation (below).

Problems with Coherence and Leadership

The focus on coherence seems like a reasonable strategy to handle the great variety of policies in the EU and its member states. At the same time, it is a simplistic solution to the tensions and conflicts over goals in the EU. The impression given by the document on Policy Coherence for Development is that development policy will always take over and that it is always clear what such a priority entails. An alternative to policy coherence would be to settle issues on a case-by-case basis or even to emphasize the internal dialogue over conflicting priorities. Such differences of opinion are built into government offices, which implies that coherence is an unattainable goal, perhaps a necessary fiction in a large bureaucracy. There is a risk that "coherence" becomes a barrier to finding smart trade-offs by concealing the diversity of opinions. Camille Adelle and Andrew Jordan show some of the difficulties in the bureaucratic procedures to reach coherence (Adelle and Jordan 2014).

Critics argue that the idea of internal coordination has become a "fetish" or a "Holy Grail" which crowds out more substantial issues (Delputte and Orbie 2020, 144). Sarah Delputte and Jan Orbie argue that the EU lacks a proper strategy, apart from adopting the UN objectives and promoting internal coordination (ibid., 148). There isn't, according to them, a discussion about the basics of politics because " . . . the obsession with coordination and the bureaucratic procedures for its implementation, as well as the current dominant discourse of coordination to strengthen the EU's external action impact, obstructs substantive discussions on what constitutes 'development' and how relations between the 'North' and 'South' should be structured" (ibid., 151f).

The alternative strategy advocated by Sarah Delputte and Jan Orbie is that the EU should become more of a forum for learning and discussion between the actors involved, that is, devote more time to bottom-up coordination than from above (ibid., 155). They put forward several arguments in this regard. One is that coordination in Brussels becomes too general and takes too little account of the context of the various recipient countries, which becomes a kind of exercise of power by the EU (ibid., 150f). Another argument is that coordination within the EU becomes technocratic (apolitical) and ignores the differences in perspective between member states, which can be relevant as well as driving new solutions. A third argument is that coordination at the European level hinders coordination between like-minded countries and the coordination which should take place at global level (ibid., 152f).

The three arguments need to be examined more closely, yet they raise the fundamental question of how an organization can balance coordination and coherence with diversity and local adaptation. If coherence is an unattainable goal, diversity runs the opposite risk of undermining strategies through contradictory behavior. This is again a fundamental dilemma of all political systems, of finding a balance between common principles (uniformity) and local adaptation (autonomy).

The dilemma goes to the heart of leadership in the EU. There is by necessity many wills in a large and diverse organization, which is coordinated in technocratic (managerial) ways as well as political (value-based) ways. A tentative implication is that the highly complex issues demand more elaborate forms of learning over time, providing more analysis and better opportunities to digest the information and form common opinions across the EU (Serban 2022). I will come back to some further suggestions.

Another observation, which is interesting regardless of whether one agrees with the criticism, is that the EU has shifted its focus in policy coordination. As I discussed in chapter three, Delputte and Orbie show that the ambition around the turn of the millennium was to achieve more effective aid, which has gradually been replaced by a focus on more effective foreign policy (ibid. 145ff, Carbone 2013; Bergmann et al. 2019). This means, quite plainly, that foreign policy has taken over and is now dominating over development policy. The follow-up question is whether this is good or bad. From a development policy perspective, it can be useful if it is considered that a broader set of instruments from more policy areas is needed to achieve the objectives of development policy.

A key question is how to deal with the development aid budget being used to handle issues which lie in the borderlands with other policy areas. More specifically, the criticism is that the aid budget is being eroded, that member states should allocate new appropriations to finance the broader missions (Delputte and Orbie 2020, 154). At the same time, there seems to be a consensus that it is difficult to solve the specific tasks of development policy (poverty reduction), without a broader set of instruments and thus coordination within the broader external policies.

ACTIVITIES BY THE EU

To understand the ambiguities and contradictions of the EU policies, it is necessary to describe in more detail what the instruments are. The EU and the member states are implementing a wide range of measures to solve urgent problems and to influence the long-term development of many developing countries. Eighty countries receive humanitarian aid, while 120 countries receive development aid (EU 2020a). The actions financed and implemented by the Commission are presented in summary form in annual reports and special comprehensive reports on the whole of operations every three years. Some reports are focused on Policy Coherence for Development (PCD) and in 2023 the EU published its first report on how the EU contributes to the fulfillment of the SDGs within and outside of its member states (EU 2023).

I will first describe the actions through the categories used in the financial statements and then broken down into the themes used to describe development policy. Lastly I will give some examples of the complex situations the

EU is involved in, which connects to the more general analysis in chapter six of drivers and barriers for development in the recipient countries.

Financial Statements

The annual report of the external financial instruments gives a rough picture of how the money has been spent. In 2019, a total of approximately EUR 15 billion was allocated to different purposes and beneficiary countries (EU 2020a). Interestingly, more themes are used in the annual report than the five areas starting with the letter P (above). The SDGs are part of a larger theme called "Delivering on global commitments,," which also includes humanitarian aid, together with the theme "The EU: A strong global actor" (on peace, security, and institution-building). A chapter on global priorities discusses seven areas of intervention, with great room for the recently presented European Green Deal. Much of the content overlaps with the PCD 2019 report (below), but the section on collaboration on technology and innovation is given more space. Another chapter gives examples of efforts on different continents.

The table appendices show how the money has been spent, including the various instruments that existed during the last budgetary period. Since 2021, these have been merged into the broader Neighborhood, Development and International Cooperation Instrument (NDICI). For the 2021–2027 budget period (seven years), EUR 79.5 billion has been allocated (OECD 2021).

The EU in total (institutions and member states) is the largest donor in the world with USD 76.1 billion in 2020 (OECD 2021). The figures below come from the Organization of Economic Cooperation and Development (OECD), whose Development Assistance Committee (DAC) collects and publishes data on aid policy in all its Member States and that of the EU institutions. The funding profile gives a rough picture of the EU's priorities in terms of who gets what.

The EU institutions (excluding the member states) were the third largest donor in the world in 2020 with USD 19.4 billion. This was a sharp increase from 2019 due to, among other things, the Covid-19 pandemic. All member states contribute via the membership fee to the EU, while many countries make additional contributions.

Most of the assistance from the EU institutions is distributed in the form of bilateral support, but one fifth is given to multilateral organizations, in particular various UN agencies, in the form of earmarked support. Of what was distributed by the EU in 2019, almost 60 (58.3) percent constituted program support to specific countries. Humanitarian aid accounted for 12.5 percent, administration 4.3 percent, NGO support 0.1 percent and "other" 24.8 percent. About a quarter were provided in the form of loans from the European

Investment Bank (EIB) and the European Bank for Reconstruction and Development (EBRD).

Bilateral aid in 2019 went mainly to African countries (42 percent), Europe (21.6 percent) and Asia. Just under 30 percent went to the ten largest recipient countries, which were countries in the eastern and southern neighborhoods. Turkey was by far the largest recipient country, with just over USD 1.4 billion. Egypt followed, with about half the sum, then Morocco and Syria. Ukraine and Serbia were some of the ten largest beneficiaries. No sub-Saharan African countries were among the top 10 recipients.

Divided into groups of countries, the poorest countries received 23.1 percent of EU funds. The largest share, 27.5 percent, went to the lower middle-income countries (LMIC). About a fifth went to upper middle-income countries (UMIC) and a few percent went to the other low-income countries (LIC). At the same time, 27.8 percent was allocated thematically, which was then distributed among beneficiary countries, of which about a third is estimated to have gone to the poorest countries.

By far, the largest share in 2019 (40.6 percent) in terms of the OECD's categories was for social infrastructure and services. The main posts were support for governments and civil society, water and sewerage, and education. The second largest category was for economic infrastructure and services with the largest item "financial and business services." Just under 60 percent of bilateral aid had a gender profile, while around 35 percent had an environmental profile.

This can be compared with that of Sweden and other member states. There are major differences between member states within the EU. Sweden was the country that provided the most aid in relation to GNI (1.14 percent) and sixth most in absolute terms with USD 6.3 billion. Just under $4 billion constituted bilateral aid. Germany was the largest donor in the EU of bilateral aid in absolute terms (USD 22.5 billion), followed by France (USD 9.5 billion), Sweden and the Netherlands (just under USD 4 billion each), and Italy (USD 2.2 billion). The five largest donors accounted for almost 80 percent of aid, while another group of 15 EU countries provided only a total of 4 percent of total EU aid (Karlsson and Tallberg 2021).

Olof Karlsson and Jonas Tallberg have analyzed the profiles of the member states to see who is similar to Sweden ("Nordic Plus") and who has a clearly different profile. In their analysis, the Netherlands and Finland are most similar to Sweden, followed by Belgium, Denmark, Ireland, and Italy. The similarities concern characteristics such as a high level of aid, a focus on Africa and the poorest countries, the development of administration, gender equality, and the environment. Germany and France have broader profiles, which can be explained by their higher levels of expenditure. The small and new member states have significantly lower levels of expenditure and prioritize other areas than Sweden does (Karlsson and Tallberg 2021, 30f).

Thematic Description

The EU provides a comprehensive description of its efforts in the reports on Policy Coherence for Development (PCD), which in addition to the financial measurements include policy initiatives of various kinds. The latest report covers the period 2015–2018 and is divided according to the five concepts starting with P, summarizing the UN Sustainable Development Goals and the European Development Assistance Agreement (EU 2019). The report is interesting since it shows the wide range of efforts made by the Commission (often in conjunction with the member states) and also shows indirectly the need to cooperate across policy areas.

There is also a recent report to the UN, a so-called voluntary review of activities by the EU related to the SDGs (EU 2023). This includes descriptions of activities to influence the global achievement of the SDG, for each of the goals. The report suffers from the same limitations as the earlier report, that it is focused on inputs rather than outputs or outcomes, i.e., what the EU does rather than its impact on Africa. There are two short appendices which open for a more analytical approach, including short points on achievements and challenges as well as comments from stakeholders.

The five Ps of the 2019 report provide an easier overview, in line with the policy goals as expressed in the policy document New European Consensus of Development (EU 2017). Table 4.1 summarizes the activities under each of the five Ps, which are indications of the focus but is of course not enough to understand the underlying idea of what is to be achieved and how this should be done in the local contexts.

It's hard to evaluate these activities without going into detail. A first impression is that the EU is making a variety of efforts which can live up to its ambition to contribute to poor countries achieving the SDGs and thus eradicating poverty. All the efforts seem laudable, but the more interesting follow-up questions are about the design and implementation of the activities, to be able to say something about their contribution to the long-term development of individual countries. A complement would be to carry out an analysis per recipient country. In the next chapter, I will discuss overall problems with the selection of measures and in chapter six I will raise some questions about adapting to the needs of the recipients.

There are indications in the Africa strategy (next chapter) that there are reasons to question the individual priorities, where researchers and interest groups have made comments on tensions between the various ambitions and that the official documents downplay the problems that exist. The discussion

Table 4.1 Summary of activities by the EU under its five themes. Source: EU 2019.

Theme	*Activities by the EU*
People	Food security: revisions of European agricultural policy and a directive on unfair trading practices between companies in food production
	Health: support to global organizations for vaccination against a number of diseases
	Migration: The European Agenda on Migration, an agreement with African countries on a declaration (the Valetta Declaration) and the accompanying action plan and the establishment of a European Trust Fund for Africa to finance its implementation, as well as various support to African countries to tackle the root causes of forced migration, including support for jobs for youth, the creation of border control organizations and cheaper means of sending money (remittances) to African countries. Furthermore, measures against trafficking, including civilian and military operations (CSDP missions and operations), are financed with a specific action plan against trafficking and a special anti-trafficking coordinator.
Planet	A clean planet for all-policy
	A decision that at least 20 percent of the EU budget, including development aid, should be used for climate-related measures
	Regional programs for "switch to green" in developing countries
	Cooperation with the UN, G7, and G20
	A policy document on International Ocean Governance
	Rules on combatting fishing which is illegal, unreported, and unregulated (IUU)
	An action plan against the smuggling of wild plants and animals
Prosperity	Open markets for exports from developing countries through the Scheme of Generalized Tariff Preferences (GSP)
	A Trade for all-strategy and related bilateral and regional free trade agreements, with sections on sustainable development and offers of financial support
	Support for the development of national tax systems, including through an External Strategy for Effective Taxation as well as a "Collect More, Spend Better" strategy for developing countries
	International agreements on common rules for the taxation of companies
	Transparency rules in tax advice
	An external investment plan to mobilize private resources to developing countries
	Africa-European Alliance for Sustainable Investment and Jobs
Peace	Support for the development of democracy, human rights, and good governance through political dialogues and support from a European Instrument for Democracy and Human Rights and a related action plan
	Proposal for a European Peace Facility for enhanced support and cooperation on conflict resolution

Theme	Activities by the EU
	Coordinated security, development, and humanitarian support measures, including Elements for an EU-wide strategic framework to support the Security Sector Reform, Joint Framework on countering hybrid threats and The instrument contributing to Stability and Peace
	A strategic approach to resilience in the EU's external action with a so-called integrated approach (between policy areas) to the complex problems
	Partnership with the G5 Sahel (Burkina Faso, Chad, Mali, Mauretania, and Niger)
	Support for the building of the rule of law and the restriction of the illicit arms trade
Partnership	Internal coordination within the Commission, including through ex-ante evaluations, coordination with EU Delegations in the countries concerned and their coordination with actors in each country (with comments on the context in which discussions are taking place)
	Examples of what is being done by Parliament, the Council, and the member states (with examples in the rest of the text)

above of the need for local coordination also indicates problems with the implementation of the EU policies.

Examples of Activities and Challenges

The following are some limited examples of activities and problems related to the first four themes, which focus on needs in recipient countries. The aim is to show some connections between EU activities and the overall objectives of eradicating poverty and achieving the SDGs. This links to the analysis in chapter six.

The theme of Peace includes activities for peace and conflict resolution, which may be the most fundamental measure for influencing the development of recipient countries. The EU is making extensive efforts in this area, alongside the UN and individual donor countries, such as France. Several analyses point to problems in the implementation of these operations. Academic literature discusses the causes of the African conflicts, which often consist of a mixture of poverty and religion. Terrorism and organized crime also have to do with this, as does the influence of major powers with values other than those of the EU.

At the global level, the UN has a mandate to intervene at the risk of war between countries and at the risk of national conflicts. There is a debate about extending the UN mandate, but it is difficult to agree globally. For the EU, it is a question of long-term cooperation with poor countries to help them solve their problems, also with an ambition to limit the flow of refugees to Europe.

In recent years, much of the focus has been on developing the EU's capacity to deal with crises in Europe and elsewhere in the world. Among other things, the problems of coordinating actions between member states and policy areas are widely discussed. Given the EU's decentralized structure, it is hardly surprising that critics find many opportunities for improvement (Bertelsmann Stiftung 2019).

An important contribution by the EU has been the financing of the African Peace Facility (APF). APF consists of one organization and two types of operations. The organization is called the African Peace and Security Architecture (APSA) and is a collaborative effort between the African Union (AU) and eight regional economic organizations since 2002. Its decision-making council is part of the African Union (AU). The operations financed consist of peace support operations and rapid response operations within what is known as the Early Response Mechanism (ERM).

The EU's involvement is part of the Joint African-European Strategy (JAES) 2007, with a legal basis in the Cotonou Agreement. Other countries and organizations co-finance the operations, while the EU has set limits on the type of costs that can be financed (EU 2019, 9). The EU has contributed EUR 2.5 billion over the period 2004–2018 (ibid., 10), but only a small part may be financed from development funds under the OECD guidelines. An evaluation in 2017 pointed to the risk that the APF is too dependent on EU funding (ibid., 13).

In 2018, seven peacekeeping operations were carried out. A total of 14 operations have been carried out in 19 countries since 2004. Each operation has its own mix of activities and forms of funding (ibid., 15ff). Two efforts were made within the ERM. In addition, APF invested in capacity building, which was evaluated by the European Court of Auditors in 2018 (ibid., 21).

Part of the conflict resolution effort is about getting groups to live in peaceful coexistence and accepting the sovereignty of the government. The problem is particularly great in Africa, where land borders were drawn without regard to national identities. Today, countries often consist of many ethnic groups, which in turn can be found in several countries. The situation differs across the African continent where, for example, Tanzania is described as a country which managed to create a common identity, while Kenya is often mentioned as a country where ethnic identities have become stronger and more conflictual over time. Burundi illustrates a situation with peaceful co-existence of ethnic groups under a model similar to "consociationalism" in the Netherlands, which means that the ethnic groups have some autonomy and self-rule (Lemarchand 2006). The latter is possibly an example that the EU can be a model for African countries, but otherwise these factors are difficult issues for outsiders to influence.

Conflict management efforts are close to state building efforts. Conflicts often take place in fragile, weak, or failed states, which have become labels for countries where the government is very weak and is unable to maintain security, law and order, welfare, or legitimate institutions. Often the cause is deep poverty combined with strong power groupings in the form of tribes, clans, and warlords. In some cases there may exist great natural resources (oil, metals, and more) and great wealth of the ruling elite. I will come back to the issue of state building and how the EU can assist.

A third complex of peace-related problems concerns the transition to democracy from all kinds of non-democratic governance, often summed up as authoritarian regimes. Most of the countries in Sub-Saharan Africa have taken steps towards democracy and are described for example as multi-party systems with a dominant party. The implication is that there are elements of democratic governance, such as multi-party elections, but these are limited by authoritarian elements which prevent the opposition from operating freely. Authoritarian leaders cling to power, but it is not a given that the situation would be better if the leaders resigned without preparing for a transition to democracy. The EU is providing democracy support in various forms, to which I will come back.

Relating to the concept of Prosperity there are measures for economic development, which include a wide range of steps, from creating a business-friendly climate to encouraging foreign investments. The emergence of a business elite can be important to stimulate an interest in better regulations. Some economists think of a globalized economy, where African companies gain by being subcontractors to global firms. Other economists believe that a more cooperative type of company can emerge in Africa, within what is known as Africapitalism (Amaeshi, Okupe, and Idemudia 2018).

Aid, trade, and technological development are some instruments with which the EU can influence economic development. High hopes are attached to the African Continental Free Trade Agreement (AfCFTA), of which the EU is a promoter, including a doubling of manufacturing and 14 million new jobs (Byiers, Vanheukelom, and Woolfrey 2018). At the same time, growth must be sustainable in the long term. The concept "Green growth" has been developed to describe some of this. For the EU, the Green Deal has become an important theme, including in development policy and the new Africa strategy (next chapter).

I will just comment briefly on what lies within the concepts Planet and People, that is, environmental policy and welfare arrangements. These are two major areas with a wide range of possible options, where a common concern is to lay the foundations for local policy development in the form of effective and legitimate states which can design and enforce policies, something which the EU is trying to support in different ways. I will come back to the importance of effective states in implementing development strategies in poor countries. The specific policies will differ according to the local situation.

In conclusion, the EU's efforts are reasonable in the sense that what is being done is relevant. There is a lot that needs to be developed in the poor countries and the EU has a broad set of measures which affect most of this. However, there is a risk that the efforts are unfocused and therefore not effective enough. To go further in the analysis, deeper knowledge of the context in which the measures are implemented is needed. How do EU activities affect local dynamics and what do the recipients do? Will there be cooperation on achieving common goals or are any of the parties acting strategically, to achieve their own goals in the first place? And what factors govern the EU's choice of measures? I will touch on some of this in the following.

ANALYSIS AND EVALUATION

There are already many analyses of the whole development policy as well as specific elements of the European policy. I will summarize some of these to show that many of the problems of the EU are actually well known already.

OECD Assessment

A reasonable starting point is with an analysis which takes in all of the relevant EU policies, by someone who broadly agrees with the objectives and ambitions of the European Union. Such friendly comments on the EU policies are made by the OECD, whose Development Assistance Committee (DAC) organizes evaluations of development policy carried out by its member states and the EU. It is the member states who are scrutinizing each other, in this case under the leadership of Canada and Japan, on the basis of a background analysis by the OECD Secretariat, which means that the comments are likely to reflect the views prevailing within the DAC.

The 2018 review praised the EU in some respects and made suggestions for improvements on other things. The initial summary was very positive:

> The European Union (EU) has shown leadership in its efforts to reach global agreements on sustainable development and climate change, as well as in shaping the international humanitarian landscape. Its extensive use of budget support and variety of delivery instruments are enhancing ownership and inclusiveness in partner countries. The EU is also working closely with member states, civil society organizations (CSOs), local authorities and their associations in building global citizenship across Europe (OECD 2018, 1).

In the following text, the OECD pointed at opportunities for improvement in terms of gender equality and the environment, but also in adapting efforts to the priorities of the recipients in migration matters. One comment concerned a lack of coherence in the choice of focus while another concerned the risk of poverty reduction becoming a lower priority with the new EU budgetary instrument NDICI (ibid., 2f).

The OECD praised the EU's trade policy measures but pointed out that some trade and agricultural policies have a negative impact on the recipient countries. There was also criticism that the reporting on policy coherence (PCD) does not describe the whole situation (ibid., 3f), which is remarkable.

With regard to the EU's relatively high proportion of aid channeled through multilateral organizations, the OECD wanted to see a more detailed justification. The EU's efforts to mobilize additional resources through its External Investment Plan were described positively, with the note to adapt the investments to the wishes of the beneficiaries and to coordinate the financial institutions (ibid., 4f).

Joint programming between the member states and the Commission was described as an opportunity for coordination, but with problems in adapting the actions to the national context, which is in line with the comments above. Another part of the planning process which received criticism was the design and use of evaluations at the overall level. The OECD wrote that it was not clear how the collected data contributes to the implementation or the policy learning, which is another remarkable observation. The OECD argued that the EU lacks criteria for assessing value for money and the OECD also wanted to make EU evaluations available to the public (ibid., 5f).

These comments point towards weak mechanisms for policy learning, which I will come back to. The problems have severe consequences and are in line with the theme of high ambitions and weak implementation.

The OECD furthermore warned that EU member states are finding it difficult to live up to the commitment to spend 0.7 percent of GNI on development aid. The reviewers argued that a larger proportion of the money should be spent on the poorest countries, while they also understand that large sums have been given to countries that take in many refugees, including Turkey.

Finally, the OECD considered that the activities were too demanding in its administration and proposed simplifications, such as using the administrative procedures of partner organizations and delegating greater powers to the local EU Delegations. The OECD also warned of skills shortages in the then DG DEVCO (ibid., 6ff).

Niels Keijzer and Simon Maxwell (2019) wrote in a commentary for the European Think Tanks Group (ETTG) that the EU policy must have improved, since the criticism was much harsher in the previous review 20 years ago. They then highlight six of the OECD's comments: that too little money is given to the poorest countries, that too much (27 percent) aid is channeled through the European Investment Bank (EIB), that too much is given without a strategy through multilateral organizations, that the various instruments are not coordinated, that there is a shortage of qualified staff in the EU (as opposed to the situation in the member states), that the administration is too cumbersome and that coherence remains a problem, with a fragmented internal organization, especially as the SDGs require major efforts in addition to development aid. These points are much in line with the analysis presented here, especially the comments on the weak coordination and coherence.

A concluding commentary by Keijzer and Maxwell points out that the Commission's share of aid will decrease if all member states live up to their financial commitments, which, according to the authors, suggests increasing the EU development aid budget to maintain the share given via the EU (ibid.). This statement makes sense under the condition that the Commission prioritizes more valuable activities or is more successful in producing the desired outcomes, neither of which is shown. The statement refers to inputs (spending levels) rather than outputs or outcomes, which is common in the public debate on development aid, i.e., a focus on intentions rather than outcomes.

In conclusion, the OECD is satisfied overall but points to some shortcomings which the EU needs to correct. These are problems the EU can reasonably agree with, since it is mainly about an inability to do what the EU has said that it wants to do. These are difficulties in living up to objectives as well as internal tensions (lack of coordination and learning, as well as a shortage of competence), much in line with other evaluations of EU policy.

Of these challenges, perhaps the criticism of a lack of coordination is the most difficult to handle. On the one hand, there is an explicit ambition in the EU to coordinate all policies, but on the other hand it is difficult to achieve such coordination in an organization with a wide range of activities. This points to the importance of the inner workings of the machinery of the EU, in Brussels as well as in recipient countries. Internal guidelines and procedures are of great importance.

More Fundamental Critique

There is more fundamental criticism of developmental policy, based on evidence from failed states like Afghanistan, Somalia, and Mali. Many countries have been involved in these operations which are highly needed but extremely difficult to succeed with. The examples suggest that it is sometimes very difficult to achieve the objectives that have been set.

Some problems of failed states are local, such as ethnic conflicts, while other problems have to do with the design of the interventions and low adaptability to changing circumstances (SOU 2017:16, cf. Pain 2021). Another example of negative outcomes is the armed operation in Libya, which has led to Libya becoming a difficult-to-govern country with a great deal of scope for trafficking and other problems for the EU. This seems to imply that it can sometimes be better to accept a dictatorship than to intervene. However, this is a complicated trade-off, balancing several objectives and making predictions on alternative governance arrangements, etc.

Here, it is relevant to mention a major evaluation of the EU's joint Conflict Prevention and Peacebuilding (CPPB) efforts in 2013–2018, which included actions worth €5.6 billion in 2011–2018 (EU 2020). The evaluation pointed to a growing understanding of conducting integrated actions, but also to the fact that it is difficult for the EU to become proactive with its efforts, partly because it has been difficult to integrate an interest in conflicts into all external policies and because it is difficult to develop learning on these issues (ibid.).

One criticism of development aid in general is that it risks becoming counterproductive, that development aid may support authoritarianism, i.e., that it contributes to the survival of poor national leaders (Hagmann and Reyntjens 2016) and that the recipient countries are caught up in dependence on aid (Moyo 2009; Glennie 2008). In this perspective, development aid must be designed in such a way as to minimize risks. The most critical authors conclude that development aid should be suspended (ibid.). Another proposal in the debate is that there must be what investors call an exit strategy, which includes, among other things, a fixed date for the end of external aid and for national actors to assume responsibility (Fee 2012). I will come back to the dilemmas which arise in the relationship between donor and recipient. The EU's ambition to move to a partnership with poor countries is a way of dealing with the problems.

The opposite position is that development aid is necessary, for example for all countries to achieve the SDGs. In this case, the implication is that objectives and interventions should be focused and simplified so that the objectives are actually achieved. It will then be important to develop instruments which are powerful enough and organizations which can implement what is decided upon. One theme of the academic debate is that development aid must be smarter (Joseph and Gillies 2009).

SUMMARY AND REFLECTIONS

The review of the various aspects of development policy shows that the EU and its member states have ambitious objectives which are implemented through a complex organization with certain conflicting objectives and wills. The objectives are the same for all the externally oriented policies, which facilitates the ambition to coordinate and cooperate. The large volume of actions across broad areas indicates that the EU is already an important player in many contexts.

The ambition to eradicate poverty and to contribute to the realization of the SDGs in poor countries is—if interpreted literally—a very high ambition, implemented with a great variety of instruments, which raises a question of what the more detailed strategies look like. It is striking that policy documents and descriptions only give a sketchy picture of how the EU (together with its member states) thinks about the means to reach the goals. The policy documents focus on intentions (values, goals, objectives) and coherence, while the strategies are largely absent. The general policy documents give little guidance and the local country strategies are underdeveloped.

Much of the strategy work and adaptation to the circumstances of the recipient countries takes place locally through the EU Delegations, which have only been briefly touched upon here. The study of the planning process in 2015 shows that there have been major problems in coordinating and adapting the strategies to the contexts. Some of the observations concern low analytical capacity and a bureaucratic approach. In a nutshell, the EU wants to have long-term strategies but is unable to do what it takes.

The focus of the policy documents is on coordinating the European instruments, while the discussion is on a general level. This discussion appears to be unrelated to the experience gained in the recipient countries. It is also unclear how the efforts relate to the specific needs of the recipients. This, in turn, can create a problem in the anchoring of common policies, both among the recipients and among the governments of the member states and the public in Europe.

The focus on intentions rather than outcomes makes it difficult to improve policies over time. There is a need to understand the local context and its drivers and barriers for development. Interventions need to be analyzed from the recipients' perspective, which is commonly known as a perspective "bottom-up," to understand how the interventions fit the local context. This is in line with the need for policy learning in large organizations. It is furthermore in line with the call for decentering analysis and interventions. It is also in line with the constructivist observation that the moral worth (legitimacy) of the EU is in the eye of the beholder, the recipient (Bengtsson and Elgström 2012).

The problem is the greatest for those efforts which have the ambition to contribute to long-term development, while the more short-term efforts can be accepted as they are. However, the selection of short-term interventions should be at least partly based on an idea of how they contribute to the long-term ambitions.

In the long-term work, it is important that there will develop well-functioning recipients in the form of governments with characteristics such as capacity, integrity, and legitimacy. A fundamental problem is that there is often a lack of such a party in the local implementation. Although it is being discussed as a problem, the texts nevertheless give the impression that the EU is facing a functioning counterparty (an implementing organization) similar to itself. There is little discussion of the chain of steps from the fundamental challenges to the ambitious goals of EU policy, which must include support for workable governance structures, to be improved over time.

Furthermore, the EU wants to work with national leaders, while some of the activities aim to counter the same (authoritarian) leaders, which contributes to ambiguity. It can also lead to problems with the confidence in the EU among the leaders of the recipient countries as well as their citizens.

The challenges are great for European development policy. The problems are complex, and research suggests that there is no obvious recipe for achieving the SDGs. This implies a need to contribute to the global learning on these matters and to learn from experience, outside and within the EU, including more academic forms of lesson-drawing, which I will return to.

The division into several policy areas within the EU is necessary but leads to an additional conflict dimension, as does cooperation with and among the member states. Learning at the organizational level is likely to be difficult, while individual employees may draw conclusions about what works in specific situations, so-called tacit knowledge. In addition, the policy is shaped through interaction with international organizations such as the UN and the OECD. The circumstances make it difficult to exercise political leadership. It is likely that it will take actors with strong will as well as an extreme situation to see new ways of action and to mobilize the energy needed to implement them.

However, it can't be ruled out that there are actors in the EU with a leadership position who are interested and know the situation in African countries. One place to look for such knowledge is in the recent Africa strategy. I will analyze the EU Africa Strategy as an example of an integrated approach of several policy areas before I turn the tables to study some key aspects of the recipient states and the relationship between donors and recipients.

Chapter 5

A New Partnership with the African Union

The European Commission shows a strong interest in improving the relations with Africa, which is the foundation for a broad strategy in relation to the African Union (AU) and its member states. The EU has proposed extensive cooperation with the African Union, signaling more of a partnership than the traditional roles of donors and recipients in development policy.

The Africa Strategy is partly a complement and partly an alternative to the more general development policy discussed in the previous chapter. The Africa strategy includes several policy areas of the EU, aiming to be an integrated approach to the ongoing relation with the African Union, which has become a hub of the relations between the governments on the two continents. The strategy consists of six themes, but development policy is not one of them, even though much of the contents contribute to poverty eradication. This raises questions about the selection of areas to collaborate on.

The chapter analyzes the contents of the strategy, especially its tensions and contradictions. Problems are identified and explanations are discussed in terms of internal disagreements. General requirements for a successful strategy are discussed, primarily in terms of developing an elaborate understanding of drivers and barriers in the African context.

THE PROPOSED STRATEGY

The ambition to deepen the relationship was most recently displayed through the high-level summit of the European and African Unions (EU and AU) in February 2022. The meeting was postponed from 2021 due to the pandemic. The Commission and the High Representative for EU Foreign and Security Policy (HRVP) set out their intentions in the document *Towards a Comprehensive Strategy with Africa* on March 9, 2020 (EU 2020). The document summarizes the situation and identifies the EU's multiple interests in a future strategy together with the AU.

In their communication, the Commission and the HRVP call for a political alliance with Africa, a partnership between equals (EU 2020). Implicitly, the Commission wants to move away from the traditional hierarchy of development policy, between donors and recipients. The new relationship will be characterized by greater cooperation, it says.

The Commission's communication is vague to some extent, which is in the nature of the matter. As one commentator wrote, the Commission's communications aim to set new directions for policy, based on existing programs and strategies, while at the same time trying to avoid offending any member state or Directorate-General (Byiers 2020). In this case, the text by the Commission points to historical ties with Africa as well as new opportunities, including sustainable development and political cooperation in global politics. The document is praised by the same commentator for its positive attitude, but also criticized for what is unclear or even contradictory (ibid.). The ambiguity is, among other things, that the strategy doesn't outline any objectives (justifications), but only a set of activities to be carried out, which I will return to.

The EU member state leaders endorsed the document in June of the same year, by a decision of the European Council (EU 2020c). There are some nuances and additions in the Council text, in relation to the original document, which is interesting to note (below). The strategy paper was also supposed to be discussed in the European Parliament in the fall of 2020, but the pandemic led to a postponement of the event.

The strategy contains a mix of new and old contents, indicating some continuation from earlier policies and strategies. The timing is also interesting. The new Commission obviously sees a need to renew its relationship with Africa, which has to do with common interests such as economic exchange and to reduce conflicts and forced migration. From the European side, sustainable development is an increasingly important issue, which makes exchange with African governments more interesting in fields like energy production (solar power). The talk about geopolitics suggests a motive of countering Chinese interests in Africa.

The diversity of initiatives and overlapping ambitions say something about the problems of the EU-Africa relationship. One wonders whether the EU's ambitions change and improve over time, whether there is learning based on experience gained or whether the EU is limited by, for example, internal rivalries or a lack of effective instruments for developing the relationship with Africa. There are also questions about where the strategy will lead. It is relevant to say something about how things will go, such as where there are contradictions, conflicts, weak points, or unsolvable problems.

The criticism now being made is in line with previous research into the EU's relationship with Africa. This is particularly interesting as the EU signals an interest in breaking old patterns and developing relations with Africa in a new way. The reshuffle of EU policies is linked to an ambition on the part of the EU to become a stronger foreign policy actor, which risks taking place without paying sufficient attention to the effectiveness of the actions implemented.

Six Themes with Comments

The main part of the document elaborates five themes which are the focus of much of the current debate in Europe and Africa. "Green transition" and "digitalization" are two of the Commission's hottest policy themes, which fall under the wider theme of "sustainable development," which is also in the strategy, while "peace" and "migration" are important themes in the relationship with Africa. In addition, there is a sixth theme on the implementation of the continued cooperation. These six themes break down into ten activities summarized in a list at the end of the document.

In a briefing for the European Parliament, the European Parliamentary Research Service (EPRS) clarified the ongoing initiatives on which the document's themes are based (EPRS 2020). As shown in Table 5.1, the number of previous instruments and agreements varies across the areas. The first two are new to EU-AU cooperation, while the others have been dealt with many times. All themes are touched upon in the SDGs, which are an agreement endorsed by all European and African governments.

One can imagine that there is a problematic history in the form of very difficult problems under some headings, such as how corruption in Africa should be dealt with, and, in some cases, conflicting interests, such as in the management of migration.

The enumeration suggests complexity on both sides, especially within the EU with its strong Directorates-General pushing different issues. The EPRS emphasizes an omission in the strategy paper, namely that of a key development policy text, the "European Consensus on Development" (EU 2003; ibid.). The EPRS has added the document to the table, but the lack of mention in the Commission's text is interesting for the interpretation of the internal decision-making processes.

The themes of cooperation listed are reasonable as examples of where the EU has placed great effort. For the analysis, it is also relevant to identify where the document is unclear and where problems can be expected to arise in the future.

The first theme of green transition to a fossil-free society has become the central issue for the EU, internally as well as externally. The Commission

Table 5.1 Ongoing activities by the EU and the AU. Source: EPRS 2020.

Theme	*EU activities*	*Activities by both*	*AU activities*
Green transition		The Paris Agreement	
Digital transformation			
Sustainable development	European Green Deal Africa- Europe alliance for sustainable investment and jobs Economic partnership agreements EU external investment plan	International platform on sustainable finance	African Continental Free Trade Agreement (AfCFTA) Sustainable business for Africa platform
Peace and Good governance	Common security and defense policy missions EU global strategy *European consensus on development*	EU-Africa peace facility EU-Africa partnership on peace and security EU-AU memorandum of understanding on peace, security, and governance AU-EU Human rights dialogue AU-EU coordination on electoral observations	African peace and security architecture (APSA) AU-led "silencing the guns-initiative" AU peace fund African governance architecture (AGA)
Migration	EU trust fund for Africa EU partnership framework on migration for bilateral relations with partner countries	Joint Valletta action plan Khartoum- and Rabat-processes AU-EU-FN trilateral task force on migration	
Implementation	Treaty on the European Union EU Global strategy *European consensus on development*	AU-EU commission to commission-meetings AU-EU political, peace and security committees Sectoral task forces under the Africa-Europe Alliance	AU Agenda 2063

document mentions Africa's natural resources, the need for innovation, a circular economy, smart urbanization, transport, energy production, and a better food production. The text emphasizes the importance of all this to cope with the strong population growth in Africa. The EU will contribute by supporting African countries in their implementation of the Paris Agreement, through cooperation on green energy and by contributing to the protection of natural resources (EU 2020, p. 2ff).

The compilation by EPRS helps interpret the short text by the Commission and the HRVP. The EPRS mentions that the parties have signed the Paris Agreement on the climate and the UN SDGs. On the other hand, the mention of the parties' individual commitments is blank, though there is a link to some of what is mentioned under "sustainable growth." The EPRS writes in its commentary that the EU hopes to have access to strategic minerals needed to reduce carbon dioxide emissions (EPRS 2020, 5). They also stress that cooperation requires that European action does not affect Africa negatively (ibid.). No examples are given, but an issue in the public debate is the risk of rich countries moving environmentally hazardous production to poorer countries.

Digital transformation is a theme discussed by the Commission and the HRVP primarily as a way of streamlining business and welfare services, while at the same time creating new jobs. The modernization of education and training systems in Africa is mentioned in particular, as is the need for investments. Technology development and safety issues are addressed (ibid., 4ff).

The Commission's text talks about digital inclusion, while the EPRS mentions that several African governments have closed the Internet during popular protests, which contradicts the wording of the document (EPRS 2020, 5). Alfonso Medinilla and Chloe Teevan note in a commentary that many African countries have invested in Chinese infrastructure and that there is a risk that they will cooperate with the Chinese on Internet surveillance (Medinilla and Teevan 2020, 9). In other words, the issue is more infected than the impression given by the European text.

Sustainable growth is a broad theme which is divided into several parts: investments, economic integration (trade) in Africa, business climate and welfare, in particular education, health, and the working environment. Here, the document points to the achievements through the alliance created in 2018, under the previous Commission. It also mentions investments of up to EUR 60 billion in the long-term budget, then proposed but not yet adopted, as well as additional investments by development banks and others. In the section on the business environment, there is a focus on improved regulation and long-term policies, i.e., issues which belong to the debate on governance (below). A commitment by the EU concerns the exchange of students, teachers, and researchers, in order to contribute to the enhancement of knowledge in Africa (EU 2020, 6ff).

The EPRS notes that there are several existing European and African economic strategies which are within the area concerned, including the new African Continental Free Trade Agreement (AfCFTA). Others have noted that the text discusses this Africa-wide FTA, while it doesn't mention the six regional free trade areas or the EU Economic Partnership Agreements (EPA) with groups of African countries. The EPRS, however, mentions that the UN Economic Commission for Africa (UNECA) has warned that the EPAs could have negative impacts on intra-African trade and that it sees an agreement with the whole of Africa as a better option (EPRS 2020, 5). In other words, the design of trade agreements is a controversial and rather unclear issue in the strategy.

The section on peace, security, and governance begins with the strange sentence "Ensuring long-lasting peace and security in Africa is as much in Africa's interest as it is in the EU's" (ibid., 10), which is a bit backwards. The interest in peace in Africa is most likely greater in Africa than in Europe.

The text has several elements: increased support for conflict resolution in Africa and for African initiatives to develop support for human rights, etc. Furthermore, it argues that attention should be paid to the interrelation between different dimensions of conflicts. Later, the text mentions cooperation which needs to be improved, such as the financing of African-led peace-promoting initiatives. One senses differences of opinion behind the desire for the dialogue on human rights to be more "strategic and structured" (ibid., 10ff), clearly an understatement.

The EPRS lists many existing commitments, unilateral as well as bilateral. Furthermore, the EPRS notes that there is tension in the approach to conflict resolution in Africa, where the AU wants Africa to make the decisions, while it is the EU which finances the operations (EPRS 2020, 6). Later in the comment, differences in the view of human rights are noted. Both circumstances are problematic for the European strategy.

The text on migration is more vague than the other texts. It begins with a description of the differences between perspectives, that Africans want to facilitate internal mobility and it has many internal refugees, while Europeans want to limit the smuggling of people from Africa. The text speaks vaguely of the balancing of efforts, "while respecting the EU's own values" (ibid., 14); again an understatement.

The text mentions the benefits of mobile labor, such as job opportunities and the sending of money to relatives in the poor home country (ibid., 13ff). The key concept of "circular migration" usually means that highly educated people from developing countries should return to their home countries after a period in a rich country (ibid., 14). The problem, which isn't explicitly mentioned, is an ongoing brain-drain from Africa to Europe, where well-educated Africans move to Europe.

EPRS describes the conflict of interest surrounding the smuggling of people, where criminalization can lead to the undesirable side effect of the destruction of local economies, as in Niger (EPRS 2020, 5). They also mention that the ACP countries want each country to decide for themselves whether to accept refugees sent back to them, which the EU does not agree with (ibid.).

The text also shows that it is difficult to maintain the idea of an equal partnership between the EU and the AU. Alfonso Medinilla and Chloe Teevan point out in their commentary that a real partnership based on common interests is not compatible with the EU's conditional support, i.e., African countries receiving rewards when they do what the EU wants (Medinilla & Teevan 2020, 16). According to them, cooperation should include African interests and should be focused on issues of commonality (ibid.). In other words, there is an ambiguity in the basic structure of the partnership; does the EU want to see the AU as an equal partner or as a subordinate?

The theme of implementation, finally, deals with efforts to deepen the further cooperation and for the EU member states to do more for Africa, as well as to act jointly in global politics in support of multilateralism (international organizations). It is highlighted that the countries of Europe and Africa have cooperated at the United Nations on, among other things, the Paris Agreement on the climate and the SDGs. The text of the document talks about enhanced cooperation between the AU, the EU, and the UN and for the EU to promote a stronger observer status for the AU in the World Trade Organization (WTO). It also promises that the EU will strive for coherence in managing its overlapping cooperation arrangements with the AU, the ACP countries, and the countries of North Africa. The EU furthermore promises to facilitate relations at the national level between the countries of Europe and Africa (ibid., 15ff).

Here, the EPRS notes that there is already ongoing cooperation, but also several examples of disagreement, which complicate the picture. One such disagreement is that the AU supports African countries which have withdrawn from the International Criminal Court (ICC), an act which undermines the position of the Court. Another example is that several members of the AU do not want to accept rights based on sexual orientation (so-called LGBTI rights) as a common value. All African countries on the UN Human Rights Council voted against or abstained when such an issue was decided in 2016 (EPRS 2020, 6f). In other words, this is a section in which the EU describes its wishes rather than what the reality looks like.

In their commentary on the document, Alfonso Medinilla and Chloe Teevan point out that African countries are more likely to vote with China and the G77 (the group of poorest countries) than with the European countries at the UN (Medinilla and Teevan 2020, 3), which is not the impression given by the Commission and the HRVP. According to Medinilla and Teevan, for the EU to be supported on more issues by the Africans, it must be prepared to support more African proposals (ibid.). This illustrates that the EU has not fully embraced the idea of an equal partnership with the AU.

Internal Disagreements

It should be added to this overview that the heads of states and governments of the EU member states have commented on the strategy twice, through the European Council. In June 2020, a rather detailed text was adopted which constitutes the Council's positions, diverging on some interesting points (EU 2020c). The original six themes of the strategy have now become nine and they come in a different order. Most interestingly, two themes have been added which do not have counterparts in the Commission's text: "Investing in people" and "Human dimension." The first of these hints at issues which belong to development policy, such as the focus on the situation of the poor and on inequality, which is what critics believe the Commission has downplayed in its March 2020 document (below).

Later in the Fall of 2020, the European Council issued a second opinion ("Council conclusion"). Here it mentioned debt cancellation as a new issue, which is an issue that is important to the AU (EU 2020d).

In conclusion, while the ambitions in the European document are high, there are also ambiguities and certain conflicts of interest in the EU's attitude towards Africa. The document is hardly smooth and uninteresting. Rather, it is interesting because it suggests disagreement and difficult trade-offs, which are relevant to study in more detail. Several issues are problematic, especially the ambiguity of which kind of relationship is desired. The EU gives the impression that it wants to see the AU as an equal partner, but in some areas it wants to decide unilaterally what should apply to the relationship.

FURTHER PROBLEMS WITH THE STRATEGY

How are we to understand the EU strategy document and the contradictions identified in the text? To get further, we need to understand more about the issues which the strategy is concerned with.

Opportunities and Risks

A first way of analyzing the strategy paper is to summarize it in terms of opportunities and risks. The question is what image the document gives of these items for the two parties, the EU and the AU.

The European text is mainly about opportunities for Africa. The EU's positions are broadly in line with an optimistic economic picture, where an expected population increase provides an opportunity for economic development, if children in the emerging workforce have access to healthcare and education, as discussed in chapter one. In addition, investment and other economic exchange with the outside world are needed to industrialize Africa and create more jobs, which the EU wants to contribute to. The green transition must be carried out at the same time, so that the industrialization of Africa does not increase the environmental problems. Growth can make it possible to finance welfare systems with tax revenues. In other words, there are several economic opportunities that the EU wants to contribute to.

For Africa, economic development can support political development. Both the EU and the AU emphasize the value of the rule of law and democracy. Peace and stability are of direct benefit to the African countries concerned and to the indirect benefit of the EU, which is winning a stable neighbor. Lastly, the text points at the opportunity to cooperate globally. All of these form opportunities for Africa which can be listed and compared to the risks of the relationship (table 5.2).

The benefits for Europe are not as clear in the text. It is only indirectly apparent that the European economy benefits from increased access to African markets and African resources. In the environmental field too, the EU is cautious in stating which specific benefits are being sought for Europe. As critics point out, Africa accounts for a vanishingly small proportion of global carbon dioxide emissions. An interpretation is therefore that the EU is partly driven by an ambition to deal with its own environmental problems, for example through access to solar energy from Africa. Security and migration policy interests are more clearly shared, although there are differences in exactly what they are and how to prioritize. Another benefit for the EU from cooperation is that the EU strengthens its global role.

The risks are not discussed at all in the EU documents. Nevertheless, some risks can be identified based on the above. It seems fair to say that Africa is taking a big risk here. On the one hand, Africa is receiving increased support, but on the other hand there is a risk of becoming more dependent on the EU, which could limit the long-term ability and willingness of African governments to take responsible actions. For both parties, there is the risk that the identified opportunities are not being achieved, which, in particular for the EU, is a political risk that cooperation will appear to be a failure.

Table 5.2 Opportunities and risks for Africa and Europe. Source: Author, based on EU 2020.

	Africa	*Europe*
Opportunities	Green industrialization	Access to resources and markets
	Welfare through domestic revenue	Stabile neighborhood
	Peace	Conflict avoidance
	Political stability	Global partner
	Global partner	
Risks	New dependence	Political failure

This is serious if the EU's ambition is to use the cooperation with the AU to strengthen its own global role. In other words, there is a political risk that China, Russia and others will benefit from a possible failure of the EU.

An Unclear Relationship

Looking in more detail at the strategy, the relationship between the parties, as described by the EU, has elements of cooperation as well as conflict, which makes its fundamental nature ambiguous. There are common positions and interests in some areas, but in other areas the EU wants to use rewards and punishments to get African countries to do what it wants. This is a contradiction which can affect the relationship as a whole.

One aspect of the problem is that EU policies in the specific areas strive to achieve different things. A fundamental problem for the EU is that the security policy implications are in part contradictory to development policy and the economic ambitions. From the first perspective, supporting undemocratic regimes can be valuable, but leads to problems of credibility. During the Arab Spring of 2013, Africans wondered why the EU supported the old regimes. One implied answer was that a dictator like Gaddafi provided order and avoided chaos.

In other words, there are fundamental differences in perspective between different parts of the EU that emphasize economic opportunities and security policy threats, respectively. The implication is that there should be more internal discussion within the EU (and AU) on how to deal with the short-term conflicting ambitions. Is it possible to reach a consensus on the path to the common goal, Africa's development and autonomy? Internationally, similar discussions are being held in terms of reaching a consensus between aid policy and security policy (e.g. Spear and Williams 2012). The lack of coordination within the EU has been discussed in terms of actorness, whether the EU is a more fragmented actor than a national government (below).

The EPRS concludes by saying that the EU and the AU have coinciding interests, but also issues where they do not think alike. The converging interests include tackling climate change and supporting a sustainable and job-creating African economy. The disagreements concern the views on migration, the handling of security issues, and fundamental values (EPRS 2020, 1).

Furthermore, the EPRS points out that the proposed cooperation will take place within the framework of the Joint Africa-EU Strategy (JAES), launched in 2007. Other cooperation with African countries fall outside, which creates further ambiguity. This applies to cooperation with the North African countries in the neighborhood policy and with the ACP countries, which include African, Caribbean, and Pacific countries (ibid., 6).

On the important question of what kind of relationship the EU wants to see, it should be noted that the document doesn't contain the phrase "partnership between equals," which was used in 2007 and which Ursula von der Leyen used as newly elected President (Byiers 2020, 1). Commentator Bruce Byiers points out that the strategy paper nevertheless seems to be less paternalistic than previous texts by the EU (ibid.).

A problem, according to Byiers, is that it is unclear who should do what. The AU is an actor with limited ability to enforce political decisions. In practice, it is individual African countries which will have to implement much of the content (ibid., 2). The AU itself has lower capacity than the EU to prepare documents with its member states (ibid., 3). Byiers also points out that the regional cooperation organizations are mentioned in the sections on security and human rights, but not in the sections dealing with economic development (ibid., 2).

Other critics see similar problems. Medinilla and Teevan point to the contradiction between talking about a partnership and the EU trying to push through its approach to democracy (Medinilla and Teevan 2020, 14). Their proposal is that the criticism as well as the efforts made by the EU need to be more selective, while the EU must make an effort to act coherently, when necessary, as was the case for example during the conflict in Egypt in 2013. In addition, the EU must ensure that its own rules are enforced in Europe, for example as regards the rights of Africans in Europe (ibid.).

Furthermore, Medinilla and Teevan argue that the parties must try to achieve effective interest-based cooperation, which means, among other things, daring to address issues of disagreement, identifying issues where the parties need each other's support, and developing solutions that work for both parties (ibid., 17). The AU and stakeholders in Africa and Europe must be allowed to express their wishes, so that the agenda is jointly owned. In addition, the EU needs to deepen its understanding of the functioning of the AU and to understand what will happen when it cooperates with other groups of African and other countries in parallel. According to Medinilla and Teevan, it should be noted that some African countries prefer to continue to live in a dependency relationship with their donors (ibid.).

These comments deal with the important issue of what the EU-AU relationship should look like. They point to the expectations raised by the idea of a partnership as well as to the EU not living up to these expectations.

Substantive Problems

The early comments on the EU text draw attention to further substantive problems. Bruce Byiers emphasizes the general risk that the visions of the document are not matched by an understanding of the situation and the incentives faced by local actors in the implementation of the vision. In other words, there is a risk that the parties will settle on the wrong things, limiting the possibilities for focused support. This, in turn, prevents reasonable objectives from being achieved. According to Byiers, there is a risk that there will be a lot of vision but little action, "also known as hallucination" (Byiers 2020, 3). In addition, the problem is that the AU has difficulty anchoring its positions with its member states (Medinilla and Teevan 2020, 4).

These comments touch upon an important issue in this relationship, i.e., whether the actions proposed will lead to the achievement of the objectives. There is also a question for the EU as to whether the counterparty (AU) will deliver what is sought by the EU. These are some fundamental problems with the Africa strategy.

Some comments given relate to specific areas. Alfonso Medinilla and Chloe Teevan note that cooperation so far is not working well on the issues of green transition. Both the EU and the AU have ambitions to be global players on climate change. Among other things, there is an African group of negotiators (AGN) that develops joint African positions (Medinilla and Teevan 2020, 8). They furthermore note that EU-AU cooperation is mostly about making specific efforts, while it is unclear what makes cooperation a more political alliance (ibid.).

Concord, which consists of organizations active in the implementation of development aid projects, presents a long list of criticisms that are in line with the above and go further. An interesting objection is that the organization misses a discussion of issues related to concerns of equality (Concord 2020, 4) and of the importance of civil society organizations for development (ibid., 13). The organization refers to several international concepts and agreements not mentioned in the EU document.

Of principal interest is that Concord dislikes the focus on economic growth and private investment. Instead, it wants to focus on sustainable development, poverty reduction, and addressing inequality (ibid., 5). It is implied by Concord that these concepts are at odds with each other—later exemplified, among other things, by the fact that investments in fossil fuels should not be allowed (ibid., p. 11). The comment is interesting, partly because it points out that the EU text is unclear as to how the two objectives of creating growth and implementing a green transition relate to each other. This is a major issue in the debate and Concord is skeptical of the pro-growth position of the EU and the UN. This in turn implies that parts of the EU text are controversial.

Concord notes in approval that the text mentions fair value chains (subcontractors in Africa), while the organization lacks something about fair taxation of companies in Africa and about facilitating the establishment of African companies in Europe (ibid., 6). This can be read as blind spots in the EU's attempts to treat the AU equally.

Furthermore, Concord points out that free trade with the EU can make intra-African integration more difficult (ibid., 10), which is a concern which other commentators have raised. Concord's comments highlight the big question of whether the right measures are being proposed or, to rephrase, that the political content is not accepted by everyone. This draws our attention to the fact that there is a political debate on these issues and that the EU's positions are not the only ones that are possible.

Further evidence for a critical discussion can be found in the research comments commissioned and published by the European Parliament (EU 2020b). Morten Bøås points out that the draft strategy underestimates the large differences among the countries in Africa. According to Bøås, several countries in Africa have "cracked the code" for state building and are now developing in a positive direction, while much of the security problems and people smuggling are rooted in the weak states, mainly in the Sahel region (ibid., 1:4–20). The EU cooperates extensively with the G5 Sahel (Burkina Faso, Chad, Mali, Mauritania, and Niger), despite their extremely weak administrative structures (ibid., 11f).

Bøås emphasizes that countries must develop from aid dependency to fiscal capacity, i.e., to make citizens willing to pay taxes and to make governments use tax revenues efficiently, which the EU document does not mention (ibid., 13), but is set out in the UN Sustainable Development Goals. He also argues that the EU is the only geopolitical player with an interest in assisting the Sahel (ibid., 16). According to Bøås, China, Russia, and the United States have a focus on other geographical areas.

In another comment, Ondrej Horky-Hluchan highlights what the EPRS has noted, that the EU's development policy positions are not discussed in the Commission document (ibid., 2:4–15). One example is that the strategy paper focuses on growth, while EU development policy focuses on problems for individuals, of which poverty is one (ibid., 4f, 12). This is seen by Horky-Hluchán as a sign that the EEAS has had more influence over the document than the Directorate-General for Development (DG INTPA; ibid., 10). This is a comment that points to an internal disagreement within the EU.

In a third academic comment, Ainhoa Marin-Egoscozabal discusses trade and other economic relations between Europe and Africa (ibid., 3:4–17). She points at the problems which arise when the countries of Africa have five different trade relations with the EU and when there are several parallel initiatives to promote investment. One solution is to bring these together in an agreement for the whole of Africa (ibid., 15). This contributes to the message that there are ambiguities on the EU side that the EU itself should be able to address.

In conclusion, the comments point to the fact that the Commission's strategy paper makes an ambitious attempt to take a comprehensive approach to its relationship with Africa. At the same time, there are unclear elements as well as elements of power talk, although the EU says it is seeking some kind of equal relationship with the AU.

The EPRS summary seems reasonable, that it is easier to reach agreement in the first areas, which have to do with green growth, than in the latter areas, which have to do with migration, security, human rights, and democracy development. Within the latter, there are larger elements of the EU's desire to have an impact on policies in Africa, leading to ambiguity about the relationship the EU is seeking and to what extent the EU can have an equal relationship with African representatives who have significant problems at home (from a European perspective).

What Does the AU Think?

The first reaction of the African Union, as expected, was that the document does not formulate a common strategy, but only the European positions before negotiations on an agreement. African priorities may be different. Already in 2018, the AU appointed Carlos Lopes as a special contact for the relationship with the EU. He presented a document at an internal meeting, which has not been published. In the absence of official comments from the AU, other commentators have suggested viewpoints for the AU to pursue to achieve its development strategy for 2063 (African Union Commission 2015) and in view of the declaration agreed between the EU and the AU at the Abidjan (Côte d'Ivoire) Summit in 2017.

An example of such comments on the strategy from outsiders is the post in which Tsion Tadesse Abebe and Hafsa Maalim (2020) analyze what should be the AU's priorities. They find a great deal of consistency between the EU's priorities and the AU Strategy for Africa's development by 2063, but also some important differences. One such difference is the conflict between the Economic Partnerships (EPA) and a trade agreement with the whole of Africa. The authors' comment is that the EPAs primarily benefit European companies and have a negative effect on intra-African trade (Tadesse Abebe and Maalim 2020, 8).

Another point where the authors see differences of opinion is in the view of migration. They point out that EU action has hampered the implementation of AU strategies (ibid., 12). The authors are making a careful understatement when they argue that the discussion must take into account global regulations beyond the EU regulatory framework (ibid.). Since this is a sensitive issue, they don't specify their criticism further.

On EU peace efforts in Africa, Tsion Tadesse Abebe and Hafsa Maalim write that the focus should shift from peacekeeping to conflict resolution and other preventive measures (ibid., 14). They find support in the wording of the European Council conclusions above (ibid.). In support of democracy development, too, the authors want an increase in ambition. They want to see support beyond election observation, to build up organizations to arrange the elections (ibid., 15). The authors also want the EU to help promote the AU's values of governance vis-à-vis their member states' governments (ibid.). This is remarkable, since it points to an internal problem within the AU and because the authors wish the EU's help in solving the internal problem.

The comment is outspoken about the problems of governance in Africa. A specific proposal is to support the African Court of Human Rights (ibid.). The text emphasizes that conflict resolution and state building measures must focus on "governance-induced problems such as political corruption . . . " (ibid.). A later section mentions the construction of the AU as an important measure (ibid., 21).

It is also interesting that the comment asks for more of what lies in the EU's development policy and from which the EU strategy document distances itself. The authors would like to see more measures focusing on the problems of the population, in particular poverty and bad health, which are supported by the European Council's commentary on the strategy paper (ibid., 15, 21). Debt cancellation is addressed as a fundamental problem, in part because it hinders investment in transport infrastructure (ibid., 16f). Here, too, support can be found in the Council text above (ibid., 19).

Furthermore, they put their finger on the problem of strategies which are endless wishlists. The authors note that previous agreements have not been implemented, partly because there are no implementation plans. This applies, for example, to the ambition to electrify the whole of Africa by 2025 (ibid., p. 9).

In conclusion, Tsion Tadesse Abebe and Hafsa Maalim, in their interpretation of the AU's position, support some of the criticisms which have been made by others and which, interestingly, have been touched upon by the European Council in its commentary. In short, it is about adding a concern with the problems of the population, which belongs to a development policy context. The conflict over migration policy has been touched upon by others, while the conflict over trade policy instruments is described more clearly here.

Some of the points put forward are calls for further support from the EU, in terms of peace and good governance. In this context, it is interesting that the authors discuss the problem of governments in Africa which have not adopted the common agenda. It is a problem, but it also has a problematic implication for Europe, that its strategy lacks realism. It is questionable for the EU to have a good relationship with the AU, regardless of the policies pursued by its members.

In short, the comments from an AU-perspective help us see weaknesses which are related to the African context. These are indirectly problems for the

EU, implying a weak analysis of the African context and a limited capability to propose actions which deal with fundamental problems. The last two points are of great significance for the analysis of EU policies in relation to Africa.

UNDERLYING EXPLANATIONS FOR THE EUROPEAN PROBLEMS

It is not enough to note that the EU's proposed strategy is vague and follows in the wake of previously identified ambiguities. The question in this section is what underlying factors can explain the choice of policies, including their shortcomings. I will return to some of the issues which were discussed on a more general level in chapter three, focusing on the perspective which highlights the role of epistemic communities (Haas 1992). This was also discussed in chapter four, in terms of a complex organization with several lines of conflict and a variety of understandings of the ends and means.

A Rational Strategy?

A first and very general observation from policy analysis, mentioned in chapter two, is that political strategies often sound rational in terms of their ends and means, while research shows that there may be problems in living up to the ambitions. Objectives can be vague and contradictory. The means allocated to achieving the objectives may be insufficient. The analysis of the problem to be solved may also be limited. Over time, there may be a stronger or weaker ambition to learn from experience and to develop the strategies. Behind these problems may be explanations in the form of competing wills or insolvable ("wicked") problems which make it tempting to pursue symbolic policies (Brunsson 2007). The cynics' question is whether a policy is intended to be taken seriously or not.

This is a watershed in the approach to understanding policy strategies. Politicians often want to appear rational, since citizens expect politicians to deal with difficult situations. Politicians are doing the best they can, but poorly designed policies can create new problems. Therefore, some researchers consider the notion of the rationality of politics to be a myth (ibid.). The willingness of politicians to appear rational makes our understanding more difficult of how politics really works and how social change takes place.

In this case, there is a risk that the Africa strategy is something everyone in the EU can agree on, a "lowest common denominator," rather than something based on an analysis of how the objectives can be achieved. The desire to agree internally can lead to differences in perspective being toned down. This may mean that the analysis of problems and measures becomes superficial.

Conflicting Wills

The above analysis has touched on the issue of conflicting wills within the EU and the AU, which is also known in terms of limited actorness of the two unions. Previously I have described the conflicting wills within the Commission (DGs) as well as other parts of the EU. A common perception among political scientists is that entities representing different policy areas compete internally in large organizations to dominate the common strategies (e.g., Krahmann 2003; Merket 2016; Hartlapp, Metz, and Rauh 2014; Gvosdev, Blankschain, and Cooper 2019; Hill, Smith, and Vanhoonacker 2017). There are different views across institutions, Directorates General, member states, and political parties in the Parliament and elsewhere. These tensions imply that the goals and interests, as well as the norms and worldviews, differ across the affected parties within the EU.

The complexity of the cooperation with Africa stems from the fact that the EU has many objectives for its cooperation, which were discussed in chapters three and four. Each member state and each policy area have its ambitions. In addition, there are the European political groupings (political parties) and their desires for relations and cooperation with external parties. The noted difference between the original text by the Commission and the final text by the Council indicates some of these complexities.

This situation is also a major explanation for why policy learning is difficult in the EU. Many organs within the EU can supply information on outcomes, but the interpretation and effort to reach consensus based on observations on what works are weak in a fragmented organization with many "epistemic communities." Research into organizational behavior point at many potential barriers, from disagreements over the kind of analysis (evaluation) needed, to vested interests in certain policies (Raimondo 2018). Pablo Yanguas talks about psychological as well as organizational factors (Yanguas 2021). More general perspectives in the social sciences focus on how new ideas are adopted, where one way is to copy behavior which is popular or seems successful, without engaging in the details of the issues, as mentioned before.

There are internal procedures in the Commission for coordination among its civil servants. To some extent the Council and even the Parliament are arenas where some consensus can be reached, depending on the circumstances. Local action through the EU Delegations and the national agencies may also provide opportunities for policy learning. This leads to questions about the circumstances under which agreement is easy or difficult to reach, which is beyond the scope of this study.

Ultimately, the present situation is complicated by the fact that the agreed objectives are not only partially contradictory and require prioritization, but also that the goals are extremely difficult to achieve. This includes the ambition to support the development of democracy in Africa and it also applies to the more limited question of how the EU should relate to corrupt leaders. From a security policy perspective, it may be desirable to cooperate with leaders in important countries, regardless of their policies, but for long-term development it is problematic to support bad leaders.

This furthermore indicates that there is a complex relationship between the EU and the AU. Both parties can choose between a relationship of "realpolitik," in which the interests of the parties are in focus, and a more normative relationship, in which the values and principles of the parties are at the center. In either case, ambiguity can lead to distrust by the other party. Leaders and citizens may have different views on the objectives and means of cooperation. Both parties signal an interest in cooperation, but the question is on what and in what ways. It is difficult to find a collaborative solution which is in everyone's interest, which I will return to in chapter seven.

EU Policy Communities

The analysis brings into focus the internal policy communities in the EU, where a number of EU policy areas handle relations with African countries. As described in chapter three, the two oldest are trade policy and development policy. In recent years, a common foreign policy and a sub-field of security and defense policy have emerged. The differences between these policies may explain a large part of the ambiguity of the EU's actions. In addition, the Africa strategy concerns environmental policy, industrial policy, digitalization policy, and migration issues, which means that many internal units (Directorates General) are involved.

Policy areas not only have separate objectives, but are also organized in different ways, as I touched upon previously. A fundamental difference is that trade and development have been integral parts of EU policy since its inception, while foreign policy rests on another legal mandate, which creates ambiguity in the internal coordination. As described before, the organization is complex and with a rather weak form of leadership in the role of the "High Representative" with two missions: President of the Foreign Affairs Council and Vice-President of the Commission (HRVP), and through a joint administration for much of the External Relations (EEAS). On specific issues, the Commission has been mandated to take action, which means that there is a weak movement towards increased supranationalism (e.g. Bergmann 2019).

I noted in chapter three that foreign policy has gradually become a dominant policy area in relation to development policy. I also noted that the permanent chair of the European Council is taking a stronger role in this issue, partly overtaking responsibilities which have been thought to reside with the HRVP.

This way of understanding the internal processes is based on describing how the relevant parts are constructed, focusing on the institutional design, where the balance of units provides the basic conditions. Within the framework of such an organizational description, it is also relevant to study what image of Africa is dominant in the various units. Their perceptions of the situation ("ideas") are characterized in part by the problems they face, but also partly by the values and interpretations of reality cultivated within the units (cf. Woolcock 2012).

It is particularly interesting that the dividing line between policy areas is cutting through all institutions and member states. For example, there are development policy and security policy bureaucracies in all member states and in all institutions (Commission, Council, and Parliament). Such "iron triangles" across the institutional boundaries cooperate to define the agenda (Steingass 2021). What makes international cooperation particularly interesting is that there are links between similar groups at different levels, where specific ministries cooperate with their counterparts in Brussels and other countries (Krahmann 2003; Merket 2016). Together they compete with other groups of ministries which prioritize other aspects of cooperation with Africa.

How Does Change Happen?

As I have touched on before, there are scholars who see an internal struggle to dominate the relations with Africa, between foreign policy and development policy (Rye Olsen 2007; Söderbaum 2013; Whitman and Haastrup 2013). A sign that new approaches have come to dominate in the EU is the change of name of the DG for development policy at the beginning of 2021. The old name DG DEVCO (Development cooperation) was replaced by the new name DG INTPA (International partnerships), which signals more of a relation between equals.

Such internal competition could explain why the development policy perspective is downplayed in the EU Communication of March 2020 and also why development policy is given more room in the comments given by the Council. People with insight into the work of the European Union confirm this picture. Several of the critics' comments mentioned above can be read as arguments in defense of a development policy perspective.

This is a hypothesis which needs to be investigated in more detail. One question is whether there are alternative explanations for the ambiguities and the changes of positions. Such an explanation could be that the member states disagree and that France in particular wants to raise the EU's foreign policy profile. Another explanation could be that there are interest groups which influence how the EU views the issues. These explanations may be compatible, which implies a further interest in the power struggle itself or on specific "norm entrepreneurs," i.e., certain "thought leaders" who influence how actors think about the issues, how they prioritize their goals and means (Finnemore and Sikkink 1998).

An additional type of explanation would point to the process of producing the Africa strategy. Who has been allowed to speak and how have comments been collected? These were important factors in developing the EU's Global Strategy (EUGS), in which the process by the member states was heavily governed by the Council secretariat, i.e., "from above," despite the fact that it was an intergovernmental process (Morillas 2018). Some researchers talk about increasing "procedural supranationalism" in the Council (Thaler 2020). The mechanisms for leadership and coordination in the Commission are at least partly different.

Policy Developments in Africa

Although the focus of this analysis is on understanding the EU's actions, it is of some interest to understand how the AU works as a counterpart, including something about its strengths and weaknesses. As mentioned earlier, there are superficial similarities between the EU and the AU. The latter organization is younger and in a weaker position, which has to do with the situation in Africa. This implies that policy areas are not as divided and fixed in their positions, but it may also imply a lack of coordinating leadership which develops and anchors common positions (cf. Karbo and Murithi 2018; Trondal, Gänzle, and Tieku 2020).

The fact that the AU itself has not expressed its positions externally indicates shortcomings in the internal machinery. A recurring criticism is that the AU allows itself to be governed by the EU because the EU usually has a long list of proposals to the joint meetings, which the AU finds difficult to match.

As with the EU, one can look for explanations in line with general social science research. The internal negotiating game can be understood as a rational and power-based process, as something influenced by the paths chosen earlier or by new ideas about what drives development in Africa (e.g. Hall and Taylor 1996). It is likely that the bureaucratic machinery of the AU is in a weaker position than it is in the EU. There is more room for national leaders to make their mark on the organization through the role of President of the AU (cf. Gvosdev, Blankshain, and Cooper 2019).

The overall picture is therefore that both organizations have problems with their internal cohesion, as is expected. They must spend time on the internal process of developing positions which bridge differences of opinion and stand a chance of achieving their goals, which could strengthen the long-term behavior of these organizations. How this can be done is the next question.

STARTING POINTS FOR AN IN-DEPTH APPROACH

A question is whether the EU (and the AU) can develop more coherent and more successful strategies. In the northern European countries, there is commonly a rationalistic view that policies should be of a "learning" kind, i.e., that interventions should be developed in the light of experience and analysis (Hallin and Svensson 2000). For example, Swedish development policy is evaluated both by the relevant authorities themselves (Sida, Swedfund, et al.) and independently by The Expert Group for Aid Studies (EBA) as well as more general auditing bodies.

Such analysis of experience is less developed in the EU. There are reviews and revisions of the instructions for the DGs etc. Independent evaluation is conducted by the European Court of Auditors (ECA). More interestingly, there are a number of evaluations of specific policies and initiatives, some of which are touched upon here. What is lacking are broader analyses of ends and means in relation to Africa, for example in the form of an evaluation of the experiences from previous strategies. There are some analytical policy documents (e.g. EU 2012c), though such reviews are not connected to the development policy documents such as the "New European Consensus on Development" (EU 2017). The key policy documents look forwards, not backwards.

Should the Strategy be Taken Seriously?

The aim of EU-AU cooperation is to achieve common objectives, although it is not entirely clear what they are since the strategy document doesn't formulate objectives for the cooperation. Rather, it contains a set of measures which are expected to benefit the countries of Europe and Africa. It may be of strategic value that the objectives are vague, since implementation can then be more flexible, but it will be more difficult to learn lessons from experience if one does not state what the purpose of the cooperation is. From this point of view, the cynics could say that cooperation is ritual; the EU proposes what is perceived as relevant or legitimate, but without an ambition to actually solve these extremely difficult problems related to African economic and political development.

Another approach is to take the strategy seriously, to examine how it can be implemented. What can be said about the relationship of the parties and their specific wishes? How should the strategy be designed to be able to function? Constructive researchers give advice on how strategies could be developed. This can be about describing and analyzing the ends and the means. It can be done with or without questioning the rationality of politics. In social science research there is often the ambition to contribute to a conversation about policy strategies.

An overarching objective of EU development policy is to stimulate sustainable development (the SDGs) in Africa. As mentioned above, Europe also needs "support" in the form of various resources. Here is the core of a win-win situation, but also the risk that either party will not have their wishes met. The parties may have objectives for their cooperation other than those stated explicitly in the strategy document and elsewhere. For example, the EU as well as the AU may have an interest in marketing themselves as foreign policy actors, since both organizations compete in part with strong member states such as France and South Africa, respectively (cf. Bickerton 2011). Either way, it is of value that the proposed measures can lead to the objectives pursued.

To increase the effectiveness of its operations, the EU needs to build its efforts more clearly on research and previous experience, to improve its learning. A short strategy document is not the place to present all the background information. Other channels can be used. For example, the Commission website refers to the work conducted in relation to Africa through its working groups (EU 2022). More such information on what the policy proposals are based on would limit the risk that the strategies are based on what is easiest to agree upon, rather than what is best for achieving the objectives. This is a part of the Africa strategy that could be strengthened.

Each policy area (DG) has its own set of objectives and means. To some extent, cooperation between the EU and the AU may fall back on the policy areas' views on these things. At the same time, there is a tension between policy areas with general ambitions and a strategy with a geographical focus. The strategy brings together actions from several policy areas to jointly influence actors in a geographical area. The coordination of objectives and means is of central importance.

The individual policy areas are linked to scientific debates on how, for example, trade policy or development policy should be designed. There is also an academic debate on Africa and its situation. What is needed in this context is more of a discussion on the impact of the various activities on Africa, especially how they affect each other, and the importance of the context of different African countries.

The choice of the AU as a partner can be seen as part of a strategy to focus on general collaboration while avoiding specific countries and issues. Trade policy is also a general kind of policy, which focuses on general impact rather than the specifics. However, the EU is much involved in specific situations through its security collaborations and its development policy.

The six parts of the strategy document raise questions about inter-connections. Is the development of effective states a prerequisite for sustainable growth and digitalization, or can these elements be achieved in parallel? How should the measures be differentiated according to the situation in various countries? Is the control of migration to Europe and global cooperation independent of AU-EU issues or do they affect the achievement of the other ambitions? None of these questions about alignment are commented on in the document. The parts stand individually, and the strategy lacks a mechanism to reconcile the positions into a functioning whole.

Should the Relationship with the AU be Differentiated?

A question of strategy is what kind of relationship the EU should seek with the AU and whether it should be uniform across all areas and countries. The strategy expresses various relationships in different areas of policy but doesn't address the question of whether all countries should really be treated equally. It is reasonable to do the opposite. Several critics have noted the problem of inconsistency between the six areas of the strategy. Only the commentary from the AU's perspective noted the second problem, that not all African countries accept the EU's values. Politics is not differentiated in the latter respect, though it makes sense to make it so.

There is a noted inherent contradiction between the EU's attempts to be equal and superior at the same time. The hierarchical elements diminish the credibility of the partnership. Partnership with an unworthy party—corrupt leaders—is also not credible. The European text acknowledges problems on the African side but is too polite to mention the problem of corrupt leaders.

One option would be to differentiate the relationship, so that deeper cooperation is reserved for democracies. Non-democracies can be treated in a tougher way. "Failed states" can be assisted as an emergency measure. Such differentiation could take place by making countries with promising development patterns into partners for green growth. Economic integration and measures for a green transition will then be central.

Countries which are not ready for economic cooperation can be treated as friends or enemies. Stefan Dercon suggests that support should only be given to countries where the elites are interested in developing their countries rather than enriching themselves (Dercon 2022). Hence, leaders who show no willingness to improve the respect for human rights, democracy, or the principles of the market economy should be seen as dictators and treated accordingly, possibly with further differentiation. Exactly how this should be done is a later question. The point in this context is that the absence of such differentiation damages the credibility of the European Union.

A difference between the EU and the AU must be noted here. While the EU only admits new members on the condition that they accept all existing legislation, the AU (formerly OAU) was from the beginning an organization for all African states. It was important to unite against other countries of the world, to gain political and economic strength, especially since global economic integration was not an option in the 1960s. This means that there is no organization in Africa for the more developed countries and, hence, no incentive for African governments to become members of a more "advanced" African organization.

Theoretically, the EU could have a new kind of "extended neighborhood policy" with the African countries and other poor countries around the world. The EU could offer several levels of partnership, as it does with its neighbors in the south and in the east. The relationship with the ACP countries is in reality an "outer rim" of the neighborhood policy.

It should also be noted that closer economic relations with African countries, treating them as equals and living up to the rhetoric of a level playing field, creates pressures on the EU, for example regarding trade in agriculture. The ambition to lower trade barriers clashes with the interests of European farmers and others. Political finesse is needed to make agreements that involve some losses for Europeans in the short term. This is probably necessary to increase the EU's credibility in the eyes of African leaders.

It could possibly be argued that, despite the rhetoric of an equal partnership, the EU is dealing in a differentiated way with African countries. At the very least, it should not be excluded that there is a differentiation in practice, based on the country strategies discussed in the previous chapter. In such a case, the question becomes why the rhetoric does not emphasize the distinction between countries. The possibility of being treated generously could be a central part of a strategy based on conditionality. Consistency then requires being clear about which countries should be under pressure and which countries should be treated as equals.

Intertwined Economic and Political Challenges

The issues which the EU wants to contribute to addressing are intertwined and subject to conflicting views. Economic development can be a cause as well as an effect of political development. In addition, the research provides conflicting advice. It is not clear how a more detailed approach should be devised, which I will elaborate in the following chapter.

Overall, Africa's development is about the grand issue of the transition from an agricultural to an industrial society (with reduced use of fossil fuels); how can this be done? What can an external party like the EU contribute? EU action needs a more developed knowledge base to start from and an ambition to contribute to learning about the complex issues involved.

What makes the situation particularly complicated is that the transition from despotic rulers to democracy and market economy can take place in different ways, depending on background factors and events ("timing"). It is therefore difficult to advise African countries on exactly what to do and in what order. Research talks about "hybrid regimes" which make up mixed forms of traditional and modern regulation and look different over time and space (Andrews 2013; Cheeseman 2015). There is no obvious model for Africa's long-term development on which the EU can rely. Instead, the EU should contribute to the analysis of what drives development in Africa and how its own efforts affect the situation.

A "Theory of Change" for the Africa Strategy

One way to develop the analysis behind the strategy is to identify the intended ends and means, as well as their causal links. This will make it easier to discuss what is needed for the instruments to produce the desired state of affairs, and whether there are any additional factors which need to be taken into account. This could be a way of showing how policies relate to each other and to the conditions prevailing in different countries.

It is perhaps utopian to expect a complete picture of how the measures of the strategy are linked. It is more reasonable to go for trial and error, but to test and improve one's efforts, one must start from a preliminary idea of what should be done. There must also be an ambition to learn from experience. It is perhaps utopian to think that EU leaders would describe cooperation in such an instrumental and technocratic way, but it is difficult to make the strategy work unless the officials do so to some extent.

It has become common to analyze strategies in development policy and other areas with instruments from project management and evaluation contexts (e.g. Burns and Worsley 2015). Among other things, expected effects of interventions are analyzed by breaking down relationships between ends and means in small steps. The result is a matrix of causal relations, a kind of social engineering's view of what is expected to happen. The causal mechanisms come into focus in what is called a theory of change, a program theory or an intervention theory (Vogel 2012).

I will discuss possible elements of a "theory of change" or roadmap in the next chapter. The complexity of development issues implies that some of the important causal relations are unclear, for example if economic development is a means to political development or vice versa. Historically, there has been a great variety of drivers and barriers across various contexts. This implies a need to structure the analysis to find out more, as well as to avoid making too firm assumptions about the African context.

Cooperation between the EU and the AU can be analyzed in terms of an exchange (chapter seven) or described as a complex system, in which the parties wish to influence their situation in a variety of respects. It is a question of jointly developing economies, implementing a green transition, creating peace, and security, etc. All of these are complex and difficult to control. Other factors affect the outcome.

One step to develop the Africa strategy is to describe the assumptions behind it, so that important points can be identified and tested. Conflicts and synergies between policy areas may need to be analyzed. Efforts can be made in different ways in different contexts, which provides a basis for drawing conclusions about what works.

A key to developing and improving strategies is to gather experience to revise the preliminary perceptions of what should be done. To some extent, research into EU actions and strategies has provided such knowledge. Politicians and officials use research as part of a review process, but other factors also influence how political change is done.

In this context, it is interesting that the EU strategy is vague about ends and means. It is also unclear about follow-up and evaluation, i.e., how experiences should be collected and used to develop the strategy. Follow-up usually means collecting snapshots of what goes on, through data on how the situation has turned out. Evaluation refers to more advanced assessments of why things are going the way they are, identifying the causal links.

Evaluation and research can be conducted to learn about causal relationships, in general as well as in specific situations. There is a great deal of similarity with research in Comparative Politics, which gives room to understand the context, why actions lead to different outcomes in different contexts (e.g., Hern 2023). Such knowledge contributes to an understanding of the circumstances in which measures are effective.

It is important to elaborate policy learning in the EU; on what foundation is the policy based and what additional knowledge needs to be developed? This implies that the EU needs to formulate a learning strategy as part of the Africa Strategy. It could also become an instrument for coordinating efforts and learning across policy areas (DGs).

SUMMARY AND REFLECTIONS

The analysis of the Africa strategy adds to the previous chapters by looking at an integrated set of policies rather than a singular area (chapter four) or three related policy areas (chapter three). The selection of policies is reasonable yet interesting, since development policy is missing from the Africa strategy and the role of the SDGs is not touched upon. This could be interpreted as a selection of policies where the relation between the EU and the African governments is of a different kind. However, the message of moving towards a partnership isn't seen in all the recommendations, which range from partnership to hierarchy, making demands on Africans to assist in the control of migration to Europe.

The specific proposals touch upon many sensitive issues, which was seen by going through some of the comments given on the strategy document. The risks and opportunities of the proposed strategy were also spelled out.

The ambiguities of the document point in two directions. They give evidence of the previously mentioned policy communities inside (and outside) the EU and how they struggle to agree on a set of policies. The ambiguities also point towards the need for a more elaborate strategic framework, based on some hypotheses on what drives development in Africa and how the EU and others can assist. This is the topic of the following two chapters.

Chapter 6

Decentering European Policies 1

Focus on the African Context

The previous three chapters have described EU foreign policy, trade policy, and development policy as well as the cross-cutting strategy for Africa. Here, the ambition is to shift the focus from the European intentions to the African context where the important outcomes of the policies are to be seen. The purpose is to identify challenges for the ambition to eradicate poverty and to achieve the SDGs in Africa, especially political and economic development.

The analysis needs to decenter away from the European context, to focus on the African situation, meaning that it must take the context as well as the will of the recipients into account. Such a focus on Africa is important for the analysis. It leads to what is at the heart of the instrumental policy, i.e., theories which can provide guidance on what the recipient countries and the EU should do. I will touch on several kinds of theories which point to various factors affecting the outcome.

Development is primarily an African responsibility, but it is also the goal of the European policies. As described in chapter four, it is unclear how much of the responsibility the EU assumes, while the EU is making efforts in all five areas starting with the letter P (peace, prosperity, people, planet, and partnership). The issues are very complex, and my ambition is therefore only to discuss overall what is happening in the African countries and how the EU's policies relate to this. General drivers and barriers will be touched upon, while I will refrain from commenting on individual countries.

As indicated in chapter two, I will focus on the achievement of the political and economic goals, since they are important for creating state capacity and resources to achieve the environmental and the social goals. This doesn't mean that the latter goals are less important, only that their long-term achievement depends on the first two sets of goals. In the short-term there will most likely be a need for external support, which raises further questions about not undermining the efforts of the African governments, a problem I will discuss in general terms in the next chapter.

The chapter starts from an analysis of the weak achievement of the SDGs in the African context, where the drivers for transformation seem weaker and/or the barriers stronger than in other parts of the world. Two alternative strategies for change are outlined, where one is an indirect, institutionalist strategy of reforming institutions in recipient countries, which is contrasted to an older, more direct and centralist strategy. The concept of a developmental state is an important intermediary factor. This is followed by a discussion of barriers to economic and political development, which are fundamental for achieving the SDGs, through an overview of ongoing research, summarized in a roadmap ("theory of change") to achieve the SDGs. A key observation is that the EU is not officially addressing these problems in its policy documents.

To place the EU policies in context, I will first give a short overview of the implementation of the SDGs in Africa. There are estimates by various organizations which can serve as summaries of the situation and a first analysis of the problems involved in reaching the SDGs. I will then add more general views from ongoing research on strategies, barriers, and drivers for development and transformation in Africa. These will serve as a context for the EU policies. To some extent, these general observations on challenges in Africa and elsewhere can serve as a replacement for the elaborate views which are missing in the EU documents.

DIFFICULTIES IN ACHIEVING THE SDGS IN AFRICA

A natural starting point for an overall picture of developments in the world is the reports made in connection with the SDGs. Three such reports are interesting to briefly summarize, as well as some of the comments published by various organizations. These are often done by researchers and with a high level of ambition.

The Sustainable Development Solutions Network (SDSN) is an ongoing cooperation by organizations which assist the UN with documentation. Its annual reports are made for the whole world and for the individual continents. Recent global reports give the pandemic a lot of space, as well as the major problems which have been exposed, such as the fact that poor countries find it difficult to borrow money for emergency measures (Sachs et al. 2021, vii) and that the poor health situation is a major problem in many countries (ibid., ix).

The report uses a global index which measures how countries relate to the SDGs. The index is topped by the Nordic countries, followed by the rich group of OECD countries which are close to 80 out of 100. Sub-Saharan

Africa is around 50 out of 100 and the other continents are in the range of 65–72 out of 100. More interesting is the trend and forecast for 2030, which is that the group of African countries will reach about 55, while the global group of low-income countries will reach about 50 (ibid., 14). The implication is that the efforts made are insufficient and that there may be reason to coordinate efforts globally, especially if low results in some countries are a problem for all countries, as it is with global warming. However, more detailed analysis of how problems and solutions are interconnected globally is needed to draw conclusions on how to step up efforts in Africa.

Extreme poverty in the world, measured as the proportion of people living on less than $1.90 a day, had fallen to 8.6 percent by the time the pandemic hit. The forecast was to fall to 6.0 percent by 2030 (ibid., 15). For sub-Saharan Africa, however, extreme poverty was at 39 percent before the pandemic and is now at around 41 percent. North Africa is at about 8 percent while all other parts of the world are lower (ibid., 21). One obvious conclusion is that the need for change is greatest in southern Africa, in a global comparison.

The report summarizes the situation graphically with red, yellow, and green dots as well as an arrow showing how each goal develops. For the poorest countries, all dots are red, except for the one showing climate impact, which is probably the result of a lack of economic growth (ibid., 31). African countries often have the same pattern, but with interesting variations (ibid., 37).

The report contains data on how countries work with the objectives, including whether there is clear political responsibility for the outcomes. However, there is no analysis of why the situation is as it is or what could be done to achieve all the objectives of each country. This type of analysis is carried out in other contexts.

The United Nations Economic Commission for Africa (UNECA) publishes reports on the green transition, giving the reader an elaborate picture of recent developments. The latest report begins with an argument that African countries already spend about 5 percent of GDP to deal with climate problems. In addition, there are the problems due to the pandemic, which has led, among other things, to the disappearance of 30 million jobs (ECA 2021, vi). More optimistic comments are about the pandemic being followed by a rapid re-start of the economy in various respects (ibid., viii).

A third group of reports is published by the African Union (AU) on its development objectives for 2063, which largely overlap with the UN objectives. A report compares the two sets of goals and discusses the status of African countries (Mo Ibrahim Foundation 2019). The picture is broadly in line with the other reports, leading to questions about what African countries can and should do to improve their situation, as well as what the EU can and should do to facilitate.

In addition to these surveys, there are various indices showing the situation in specific countries regarding the development of the economy, welfare levels, the environment, and political factors. The World Bank and UN follow-ups on the SDGs report a large amount of data, published in the series "World Development Indicators" and "Atlas of Sustainable Development Goals" (World Bank 2017). The more interesting follow-up question from a policy perspective is which factors are obstacles or drivers for improving the results. These are major research issues in development economics and comparative policies. All in all, the reports show that the efforts to reach the SDGs are much too weak.

Policy Proposals

In 2015, the British think tank Overseas Development Institute (ODI) released a report predicting that none of the UN's targets would be achieved globally by 2030. Each goal received a rating and was followed by reasoning about how much change in ongoing trends would be required to achieve them. Some economic objectives were considered quite easy to achieve—including poverty reduction—while some of the environmental objectives were judged to be the most difficult. Items like peace and industrialization ended up in the middle (Nicolai et al. 2015).

One of the most interesting observations in this context is that the authors identified six key drivers for better outcomes: political leadership, effective policies, a well-functioning implementation organization, good finances, partnerships with donors, and citizens' responses (ibid., 36). The list is almost tautological, in the sense that they ask for some fundamental problems to go away. It begs the underlying problem of finding solutions to these problems. Another reading is that there is a need for a two-step approach, where a first focus should be to improve these instruments to guide further policies. This is essentially a call for "good governance" (SDG number 16) to make other policies more effective, which is very relevant for example where corruption is a major source of inefficiency.

In the same vein, ODI publishes assessments of what is needed to eradicate global poverty. In 2019, there was an argument that most of the countries on earth will be able to finance a basic level of welfare through their own taxes, while 46 countries (mainly in Africa) will not be able to do so. For these, half the solution is to streamline taxes and expenses, and the other half is for international donors to contribute more. The latter "only" requires all donors to meet the commitment of 0.7 percent of GNI to aid, and for all donors to focus half of the aid on poverty reduction (Manuel et al. 2019). This is a thought experiment to show that money is available, rather than a proposal to be taken literally.

The International Monetary Fund (IMF) makes similar predictions for individual countries, which show the variation in national contexts. An example shows that countries like Benin and Rwanda need to set aside about 20 percent of their GDP by 2030 to meet the targets (Prady and Sy 2019). The countries differ in their development history, while both are judged to be on a path of good development and take the SDGs very seriously (ibid., 5). This implies that the needs are larger in other countries.

Reports commenting on what should be done are published by the Brookings Institution under the theme "Foresight Africa." Some of the chapters in the latest reports deal with the post-pandemic situation and the situation in healthcare, education, and business. The reports analyze governance issues, such as the confidence of the population in their leaders of different countries (Ordu 2021). This relates to one of the fundamental issues, that the citizens need to have confidence in their leaders and the state bureaucracy to be willing to pay taxes and to accept other policies which go against their individual desires or traditional ways of dealing with social issues.

The reports touch upon some key issues in the popular and academic debate on development. One issue is whether states (collective leadership top-down through a bureaucracy) are necessary to guide social transformation. There are many examples of great leaders or social movements which have modernized their societies, but also of failed dictatorships. There are furthermore examples of order without states, which add nuance to the analysis (Risse 2011).

Another issue is that these states must be accepted by the population, which in modern times means that there must be some inclusion or consent by the ruled. The normative concept of legitimacy points at characteristics which make the leaders worthy of acceptance, such as consent, fair regulation, and an impartial and altruistic bureaucracy to carry out the decisions ("rule of law"). This is not to exclude that other forms of leadership will continue to be important for some time, for example the rule by clans and other elites.

Other commentary highlights specific issues, such as trade policy. A European think tank which has made contributions on developments in Africa is the European Union Institute for Security Studies (EUISS), including giving comments on what is needed for the African Continental Trade Agreement to lead to the desired economic development (Faleg 2021). The report is an example of so-called backcasting, showing which changes are necessary at present to achieve a future goal, in this case to increase trade to make economies grow. Economic growth is a fundamental driver of change in the SDGs although there are risks of negative impact on the environment (chapter two). Some theories see economic development as a driver of political development, rather than the other way around.

The American Carnegie Endowment for International Peace ("Carnegie") publishes reports on developments in poor countries, most recently on why economic diversification is important in Africa (Usman and Landry 2021). This adds to the picture of which policy changes are important to make the economies grow faster.

An African think tank with many contributions to the debate on the situation in Africa is the Institute for Security Studies (ISS), not to be confused with EUISS. One report claims that economic development is taking other paths in Africa than in Europe, partly because the states don't function as the development theories assume. The argument is that African economies develop informally and with elements of organized crime. The authors argue for a greater role for local actors and a more limited role for the state (Scheye and Pelser 2020). Another of their reports points to the need to simultaneously develop entrepreneurship and democratic leadership (Cilliers 2020). Both observations are in line with the research on the drivers of development, which I will come to.

All in all, the reports show that the countries of sub-Saharan Africa are a long way from achieving the SDGs. They also indicate that the eradication of poverty is not one of the most difficult objectives to achieve. However, the large difference in poverty rates compared to the countries of North Africa and to the rest of the world suggests that major changes are needed in the economic and political situation of Sub-Saharan Africa. This points to a need to rethink national strategies and donor strategies.

This picture of slow achievement of the SDGs is not an overall picture of the impact of development aid, but it does point to a need to understand how overall changes are taking place. The long-term perspectives need to be strengthened and the role of the EU specified. This needs to be elaborated by the EU, shifting its focus from intentions to outcomes.

INSTITUTIONAL AND CENTRALIST STRATEGIES

The fundamental question for Africans and their European supporters, through the European policies and the Africa strategy, is what should be done to achieve the desired results, especially when there is competition between donors with different orientations, such as the EU and China. Development is at heart a long-term process of political change (Yanguas 2018). The national economies and the political systems need to change, often in radical ways and often under opposition from existing (undemocratic) rulers. These are highly complex issues for a strategy.

For today's developing countries, the UN vision expressed through the SDGs is to implement several large-scale changes at the same time (chapter two). Industrialization needs to be carried out in an environmentally friendly manner and, at the same time, good governance in various aspects need to be introduced, with rights and freedoms and a well-functioning state apparatus capable of administering the desired measures. The UN sets the target for 2030, but it is unrealistic that all the transformations will be achieved by then. In today's rich countries, the processes of industrialization and development of good governance has taken decades, if not centuries.

As I discussed in chapter four, the activities by the EU, reported under the five themes used by the UN, starting with the letter P, can be seen as elements of a strategy to change the situation in poor countries, where "peace" is about resolving conflicts, building states, and moving towards democracy, the rule of law, etc. "Prosperity" points to the need for industrialization of poor countries. The EU as an outsider can be perceived as having a responsibility to help kick-start development, including through "partnership." These three seem to be the reasonable focus of the EU's efforts.

As pointed out above, "people" (welfare) and "planet" (environment) are more clearly the responsibility of the poor countries when their economies and state capacity grow. Admittedly, for the foreseeable future they will need support, but the long-term ambition of the SDGs is that the poor countries will finance their welfare and pursue their own environmental policy. Both elements point back to good governance (including "state capacity") as an important prerequisite. A key, then, is to contribute to the construction of states which can deal with their country's challenges. For long-term legitimacy, states need to be more democratic and less corrupt. Hence, I will focus in the following on the drivers and barriers for the political and economic goals of the SDGs.

In terms of modern research perspectives, there is a need for rules (institutions) which encourage political and economic development. I will come back to regulatory frameworks which support economic growth as well as to the value of political debate and competition among political parties to provide programs of modernization.

What makes the situation particularly complicated is that the transition from dictatorship and a centrally controlled economy to democracy and a decentralized market economy can take place in different ways, depending on background factors and events. There is no obvious model for the long-term development of poor countries on which Africans or the EU can rely. Instead, the implication is that the EU should contribute to the analysis of what drives development and how its efforts affect the situation. This is to place EU policies in the context of the recipients rather than focusing on intentions.

The Importance of Institutions to the SDGs

Daron Acemoglu and James Robinson as well as other researchers on economic history have highlighted that modernization and industrialization are based on the emergence of new "rules of the game" (Acemoglu and Robinson 2012). The perspective which has become dominant among economists and political scientists highlights the rules of the game for economics and politics, the so-called institutions (rules and norms). The key argument is that stable rules which provide openness is of great value in the economy as well as in politics, allowing for challenging and competing views (new firms, new political opinions) under conditions which provide stability and allow such dynamism. In essence, most of the relevant institutions are part of the concept of the rule of law (Carothers 2006).

This institutionalist perspective isn't a blueprint, ready to use for development policy, but rather a framework for thinking about what is important to drive transformation in African countries and elsewhere. The institutions guide actions, at the national as well as the global level. I will come back in the next chapter to the importance of foreign policy and other external factors.

In the institutionalist perspective, it is understood that the economy and politics are self-sustaining systems in which individuals act autonomously but are guided by the framework conditions (rules and norms). The institutions give indirect guidance by making certain actions easier, higher rewarded or normatively endorsed. This contrasts with the more direct forms of central control which were popular before, to be discussed below. The follow-up questions for donors and national leaders are what the good rules of the game are and how to introduce them in countries where they do not already exist, with the help of the EU and others.

This is a perspective in ongoing research and not necessarily the best way to frame a set of policies. Nevertheless, one would expect the EU to show some awareness of the implicit recommendations on what is important for transformational change.

In short summary, the good institutions include rules for a market economy, such as rules for owning and operating businesses, trading, and making long-term investments (freedom to conduct business, ownership, etc.). Acemoglu and Robinson point to the value of clear rules which make it easier for individuals to start a business and thus take financial risks. Part of this is to have trust in other individuals and in public authorities (Acemoglu and Robinson 2012). With the establishment of such institutions follows economic development.

In a wider range of important institutions, one could include factors which relate to norms and values which are relevant in the transformation from an agricultural society to an industrialized society. Two focal points are education and religion. Education provides basic skills such as reading and writing and also knowledge about the sciences, history, geography, and so on. It is noteworthy that compulsory schooling played an important role in Europe, "turning peasants into Frenchmen" (Weber 1976). In some developing countries, a weak educational sector is a means for the ruling elite to maintain control (Elayah 2016). Religion is a more traditional set of beliefs, partly in conflict with education. There is a long debate on the importance of certain religious beliefs, for example in the hypothesis that Protestantism was important for capitalism (Weber 1930).

An important issue concerns the role of trade, whether trade can lead to companies in poor countries becoming subcontractors for international companies, which was an important part of the development of Southeast Asia. This can be seen as a fast track to economic development, as international markets are larger than national ones. One effect may be that the companies which are subcontractors embrace new technologies faster than other companies. Hence, trade policy can be a form of indirect aid to poor countries. This is in contrast to earlier economic theories which emphasized self-sufficiency ("import substitution") and the need to develop domestic production in all areas, a mercantilist strategy.

There is at the same time a risk that the potential of trade agreements such as the African Continental Free Trade Agreement (AfCFTA) will be overestimated. Previous research has shown that regional free trade agreements didn't work as intended. One reason was that governments chose to protect their national companies from the new competition (Byiers, Vanheukelom, and Woolfrey 2018).

Other rules lay the foundation for political democracy, for example through limited (constitutional) exercise of power, elections, freedom of speech, and more. The possibility of holding leaders accountable is a central part of democracy as a system of governance. Another aspect is to have political parties with competing visions to seek a mandate from the voters. The high ambitions of the SDGs presuppose that there are organizations which can deliver advanced regulations and services, as well as manage trade-offs against other ambitions, such as maintaining growth and democracy.

Environmental policy presupposes that there are analytical capabilities, for example within a ministry of the environment or a ministry of finance, which can adapt instruments to the situation and strike a balance with the equally important economic policy. In the areas of welfare, funding is a key issue, which is dependent on acceptance by the citizens to pay taxes. This leads to another big issue of how welfare systems can be designed under emerging industrialization (Rudra 2008).

The institutionalist perspective is a theory about the importance and origin of the institutions, but it isn't obvious how the historical descriptions can be turned into a strategy for all poor countries, how they can redesign their institutions with the support of external donors such as the EU. The long list of possible institutions of relevance implies a need for priority and a need to deal with multiple pathways to the desired end, the achievement of the SDGs.

The emergence of the beneficial rules has taken place over centuries in Europe and under great suffering in the form of wars and other conflicts. Today's poor countries are in other situations and must make several changes at the same time, while maintaining peaceful relations (Carothers 2007). A particular question is whether today's dictators ("autocrats") have the will and ability to devise appropriate measures to kick-start the economy, without threatening their own hold on power. The SDGs appear to be written for a benevolent leader with the sole focus on solving the problems of his citizens. In reality, some leaders prefer to stay in power to enrich themselves and their supporters.

This summary describes a view which is in fashion academically and is likely well-known in the EU.

How to Change the Institutions?

Economists from Karl Marx to Mustaq Khan describe the political process in which new rules of the game are formed, often under opposition from old elites (Khan 2011). For example, Karl Marx noted that companies play a central role in the modern economy ("capitalism") which emerged in the nineteenth century and that it was the entrepreneurs (the "capitalists") who pushed forward the new regulations which favored companies and limited the power of the kings over the economy of England. There is some similarity between the situation in Europe in the Middle Ages and in Africa now, in the form of autocratic rulers trying to control the economy, instead of creating regulations which unleash economic drivers (Brett 2009; Ayittey 2005). Trade can create interest among leaders in making their countries attractive to investors.

One view is that there must be people who push for a new order. The "capitalists" wanted greater freedom. Other examples may include people who want to uphold a legal system, a fair bureaucracy or the free thinking of Academia. The term "pockets of effectiveness" refers to groups that function relatively well and uphold good values, for example in finance ministries, courts, and universities. Even the military can be a positive force if it is free from ethnic conflicts. In terms of economic development, companies and their owners can be a positive driver. This is part of the answer to the important question of who can push the rules of the game which lead to the achievement of the SDGs. The follow-up question is how the EU can support such islands of individualism in other countries.

The process of change is extremely complex. Starting points as well as endpoints vary by country. Even in Western Europe today, there are major differences between the economic and political systems, despite the fact that all countries are democracies and market economies (Schmidt 2002, 2006). The development paths can be varied, with mixed forms and "hybrid regimes." There is extensive research on the path from authoritarian to democratic governance (Landman 2003) and how a modern market economy can emerge in developing countries (Whitfield et al. 2015).

One question is whether this should be seen as a large-scale transformation or whether it is reasonable to divide the problems into an agenda for the individual items in the SDGs: a well-functioning legal system, a professional and corruption-free bureaucracy, human rights and freedoms, independent media, independent organizations (civil society, trade unions, religious communities), school systems, healthcare, freedom of enterprise, financial markets, infrastructure, environmental protection, etc. The SDGs are built on the thinking that all issues are related, which produce an almost infinite number of possible paths of transition.

For each component, there is extensive research on development pathways, but what are the effects if some issues follow democratic principles when others do not, in a hybrid manner? The literature on institutional models in Europe emphasizes that the effects of specific rules can be limited in such a situation (Schmidt 2002). A social model can have a balancing point which means that minor changes do not affect the model as a whole (Streeck and Thelen 2005). This implies a need to separate African societies into several models, for example based on the kind of state (legal system) it has in place.

Finally, it should be noted that the institutional theories are basically a stylized description of the historical developments in Western Europe and the United States. Critics argue that states played a more governing role than these models show (Chang 2003). It is not clear how poor countries with alternative conditions will transform themselves to resemble the model, especially if other major powers such as China are trying to influence them in a different direction. The analysis needs to say something about alternative strategies and factors that are outside the model.

To summarize, the institutionalist perspective focuses on rules and norms. It helps us understand barriers and drivers for transformation. The basic elements are general to many contexts, while the specific issues differ, especially who is in a position to transform the rules from the inside. There are no blueprints to be used for specific countries, which implies that policy and research need to be open to learn from experience.

Centralist Strategies: The Authoritarian Alternative

The alternative to focusing on the institutions as a means of indirectly promoting economic and political development is to pursue a more direct approach, in which actions are directed from a national center. Older theories of development pointed directly to things which need to happen in lesser developed economies, such as raising the productivity of the economy by investing in machines, better crops, better education, or better technology. Such political programs can be implemented by benevolent leaders or competent bureaucrats. Historically, they were often pursued by non-democratic leaders.

The model has been successful in Asia under different circumstances. Some Asian countries were democracies (Japan), became democracies (South Korea), or remained dictatorships (China), raising questions about causation. Democracy is neither necessary nor sufficient for modernization. Fortunately, dictatorship is neither sufficient nor necessary either.

For a long time there has been a perception that poor countries must first introduce democracy and the rule of law ("good governance"), before economic development can take off, or at least some such elements (Grindle 2004). Other scholars have argued that democracy may be the result of economic development, as South Korea is an example of. A further variation is that some leaders have been benevolent dictators who have used their control over the economy and politics to develop the economy and limit corruption (Kelsall 2013). This is seen as a possible development path for weak states in Africa, but the risks are great, including the risk that this will become a defense of dictatorship (Niklasson 2019).

The EU supports democracy because it is good in itself. It is difficult to see how the EU could support dictatorships in order to achieve growth, prosperity, or more effective climate action. When the EU cooperates with dictators for security policy reasons, it receives criticism. There are also arguments that democracy will improve the workings of a national government which is not a democracy today. The argument is that democracy has long-term positive effects, for example that a free debate would make China's policies more effective.

Centralism points to key issues and can be of value in some contexts but is likely to fail by not allowing competition over economic policies or political visions. With dictatorship, there is, for example, a risk that the government strikes deals with companies to the detriment of the citizens. The examples of Europe and Asia point to the possibility of finding rational "middle ways" of states.

Developmental States

The comparison with the countries in Asia has led to a discussion on the possibilities of creating so-called developmental states in Africa. The problem discussed above is that states must have many good qualities which they lack at present. The rule of law and the absence of corruption have been mentioned. The debate on Asia stressed that their states were intertwined in the economic system, but at the same time independent from the dominant actors of the economy. The ideal was that bureaucrats understood and influenced economic development without listening too much to the interests of existing companies, a situation described as "embedded autonomy," practiced by bureaucracies such as the Japanese Ministry for International Trade and Industry (MITI).

The literature emphasizes that state-building in Africa and other parts of the world is different from the conditions in Europe. One difference is that states are not based on nationalism to the same extent. Often the states in Africa are large with small or heterogeneous populations (Herbst 2000, Thies 2009). Another difference is that today's states are affected by an international context which is different from the European older context, partly because today's states are not always good role models.

The last observation belongs to a group of sociological theories, which point out that state building is influenced by norms from the outside world. A further theme is to compare the current situation with European state building in previous centuries, especially the importance of wars and rivalry to make states efficient (Tilly 2004). Cameron Thies (2007) examines whether there are circumstances which create a development-driven competitive situation, similar to that between the European states, but peacefully, which could have a positive impact on development in Africa. His short answer is no.

One underlying explanation for the emergence of effective states in Europe is that Europe was densely populated and became the scene of many wars, while Africa was sparsely populated and more peaceful (Thomson 2010). Charles Tilly and others point out that it was the wars which laid the foundations for the effective states of Europe. There were some independent states in Africa, such as Ethiopia, but it didn't develop in conflict with other states. The British sometimes ruled through traditional kingdoms (Scott 2017), which were weaker than the European states at the time.

Further theories highlight the interests and incentives of individuals in key positions, such as how informal leaders make up their mind about power and the distribution of resources, including the role of development funds (Anten, Briscoe, and Mezzera 2012). There is a risk that development funds will become a loot in a power play between groups. This approach may be consistent with the sociological approach, but points to different ways of influencing the situation, with new norms or incentives.

The problem of leaders enriching themselves is part of the grand issue of corruption. The discussion on the causes of corruption points to low salaries for government employees and/or personal loyalty relations (patrimonialism). Massive changes are needed to move from a situation where almost everyone is corrupt to almost no one. The measures range from the creation of anti-corruption authorities to social contracts which make citizens see the state as beneficial (Rothstein 2021).

The situation is complicated by the fact that dictators (autocrats) at the same time have an interest in remaining in power and have therefore often developd what is known as survival strategies, which include limiting the opposition's space in the political system (Bader and Faust 2014). This clashes with the EU's democracy objectives and raises the question of how the EU should relate to autocrats.

A special literature deals with measures after an invasion with the aim of changing government. The failures of the United States in countries such as Somalia and Iraq have given rise to a theory of the "state builder's dilemma," that it is difficult to find a new leader which the people as well as the intervening superpower will accept (Lake 2016). One variant of this is that foreign financial support for a government can make it less interested in anchoring its measures with the population (Moss, Pettersson, and van de Walle 2006).

For donors, it sometimes makes sense to provide financial resources to informal leaders (e.g. warlords), if it is believed that their supporters have the opportunity to demand responsibility for how the funds are spent, instead of cooperating with a legal but weak government, from which no one demands responsibility. In other words, unconventional action may be required to deal with extreme situations.

In conclusion, the lack of effective states is a major obstacle to economic and political development in many of the poorest countries. It isn't certain that the political instruments will have to be developed before growth can take off. Modern research points to complex causal relationships. On the other hand, it seems inappropriate to turn this into a principle of cooperating with dictators, in breach of the SDGs. For the EU, it seems more reasonable to continue to support those who are pushing for the establishment of democracy and a market economy in the poor countries. Indirect aid in the form of extended trade may also be important in stimulating the processes of change.

BARRIERS TO ECONOMIC AND POLITICAL DEVELOPMENT

The choice of development strategy must be based on an inventory of barriers, but it is not entirely clear what factors are hindering economic and political development. A review of such obstacles will be a list of some of the problems that EU policies seek to help solve. The obstacles are part of a larger analysis of what is being done and what can act as drivers or barriers to economic and political development.

Barriers to Economic Development

Behind the reasoning for stimulating change in poor countries lies a question of why they are poor, why they have not developed as quickly as the countries of the "North." One answer mentioned above is that the rich countries have held back development and made them poor. Colonialism comes into focus and there is an academic debate about the effects of colonialism. Atul Kohli calculates the economic losses for India by belonging to the British Empire (Kohli 2020), but he also sees advantages in some of the British constitutional principles (cf. Lange and Rueschemeyer 2005).

The reasoning may lead to the conclusion that the EU should help its former colonies to a larger extent, but it doesn't say much about what should be changed in the poor countries today to move on to a different development track. There is a risk that development aid will be poorly designed if the motive is primarily to repay a debt.

A possible alternative is to see the countries of the South as unintended victims when the countries of the North increased their trade (Williamson 2011, Kvangraven 2020). According to trade theory, the prosperity of the countries which trade with each other is increasing. One effect is that these countries are becoming richer in relation to those which don't trade, where the latter suffer a kind of negative side effect from others reforming their policies. If this is a moral problem, the implication is that all countries must be offered to participate in the global trading systems. Otherwise, they will be held back and economic gaps will arise.

A more tragic explanation to the problems in some countries is that access to natural resources such as oil and minerals can create problems. One type of problem is that there are conflicts over assets, which makes the situation unstable. Another type of problem is that governments can distribute favors to citizens instead of financing public activities through taxes. This, in turn, weakens the demands for democracy and modernization. This is the core idea of "rentier states" (Walker 2023). An extreme example is Angola, which is considered a failed state which survives thanks to its oil (Soares de Oliveira 2007).

Dani Rodrik (2015) is pessimistic for other reasons, arguing that industrialization requires advanced skills and abilities of the workforce, which in Rodrik's view means that today's poor countries can only develop simple service jobs, where they end up in a kind of "premature deindustrialization." Other economists are more optimistic and see great development opportunities in Africa (Signé 2019a). Landry Signé focuses on political factors to explain why African governments repeat failed strategies. His argument is that they are stuck with old policies ("paths") since they are too weak to design and implement new policies (ibid.).

A further explanation is to say that today's development aid policy creates or exacerbates problems in poor countries, even if the aim is to help. The problems of fragmentation of aid and the focus on helping where it is easiest, rather than where the needs are greatest, have been mentioned above. For a period, the EU sent part of its surplus agricultural products to the poor countries, helping consumers in poor countries but hindering the development of African agriculture. Contemporary politics has identified several of these problems and has an ambition to avoid past mistakes.

A further objection is that postcolonial leaders destroyed their countries' development opportunities by changing too much and unleashing new conflicts (Cooper 2002). However, there is a wide range between leaders who enriched themselves and those who had visions for the country's development, for example in Ghana and Tanzania. Economists point out that the new states often followed paths created by the colonial powers which limited the options for action of the new leaders (ibid.).

Underlying Factors

An underlying factor is the large and often unnatural African states created at the Berlin Conference in 1884–1885. These states were generally difficult to govern. In addition, they did not coincide with national identities (Herbst 2000). Conflicts between ethnic groups contribute to political conflict because politics is often focused on ethnic identities, not on mobilization around interests in the industrialization process (as in Europe), such as "workers versus capitalists." One view is that a national identity is needed to push through the changes that lie in the concept of modernization.

A supplementary question is whether the African Union or the regional economic communities (RECs) can replace or complement the African states; can political loyalty be directed towards a supranational organization, when there are few functioning nation states? It is not obvious that developments in Africa or other poor areas must follow the models that were common in

Europe, where the EU started as an intergovernmental arrangement, based on well-functioning states.

A hotly debated question is whether traditional African rules and norms hindered or facilitated economic development. A common view is that ownership was collective in the villages and that there were therefore no rewards for individuals to develop agriculture and other economic activities. Economist George Ayittey (2005) argues against this, that the traditional rules of the game included incentives for individuals to improve their situation, which means that African countries could have developed economically under such circumstances.

The relevant question in modern times is whether there are norms which benefit growth if the conditions are right. A very basic observation in African countries is that the extensive sales of agricultural products and handicrafts and a comprehensive informal economy are signs that this is the case. Rather, the obstacles lie in the regulations of the economy, as suggested in the institutional analysis.

Another fundamental factor is what is called neopatrimonialism, where what on the surface looks like modern states is governed by personal loyalty ties ("patrimonialism," "clientelism"), as in the mafia or during feudalism (Kelsall 2013). Citizens give loyalty to local leaders and receive protection in exchange. Local leaders, in turn, can make trades with senior leaders and the national leader. One variant is that the local groups are made up of clans that are held together by family ties and provide protection in troubled situations. This is a common and "simple" model for creating order in societies without a state, such as Afghanistan, Mali, or Somalia (Weiner 2013).

Neopatrimonialism is often equated with kleptocracy, where corrupt leaders enrich themselves. For a long time, this has been regarded as a fundamental problem for poor countries in Africa and elsewhere. The loyalties are a restriction on a modern economy but also on democratic governance, in which citizens are assumed to act freely and without risk to their security and livelihood.

With a famous formulation, many poor countries are characterized by having "weak states but strong societies" (Migdal 2001). In Europe, such social power was replaced by what Max Weber called a legal-bureaucratic governance model, with officials following general rules. The origin can be sought in the Catholic Church, army, and courts.

In the short term, the underlying factors constitute significant obstacles for the EU and others to influence the situation. In the longer term, these can also be influenced, through direct action and indirect changes through mechanisms such as growth and influence from other countries.

Barriers to Political Development

Many poor countries are dictatorships ("autocracies"), but not all. Most countries in Africa are described as "multi-party systems with dominant parties," which means that they have some similarities to democracies (general elections) but are limited in their public debate and other background characteristics. Autocrats govern their countries through political parties or states which distribute benefits to supporters (Svolik 2012; Geddes, Wright, and Frantz 2018). Many countries are characterized by corruption, nepotism, and neopatrimonialism, but what is interesting is whether developments can be reversed, in order to lay the foundation for achieving the SDGs. The goals require a certain capacity to decide on and implement rational measures.

Nic Cheeseman has summarized six pathways to democracy and their likely outcomes, which captures some of the key processes of change (Cheeseman 2015, 96). A problem is that the mode of transition has impact on the regime that follows, where the democratic regime can be very limited or fragile.

Cheeseman describes stylized patterns of the transition to democracy, which illustrate many situations in Africa. The transition can be driven from above by the leader, who then retains power through a dominant party. The opposite is change driven from the bottom by protest movements and ending in a potential democracy.

Four intermediate situations consist of some form of conflict resolution, involving the leader and the protest movements, where the process is influenced by different parties. Two forms of externally influenced conflict resolution lead to weak democracy or an authoritarian regime. A national coup or negotiation has greater potential to lead to democratic outcomes. There is no guarantee that the patterns will eventually lead to democracy.

Nic Cheeseman is also a leading name in the research on the impact of formal regulation on democratic transitions (Cheeseman 2018). This contrasts with older perspectives, which held that neopatrimonialism and other state characteristics prevented gradual transformation. Modern research shows that it makes sense to support development by introducing democratic rules of the game (ibid.).

The focus on development paths highlights slow transformations, but there is other research on the spread of ideas which points to the opposite, that leaders are happy to copy popular politics from other countries. The rapid spread of the ideas of democracy and market economy in the 1990s can be seen as evidence that there was a relatively superficial embrace of modern ideas (Simmons, Dobbin, and Garrett 2008). Here the implication is that development policy can spread the ideas of democracy, while there is a risk that the copied constitutions are ill-suited to the situation in the specific countries. The so-called third wave of democratization around 1990 had to do with the end of the Cold War. Countries supported by the United States or the Soviet Union changed when one of the superpowers disappeared.

The paths limit the actors, while the global exchange of ideas opens up for new ambitions. In addition, there are perspectives which treat leaders as rational actors in a negotiating situation. Robert Bates has used game theory to show that it is possible to understand farmers and warlords as rational actors within the framework of the rules of the game (Bates 2008). Similar reasoning can be used to understand the leaders' propensity to reform and/or cooperate with the EU and China, which I will come back to in the next chapter.

Two circumstances are often mentioned as obstacles to democratization. One is the lack of a liberal tradition with its ideas of democracy and political rights. This includes, for example, the idea that it is important to have a functioning political opposition (Uddhammar, Green, and Söderström 2011). The second is the one mentioned above, that the dominant line of conflict is about ethnic identities, not about "class conflicts," i.e., the economic conflicts of interest that usually arise when a country is industrialized, and which are suitable for dealing with in a democratic system. Industrialization is a basis for the development of political democracy (Rodrik 2016).

Dani Rodrik points out that there may be other paths to democracy than those which have been common in Europe. The ruling elite can support a transition to certain forms of democracy (separation of powers) if the elite is divided or if mass protests threaten (ibid., Sebudubudu and Molutsi 2011). Rodrik also points out that some authoritarian states, including China and Singapore, have been adept at creating rules of the game for economic development and have given some (small) room for dissent (Rodrik 2016). Another example is the division of offices in Lebanon between Christians and Muslims, as a way of dealing with ethnic divisions. In Africa, Mauritius is a successful example of democracy in an ethnically divided country.

Rodrik's reasoning runs partly counter to the interpretation that has been dominant. As mentioned earlier, the World Bank and other organizations in the 1990s argued that good governance is a prerequisite for economic development. Some scholars have argued that it may be the other way around, that political democracy is driven forward by the demands of the population arising from industrialization, while some basic rules of the market economy are necessary to begin with (Kelsall 2013).

The follow-up question is what external parties such as the EU can do to support the democratization processes. The EU gives support for economic development and for actors who can influence the political system, including civil society organizations. Another dimension is to make demands and to reward and punish through financial support (Godfrey and Youngs 2019). A particular issue concerns the emergence of a well-functioning administration capable of implementing political decisions. Comparisons between Africa and Asia point to the lack of a well-functioning bureaucracy which can drive economic development in Africa, a developmental state (above). A theme of research is the possibility of developing bureaucracy, sometimes with Botswana as an example from Africa (Meyns and Musamba 2010).

I mentioned the problem of corruption above. Here too are several interesting development paths. Countries such as Rwanda, Uganda, and Ghana have reformed their administrations, but in different ways and under different circumstances. As with the emergence of democracy, the interests of the elite are central, but also the ideas that dominate the elite's thinking on the need for reform (ESID 2017).

Tax systems have come into focus with the SDGs. The EU and international organizations want to help developing countries "collect more, spend better" (EU 2015b). The European information material is technically oriented and shows, among other things, how European countries handle taxes and expenditure. It only hints that there may be fundamental problems in the legitimacy of governments, that citizens do not want to pay into a system in which they do not have confidence.

To summarize, there is a vast set of potential drivers and barriers. Some are close to the economy and the politics, while other factors are underlying and part of longer causal chains. The policy implications aren't obvious for the EU or for national actors, including the opposition. One way to focus the analysis would be to look more closely at particular cases where reforms have been made (or stalled) with or without external support. Another focusing device is to place the drivers and barriers in a tentative temporal order through a theory (hypothesis) of how the factors are linked.

A ROADMAP FOR THE SDGS?

I will summarize the analysis in a roadmap ("theory of change") by turning the examples from the overview of research above into a simplified causal chain, even if this risks over-simplification. The model is intended as a first example of how to integrate issues discussed in earlier chapters, with the further aim to show a tool to focus the analysis and the development of policy. Needless to say, there are many alternative views on how poor countries could develop (e.g. Cheru 2002; Andreasson 2010. See Odusola 2017 for an analysis of reaching the SDGs in Africa similar to mine).

A Heuristic Device

The theory of change is intended as a stylized hypothesis, a heuristic device to simplify the description of the causal relations and the analysis of real examples (countries). It shows a process of events, how small steps are related in order to lead from the present situation to the achievement of the SDGs, making up a roadmap of desirable steps (Burns and Worsley 2015). It is one of a group of heuristic devises aimed at bringing in an improved understanding of important factors for aid effectiveness (Copestake and Williams 2014).

Historical chains of events can be analyzed by means of process-tracing or some model of cumulative causation (Tilly 2004), while the theory of change extrapolates and simplifies to form the heuristic device. It is slightly abstracted from reality to form a general image of a transformative process into the future, based on what we know of the past. This is intended to open up debates on specific cases, to inform the details of the specific set of changes which need to take place, as well as the role of the EU.

This can be used as a planning instrument or a means to structure an evaluation of interventions (policies) at a later stage. It is a common instrument for project management and the point in this context is to treat the road to the achievement of the SDGs as a very large and complex project in its key steps. An advantage is to see events as related over time, which can lead to the prioritization of early factors which can have long-term effects and to avoid the opposite, events which depend on other circumstances. Roadmaps are common in climate policy and technology policy (e.g. Stern 2006; Miedzinski et al. 2022).

This is similar to the debate over "good governance," where an early view was that good governance (democracy and the rule of law) is a prerequisite for economic development. This was challenged by the view that "good *enough* governance" is more reasonable (Grindle 2004). The argument was that too much energy is put on the high ambition of "good governance," while "good enough" will take societies in the right direction with less effort. This can be combined with the view that economic development will lead to good governance in the next step (Niklasson 2019).

Roadmaps and "theories of change" are mainly instruments to help the development of policies, which differ from methods of research. Traditional social science methods look at past events, a single or a short but complex event, such as a popular uprising. The significance of relevant factors can then be estimated through statistical or comparative methods. The methods can provide deep understanding of a limited range of issues or a shallower understanding of a larger number of issues (Landman 2003). The analysis of events which unfold over time is generally more difficult.

The Model

One of the obvious simplifications in this roadmap (theory of change) is that events are placed in a linear order, in rows, which imply that events have to follow a certain sequence, while in reality one would expect some overlap and some alternative causal pathways. A more realistic "theory of change" for the SDGs would include a set of events with only few assumptions of causality, for example as a set of dots to be connected. This would be much more difficult to grasp, but would leave room for various drivers, such as political reform or economic growth as the fundamental drivers. A justification for the simple outline is that it helps aggregating some of the previous points in this chapter and that it is meant to be the start rather than the end of this research.

There is a main block of political transformations in row 2–7 below and a main block of economic and related issues in block 8–13. The first row contains triggers to set reforms in motion. Some elements have a logical order, for example that "freedom of enterprise" leads to a more dynamic economy (under certain circumstances), which doesn't rule out that some early economic growth can take place without freedom of enterprise (a trigger) and then lead to the introduction of such freedom. At this point, the order is based on an interpretation of the literature, which needs to be elaborated further.

The table has three columns, to illustrate the key events, important assumptions, and the role of external actors. The last column contains the roles which the EU could play, which in turn could be used to revise European policies. This is not to say that all policies should only be based on the situation in each country. It is more reasonable to think of some policies which are general and some activities which are adjusted to the local context, which is how the EU aims to operate today. The difference is in the decentering of the policies, to pay greater attention to the context and the causal links.

The middle column contains important assumptions, which is a common element in a theory of change, with the purpose of understanding the finer causal relationships. The assumptions are the necessary but often neglected steps which are needed to get from one stage (row) to another, i.e., other things which need to happen for the causal links to work.

Two key assumptions are not addressed fully. One is the capacity of African governments to lead the transformation, which is treated as something which grows over time. The other is the capacity of the EU to make positive contributions to the African transformations. The evidence in chapters 3–5 indicate that this is difficult. Decentering is seen as a way to improve the odds of making positive contributions.

The model is compatible with a focus on elites, as in recent theories by Douglass North and others, who argue that the key to development is the evolution of the role of elites in society. Their core is a hypothesis that the relation among the elites evolves over time and that this is the explanation of the transformation from enrichment to the adoption of the rule of law, which is to the benefit of the elite (North, Wallis, and Weingast 2009). This is compatible with, but not addressed in this highly simplified model.

Table 6.1 A tentative roadmap to achieve the SDGs in autocracies. Source: Author.

A causal chain of events	*Important assumptions*	*External support*
1. Triggers: • Economic growth/recession • Peace/war • Leadership strong/weak	Some elite rivalry	Peacekeeping
2. Freedom of expression: A public debate on development strategies	The formation of social movements and political parties Production of localized ideas Foreign academic support	Funding, ideas Academic exchange
3. Democracy: Governments are elected by the citizens with a mandate for change	Elections are fair Parties are not controlled by elites	Elections
4. Central government policy capacity • Economy • Environment • Welfare	Available economists etc.	Advice by the EU & AU
5. A professional bureaucracy where the rule of law is assured (corruption and neopatrimonialism are abolished) • Digitalization	Meritocracy Available trained civil servants: education, returning diaspora. No clientelism	Advice Secondments
6. The government is accepted/ legitimate, efficient	Citizens notice the difference Policy learning	
7. Peace: Conflicts are solved - Foreign negative influence limited	Local willingness	Security cooperation
8. Freedom of enterprise: new firms • Digitalization	Available skills, business opportunities Strong work ethic	Advice
9. More efficient agriculture	Technological development	Technology transfer
10. Foreign investments	Available investors and objects Fair trade with the EU and others	Trade agreements
11. Environmental protection (Green transition)	State capacity through trained staff Citizen acceptance Fossil fuel subsidies abolished	Professional networking
12. The dominance of a middle class	Economic growth Political freedom	
13. Welfare systems are developed (Eradication of poverty)	State capacity through trained staff Citizen acceptance of taxes	Professional networking

Thirteen Steps

The theory of change is outlined in 13 steps based on the institutionalist perspective, which is also the implicit model of the SDGs. This is intended as a helpful simplification, but is also a potential weakness, for example where economic growth drives political development. I have placed "triggers" at the beginning, without explaining how they arise in particular circumstances. This is intended to open for a variety of "logics of development." The context is generally one of strong elite rivalry, perhaps even war, possibly with some foreign intervention.

Three types of triggers are particularly important. One is the beginning of economic growth, another is a peace settlement and the third is some kind of benevolent leadership (Mandela, Kagame, Nkrumah etc.). To leave all options open, it is noted that negative events can trigger change, as well as positive events.

The rows 2–7 are a set of political transformations, where peace (number 7) is treated as an outcome at a late stage, a result of a transformation of the national government. Peace can be introduced earlier, especially by foreign intervention. In the SDGs, it is placed at the beginning (chapter two).

A standardized pattern of political reform would be to allow freedom of speech, to give room for debate on development strategies. It is necessary that there are alternative opinions to the ruling autocrat's views. It is assumed that there can be some debate before economic development takes off, when interest groups arc formed. This eventually leads to multiparty systems and competitive elections, while in reality there are many examples of fraud in multiparty systems. These distinctions are important in Africa and elsewhere today. One interesting pathway is to adopt democracy through a national conference, as in West Africa.

Transformation of the bureaucracy is an important step which is assumed to come after democracy, while in Europe it came under the authoritarian kings. This indicates that the need for meritocracy, impartiality etc. is more general and that the causal mechanisms don't depend on democracy. One observation is that there are "pockets of effectiveness" in African bureaucracies. This indicates that there are at least two major steps with slightly different consequences. One is to develop policy capacity at the central government. Another is to have a bureaucracy to implement policies in relation to the citizens. Here, the supply of educated staff becomes very important. This is where trust, authority, and legitimacy are created, away from a partial and corrupt bureaucracy. This is of course a major step which may never be entirely completed.

The rows 8–13 relate to economic transformations, including environmental protection and the creation of welfare systems. There are three basic items which are important steps, though they can to some extent be parallel: more efficient agriculture, the setting up of new firms, and foreign investments. Environmental protection is treated as a separate step, while it should be parallel. It is also dependent on an efficient machinery of government to design and implement policies.

Welfare policies are something of a final end in the theory of change, dependent on economic resources having been created. This is described as a dominant middle class which can afford welfare and an affluent lifestyle. This is in the future for most Africans. Other models of welfare, partly based on development aid and remittances, are necessary at earlier stages. The SDGs point at domestic revenue mobilization, which could be through taxes or other forms of welfare payments. Such issues of design are a later question, even if certain steps and traditions may form paths for welfare services.

Assumptions

One of the benefits of constructing a theory of change is that assumptions must be made explicit. They can have great importance for the coherence of the "theory." There are often lots of steps (smaller items) which are taken for granted or perhaps forgotten, such as the importance of certain kinds of actors and resources.

One such general item is to have political leaders with useful skills, including knowledge of how to lead social transformation, or at least key aspects of such leadership. Democracies depend on political parties which can articulate political platforms and who know some alternative visions. Education and foreign support can be important for the supply of candidates and programs.

Another similar factor is the supply of an educated workforce to hire as teachers, lawyers, doctors, or bureaucrats. Building meritocratic systems of governance presupposes the existence of education and training at universities, which in turn presupposes investments and training for their staff. The SDGs mention knowledge exchange, where advanced technologies should be transferred from the rich to the poor countries, which creates a need for skilled staff and facilities at universities and firms, for example.

A more controversial issue is the contents of the necessary skills. There is a European argument that political and economic development to a large extent was the result of a struggle for individual freedom against repressive mercantilism in the eighteenth century and onwards. Classical liberals like John Locke, Adam Smith, and John Stuart Mill articulated principles of individual liberty. Nowadays, liberalism is used as a label for very harsh programs of reform, based on economic theory and imposed by international organizations in one size to fit all contexts. In addition, the Marxist critique of dependency has a long tradition in development studies. This is something which could form the basis for separate political parties to compete for popular support. Put more forcefully, an exchange and import of norms and values may be more important than taking a post-colonial stand, if that means to abolish all ideas invented in Europe. The influence from China and others can also be dealt with as a competing ideology.

Even more speculative, one could argue that it is necessary to shift from a situation where elites are short-sighted and selfish to a situation where they value long-term cooperation and see win-win situations. This is important for the reduction of corruption and personal bonds of loyalty such as neopatrimonialism, which are sometimes seen as fundamental barriers which are very difficult to reform, which pose dilemmas for development policy, how poor people can be helped without indirectly supporting a corrupt regime.

External Support

This rough draft indicates a rather limited role for external support. The main responsibility lies with Africans to find solutions, which illustrates another aspect of decentering, that the EU should play a limited role, except perhaps in situations of emergency or wars. Development policy must be designed so as not to limit the responsibility of African governments and people.

It is difficult to draw conclusions from the overview. The activities organized under the five "Ps" could still be relevant, especially to assist in helping peace, people and planet. Prosperity is also very relevant and provides public as well as private motives for engagement with the situation in Africa. Foreign investments are important to develop the economies.

The theory of change points towards a new European role in assisting education and skills development, technology transfer and advice on many things by including Africans in professional networks. This also points in the direction of specific partnerships, as in the Africa strategy.

A final question is if the EU is fit to play a more subordinate role. Its support for the African Union can be interpreted as an effort to support African leadership on a continental basis. The European relation to individual governments is more complex. Some problems with local learning have been noted in chapter four.

SUMMARY AND REFLECTIONS

The chapter has pointed at many problems related to barriers and drivers in poor countries. The starting point was the problem of achieving the SDGs in the poor countries. The short overview gave some examples of general problems, while the specific drivers and barriers differ across countries.

Development policy requires extensive knowledge of how processes of modernization can be supported in poor countries. The issues are complex, and researchers are divided over what to do and how to understand the causal relationships. These debates relate to classical conflicts over planning, to what extent societies can be transformed according to a rational (preconceived) plan from the center, and to what extent societies must evolve in a spontaneous fashion, without a plan.

The institutionalist perspective is something of a middle position, focusing on key elements of regulation (institutions) while leaving the details open. This gencrally refers to the regulation of material things, based on an image of interest-driven individuals, but can also include norms and values. The institutionalist strategy, which dominates research into economic and political development, was then analyzed and compared to an older perspective of centralist control, where it was assumed that governments in poor countries could control specific items of the national economy.

The analysis pointed to a variety of underlying barriers to development. As a rough outline, a set of barriers for economic and political development were mentioned. This included a typology of transformative processes, from dictatorship to democracy, where the circumstances have great importance for the depth and stability of the new regime.

Lastly, these issues were integrated in a tentative theory of change (roadmap) for the achievement of the SDGs in Africa. The point of rearranging the analysis in a temporal form is to make specific items more useful by highlighting the means-ends relationship of the activities to reach the SDGs. The ambition is to focus the analysis and to enhance learning from experience. In the next chapter, I will analyze factors related to inter-party relations, which add complexity to the EU policies.

The EU's most important document on the New European Consensus on Development (EU 2017) does not provide clear answers as to how the EU thinks about these issues, other than that the EU agrees with the SDGs, which may be broadly considered to be an institutional strategy as set out above. Several specific issues are discussed in the policy documents (chapter four), but they are not connected in a causal fashion or related to contextual factors.

The differences in approach between member states and between policy areas have to do with the issues and strategic choices that have been discussed here, but it is unclear to an outsider how the EU views barriers and drivers of development in poor countries. The country strategies are meant to express more developed perspectives on the specifics of the countries concerned. Alternative knowledge of causal factors and the design of external support may be available in the national organizations for development aid.

The absence of analysis in the key documents gives some support to Sarah Delputte's and Jan Orbie's view that the focus on internal coordination has crowded out a discussion about the basics of the policy, what to do in specific situations (above; Delputte and Orbie 2020).

Chapter 7

Decentering European Policies 2

A Cooperative Relationship?

While the previous chapter was a broad overview of contextual factors, this chapter will focus on two relational issues. The first of these issues zooms in on the link between the donor and the recipient, where the context makes the two depend on each other, which is a point easily overlooked. It is easy to see that the EU is a dominant party in the relationship, supplying much needed resources, while it is more difficult to see how the EU is dependent on the African partners to reach its goals. This dependency has to do with the necessity to cooperate to make use of sensitive information and to make commitments. Trust is a prerequisite for efficient supportive interventions.

The second type of relational issue brings in foreign policy. While most analyses of economic and political development focus on internal factors, with a foundation in Comparative Politics, the discipline of International Relations adds important international dimensions, such as the relevance of relationships among states. This leads over to development policy conceived of as a tri-partite relationship, where competing powers such as China have an impact on EU-Africa relations. These relations are complex but important to understand to increase the efficiency of the EU policies. One implication is that the EU should play with more instruments than those included in traditional development aid.

COOPERATION AND DEPENDENCY

A factor which is outside the focus on good institutions (chapter six) has to do with building trust in the relation between donors and recipients. Development aid is a multi-step intervention, from donor to recipient and then among parties in the local context, even more if projects are contracted out to NGOs and other organizations (Wong 2012). Policy implementation can be seen as several successive steps of influencing other parties in certain ways, from the donor agencies to the African recipients (Lynn 1993; Gibson et al. 2005). The African governments play a key role in bridging the parties of the transaction, for example by supplying qualified contextual information.

The general problem of designing smart policies to reach the SDGs in Africa is very complex and presupposes not only capacity by governments and their external supporters, but also information about available options and about the motives of the parties involved. This has implications for voluntary cooperation by two parties, especially when cooperation is highly demanding, for example to transform African societies and, for the EU, to support such difficult policies outside of one's home country.

The situation is riddled with a structural problem common to many situations in which the parties are uncertain of each other and where there can be cheating on both sides, which produces fear of being used. Common interests are difficult to reach under situations of interdependence, lack of information, and lack of credible commitment. The logic of the situation must be addressed to reach beyond an interest only on the surface by the African and European leaders, i.e., to look as if cooperation is running smoothly.

Critics point to problems such as recipients and donors having other intentions than the official ones, including domestic goals and self-centered goals. The presence of such motives enhances the risk of being used by the other party. Furthermore, economists point to deadweight effects and "fungibility" (exchangeability) effects of aid, i.e., that donors fund activities that would have been carried out anyway or that allows the recipient to use their limited funds for something else (Rana and Koch 2022). These problems are given large room, for example, in the debate on industrial policy, where the recipient of subsidies is often companies with large assets, but they can also exist in the relationship with the leaders of poor countries.

The Dilemmas of Giving and Receiving

The situation described is called a "Prisoners' Dilemma" in the game theory literature which analyzes relationships between parties which are assumed to be rational utility maximizers. The name comes from a situation where two prisoners are interrogated separately and offered a change to cheat on each other. This is a general literature on all types of situations of cooperation. Researchers like Robert Bates use it to explain how warlords think in fragile states (Bates 2008). Other researchers have applied it to forms of EU development aid (Grigoriadis 2013) and to development aid in general (Pomerantz 2004; Gibson et al. 2005). The implication is that the parties should make efforts in different ways to build trust which can form the basis for long-term exchange. They must prove themselves reliable in the long term.

Table 7.1 The relationships between donors and recipients as a "Prisoners' Dilemma." Source: Created by author.

	Donor cooperates (altruist)	*Donor does not cooperate (egotist)*
Recipient cooperates (altruist)	3,3	1,4
The recipient does not cooperate (egotist)	4,1	2,2

The figure describes a highly simplified situation, in which two actors have a choice between cooperation or not ("defecting") in relation to each other, i.e., to aim for common goals or settle for what is best for oneself. There are four possible outcomes, which are ranked in the order of a self-centered actor, where (4) is the highest value. The best for an egotist is to take advantage of the other actor (4,1), while the worst is the reverse (1,4). The risk of being used by the other actor leads to low-risk strategies, while better alternatives are unattainable under the logic of the game. The dilemma is rigged towards defection, which is implied by the numbers (below).

The dilemma describes a situation (a relationship, a structure) which is common in many situations which have to do with cooperation with strangers. A version called "The Tragedy of the Commons" is often used to illustrate the problem of overusing environmental resources; "why should I restrain myself, if there's no guarantee that others will do so too?" (Gibson et al. 2005, 37f).

The two options are in principle the same for both actors, while they mean different specific things. The most obvious self-centered temptation for the recipient of development aid is to take control over some of the funding (corruption) or to pursue other goals than development (Booth 2012; Elayah 2016). The European donor, on the other hand, might be tempted to serve other and partly conflicting goals (to win elections or win profits) or to run uncoordinated programs which create a mess in the local context (Brown 2005).

Either side can "defect" by settling for ritual behavior, playing things safe rather than pursuing more demanding strategies which involve risk-taking. This is the combination (2,2), which describes a low-ranked outcome of mutual defection. Donors get to spend their money while recipients use the funding to look good. Aid becomes a ritual and the achievement of the SDGs is not affected very much.

More interestingly, rational actors end up in (2,2) when they realize that they can be deceived in (1,4) and (4,1). The "don't cooperate" ("defect") option is always better than "cooperate," no matter what the other does. The players receive (4) or (2), which is better than (3) and (1) and the situation is the same for both parties. This is in technical terms called a dominant strategy, which is also the key characteristic of this game, the most challenging of all games.

At the heart of the "Prisoners' Dilemma" is the fear of being exploited, without the opportunity to retaliate, which leads the actors to mutual defection (2,2). At the same time, there is a better outcome for both actors in cooperation (3,3), which can only be achieved if they trust that they will not be exploited. This is the collaborative combination where the recipient is creative and is putting the resources to good use, while accepting some limited control by the donor, who is happy that the recipient is creative. To reach this mutual gain, a balance between control and creativity, the parties must resist the lure of deceiving the other and the fear of being exploited. The win-win situation of (3,3) presupposes confidence and a long-term perspective in the relationship, which is impossible in the narrowly defined game.

The literature on game theory points out that the simplified description captures a general logic which is seen in a variety of situations where it is difficult for actors to cooperate because there is a temptation to deceive each other. With a technical formulation, the problem is that what is rational for each player individually isn't rational for the group.

Implications and Solutions

The solution to the dilemma is the outcome (2,2), which is clearly inferior. To reach (3,3)—which is an improvement for both sides, a win-win situation—there must be repetition or some way to make a binding agreement. If the parties meet several times, there is the possibility to opt for a conditional strategy, to cooperate if the other does too. Part of the conditional strategy may be to signal the intention of such a behavior. If both parties do so, this can lead to some trust in the relationship, that the other side will not take advantage of the inherent weakness. Such trust can develop over time if there is knowledge of the situation and a desire to prioritize the mutual benefit. There must also be some means of retaliation if the other defects, which sounds a bit odd at first. The message is "to speak softly and carry a big stick." Over time, this long-term rationality can support a norm of generosity towards strangers.

A common instrument ("stick") in development policy is so-called conditionality, where aid is increased or decreased in response to recipient behavior. There are many problems with this strategy, for example that it doesn't work in relation to governments with access to resources and that it goes against the image of a cooperating donor (Börzel and Hackenesch 2013).

Another version of conditional cooperation is in a situation of a large population, where those who are conditional cooperators can find each other and avoid the pure egotists. One question in game theory is what it takes for conditional cooperators to survive in a hostile environment (Axelrod 1984). Such donors and recipients can survive in a "sea" of egotists under certain circumstances.

The "shadow of the future" (and repetition) is the key to cooperation. In other situations, however, it may be of benefit to have a "shadow of the end" as a key element. There is an argument that donors need "exit strategies" to signal limited responsibility, that the recipient must accept responsibility of certain activities at a set point in time (Fee 2012). This reduces the incentives to cheat on the donor by doing ritual activities. The two recommendations are compatible, if the exit is only about specific projects and the future is about the relationship in general, where new projects can be launched. In the language of game theory, the exit strategy is a "stick" carried by the donor to discipline the recipient.

A problem is that "the sticks" carried by the recipient are less visible. On the face of it, the African governments are in a much weaker position. However, there are two sticks, which I will come back to. One is to have other partners, like China, to gain some independence from the EU. The other is the qualified contextual information which the donor is dependent on to assure efficiency in the specific projects. The donor (the EU) may mistake the situation for one of pure hierarchy, thinking that the donor isn't dependent on the recipient (cf. Ayres and Braithwaite 1992).

Others have expanded the dilemma to include norms, such as a choice between acting "rationally" (utility-oriented) or norm-based (Kratochvil and Tulmets 2018). The dilemma may go away if the actors are altruists rather than egotists. A strong sense of common purpose would lead the actors to find a cooperative solution, but it only works if everyone is an altruist or if it can be known who is and who isn't. Some norms can support the long-term rationality of treating others fairly, for example. More interesting situations is where rationality and norms (such as politeness) imply different actions.

There may be other situations in the relation between the EU and African governments where shared norms play a larger role than in my general description of development aid. Toni Haastrup describes the new relations in the area of peace and security as built on common norms which seem to lead to common interests (Haastrup 2013).

Other norms can make the dilemma stronger, for example if there will be punishment in another context for cooperation. This is, for example where "the prisoners" are members of the mafia and will be killed if they give evidence on the other to save one's own skin. Theoretically, outsiders could threaten the parties in development policy not to take certain courses of action. This is a risk taken by placing development policy under the control of foreign policy and other goals.

It should be mentioned that there are heuristic devices based on norms too, such as role conceptions which inform actors on expectations, i.e., what is appropriate to do in certain situations (Bengtsson and Elgström 2012). The role conceptions are not based on interests (utility-maximization) and are therefore an alternative mechanism to influence behavior. However, they are likely not as important in situations where money and influence are at stake and where coordination with limited information is needed. The games capture this kind of situation.

There are two other ways to revise the situation to break out of the Prisoners' Dilemma. Sometimes it is possible to divide a collective good into smaller private goods. One example would be to divide a common into individual plots, to avoid conflicts in collective farming. This thinking can be applied to divide land which is owned by a tribe into private lots. More generally, it implies the search for market-based solutions to development problems, where private incentives are beneficial. This is of course controversial, but in line with an argument that economic growth in Europe was based on certain legal inventions like ownership, loans, insurance, market transactions, and companies with limited liabilities (shareholder corporations).

The other option is a political solution, to make a binding agreement through a contract or an organization where collective decisions can be made and enforced. This is impossible for the two "prisoners" but may be a reasonable solution in other contexts, for example to split water resources between upstream and downstream users (Ostrom 1990). A joint agreement with means of enforcement may be the only acceptable solution. The African Union can be seen as such a collective arrangement to deal with common problems in Africa, and the European Union likewise in Europe.

In development policy, the game model has been used, among other things, to analyze the recipients' problems in dealing with donors who are not cooperating. Lyndsey Whitfield has developed a multi-step rationalist model and uses it as a basis for understanding development policy from the African side, through African countries' donor management strategies (Whitfield 2009). Her additions to the model include the fact that the expectations of the recipients are shaped by their previous experience and how the overall aid system is constructed. The "game situation" between donors and recipients becomes more complicated but also more realistic when norms and other factors affect the actors.

Stephen Howes has developed the rationalistic analysis into something of an "impossibility theorem of aid effectiveness" (Howes 2013, p. 70), where donor governments must make a trade-off between possible actions to improve the relationship. Howes shows that stronger political control of the donors through feedback mechanisms may lead to lower quality on the recipient side, i.e., a stronger focus on what is measurable means less focus on transformational projects. Furthermore, increased donor coordination leads to less innovative programs, i.e., "central planning" becomes a "cartel of good intentions" (ibid., p. 69). None of these risks are discussed by the EU.

Ambiguity of the Parties

For the donor, it can be difficult to judge whether the recipient is honest or corrupt. Will the dictator continue to invest in the welfare of the population, if development aid is given, or will the dictator use national funds for something else, such as buying weapons? One solution is to provide support to organizations independent of the dictator, but it also risks reducing the pressure on the dictator to address the problems of the population.

Another situation is if the recipient becomes so dependent on the EU that the recipient turns passive. Too much commitment on the part of donors could result in a reduction of the recipients' will and the space to act, a kind of "acquired helplessness" in (1,4). On the receiving end, there are also the problems of governments that no one listens to and warlords competing to have access to goods which can be distributed to supporters. Should the EU deal with clan leaders instead of governments, if it is the clan leaders (but not the government) who feel pressure to deliver to the public (the clan)? It would be a kind of accountability mechanism on the part of the local population.

For national and local leaders, there is a temptation to use aid for their own gain (4,1). Mikkel Funder, Carol Mweemba, and Imasiku Nyambe describe how the implementation of the SDGs has become an instrument in the power struggle of local politicians (Funder, Mweemba, and Nyambe 2018). Local leaders may have an interest in enriching themselves and their supporters, even by getting control over development funds. In a corrupt environment, it can be irrational to oppose corruption.

It can also be difficult for the recipient to know if the donor is honest and has long-term intentions or if the donor primarily wants to achieve quick results. Will the donor stick to his or her promises over a reasonable period? Will several donors coordinate, or will they make conflicting demands for their efforts (for example, through different indicators to follow up funded projects)? The coordination problems can be credibility problems from the perspective of the recipient.

Both parties can influence how they are perceived, but if there is a great deal of uncertainty, they end up in a dilemma, where they must choose between trusting the other or acting so that their own risks are minimized. With a technical term, there is a problem with information between the parties in that they don't know each other's real intentions. The information may even be asymmetric, if the recipient knows more about how to design projects and this information is vital to the donor. In such a situation, the recipient becomes more powerful in relation to the donor. To put it bluntly, one has the money and the other has the information on how to design projects and execute projects. Both resources are needed for efficient projects.

Such a situation implies dependency and a need to strive for the optimal (3,3) rather than to go for the higher ranked but unattainable (4,1). What looks at first like a pure hierarchy with one dominant party may in fact be a situation of mutual dependency. It implies further action to make the recipient willing to share or utilize qualified information (Akerlof 1970). This can be the case in the relation between governments and their agencies as well as between donors and recipients.

The Prisoners' Dilemma belongs to a rationalistic research tradition which has been criticized for becoming self-fulfilling. One can perceive a hidden message that all donors and recipients are cynical or that the rational thing is to act like a cynic so as not to be exploited (Ellis and Thompsson 1997). In line with this, constructivists argue that it is generally more interesting to study what makes individuals perceive themselves to be in this situation, because it is the short-term rationality (egotism) which creates the fundamental problems. One way out is to support more altruistic values, such as the norm that it is good to trust others and to cooperate, which makes it easier for the parties to cooperate in good circumstances. Whitfield's model is a hybrid model which handles this.

The Prisoners' Dilemma implies the utility of "carrying a stick" to raise the stakes in a situation where the other is tempted to defect. This is close to the practice of "conditionality," where development aid is based on making demands on the recipient. Such policies may be difficult to apply in practice, for example where strong enforcement by the IMF was seen to hurt the poor rather than the leaders, who were the targets of the policies (Williams 2012).

Elinor Ostrom investigated how collaboration can occur in the circumstances where a time dimension changes the character of the game (Ostrom 1990; Shivakumar 2005). Long-term rational egotists can in practice adopt altruistic behavior as long as it works. In a conflict, it can be a matter of getting the warlords to see their long-term interests, such as peaceful behavior opening for a higher standard of living for the family than continued conflict, which seems rational in the short-term (Bates 2008). Women are considered better at choosing long-term strategies, which have led to proposals to include women in negotiations in male environments as part of a "feminist foreign policy" (Thomson 2020, 430). In the debate on peacekeeping operations, Yaroslav Tir and Johannes Karreth (2018) have suggested that the responsibility should be placed on the international organizations if they have the greatest interest in maintaining peace.

A further complication is that there are risks built into the relationship that the EU and other donors need to manage. I mentioned earlier that the EU has several relations with the recipients, that it wants to cooperate globally with the countries of Africa, at the same time as it wants to give money and (to some extent) make demands. The member states want to do business with poor countries as well as make them adopt our view of democracy and human rights. These aims may imply different relations ("games"), which would then produce contradictory strategies for the EU.

In addition, the EU is made up of a number of actors. The EU delegations are conglomerates of several parties on the EU side. Ambiguity can confuse the counterparty and cause a recipient to choose something other than pure cooperation. The recipient can also take advantage of disagreement on the EU side. This has led, among other things, to a debate on whether aid should be given unconditionally or as a reward for behavior which the donor deems desirable.

The EU's ambiguity as a donor may have to do with mixed motives. Officially, aid policy is an altruistic policy, but there may be egotistic motives, such as favoring the export industry or attracting altruistic voters at home. The economic motives may be based on the notion that they should lead to mutual benefit. The same applies to cooperation in environmental policy. Security policy can be both altruistic and selfish. A major discussion is about the observation that the EU's foreign policy perspective risks shifting the focus away from the situation of the poor population, which was the hallmark of development policy. This shows that the nuances of the motives can be important in laying the foundations for trust and cooperation.

The difficulties in devising a functioning development policy are another problem that can lead to "ritual" policies which follow dominant ideas in order to avoid criticism. This makes it difficult to adapt the efforts to the specific situation in each recipient country, to "play with a responsive approach" (Yanguas 2018).

The aforementioned "state builder's dilemma" can be interpreted as a game between three parties, in which the designated government seeks to gain trust both from the occupying power and from the population. The dilemma lies in the conflicting requirements. The people find it difficult to have confidence in a person chosen by the occupying power, while the occupying power finds it difficult to have confidence in a person chosen by the people through free elections (Lake 2016).

For an outsider, such as the EU, it is difficult to influence development in a way that is "fair" and accepted by the local population. There is a general problem in all situations where one party tries to influence another party to change. In the worst-case scenario, external aid creates new dependencies and helps preserve existing power structures.

It should be said that game theory is close to versions of principal-agent analysis, which is another rationalistic model to understand relationships

(Rana and Koch 2022; Jakupec and Kelly 2019, chapter nine). It starts from a hierarchy where the principal tries to control the agent. Under assumptions of limited access to information it will become a game where interdependence rather than hierarchy becomes dominant.

The metaphor of a game suggests that the situation can be analyzed as a relationship between two parties or a small set of actors. An opposite approach is to focus on the plurality of overlapping policies and regulations which have impact on development policy. Fru Norbert Suh I (2020) applies the concept of regime complexity to bring out how the situation becomes vague when there are contradictory contexts which guide actions in this area, as in other areas.

THE IMPACT OF THE INTERNATIONAL SYSTEM

The relation between donor and recipient can be further elaborated by bringing in factors from foreign policy. The analysis in chapter six focused on economic and political development, but some aspects are missing, which have to do with the context and actors who can influence the relationship between the EU and its African partners. This adds further complexity to the situations where the EU is operating.

Economists analyze internal and external economic factors, such as national production systems and trade with other countries. Political scientists focus on internal political developments. Both are interested in the relationship between political and economic development. External political factors are often lacking, which are analyzed in International Relations. This suggests that there are four kinds of factors which need to be considered (table 7.2).

IR brings in questions about geopolitics, the international context and the survival strategies of the African governments, where the point is that the governments are involved in relationships beyond development policy. Poor country governments may feel constrained or even threatened by their neighbors. This is a dimension which to a large extent is overlooked by studies which focus on internal processes (in Comparative Politics; Landman 2003). It makes a great difference if African governments are assumed to be only concerned with domestic policy and its relations to donors like the

Table 7.2 Internal and external factors affecting the economy and politics. Source: Author.

	Internal factors	*External factors*
Economy	Productivity, regulatory framework	Trade
Politics	Protest movements, media	Hierarchy, alliances

EU. Bringing in their foreign policy shows the complexity and implies other instruments (and limitations) for the EU to influence the African governments.

The question of China's role puts its finger on the relationship of poor countries to major global powers beyond the EU. Literature in the field of International Relations focuses on the importance of such external factors. One type of theory highlights the global structure and the role of states in it, including that it matters how many "poles" (superpowers) there are. Several scholars have noted that development policy changed at the end of the Cold War when global power relations changed with the disappearance of the Soviet Union (Williams 2012; Quinn 2016). Such issues matter to African countries and to other parts of the world.

I have discussed in chapter three how foreign policy, trade policy, and development policy have become intertwined within the EU and that European strategies are about supporting the poor countries and cooperating with them. There are also elements of hierarchy and power play in the EU-Africa relations, through military action and by calling for poor countries to comply with EU norms for migration. Despite this, the EU essentially sees itself as a helping superpower. Others have noted that American development policy is based on more of a great power policy (Malacalza 2020).

The literature in the field of International Relations points to power relations, where the big and strong countries want to dominate the small ones. Some versions ("realism") see states as power-hungry "utility maximizers" while other theories ("liberalism") see a desire for cooperation to get out of what would otherwise be a situation of anarchy. The two correspond to short-sighted and far-sighted strategies, respectively, in a situation of the Prisoners' Dilemma. These perspectives are often used to analyze the actions of the United States and other major powers, while it is relatively rare to analyze the relationship of the weaker states with the major powers, such as what they can do to increase their room for maneuver. Such perspectives have been common in the discussion of what small countries can do to increase their room for maneuver in relation to the global economy (Katzenstein 1985).

For the leaders of poor countries, the weak economy is a limiting factor in their foreign policy action. Poverty puts them at a disadvantage vis-à-vis the EU and countries which are richer (Clapham 1996). The lack of resources can manifest itself in low capacity to produce proposals and difficulties in attending international negotiations. A side effect could be a strengthened conviction to show independence.

Another difference with European countries is that poor states are often weak in what is known as sovereignty (ibid.). They do not have control and do not enjoy authority or legitimacy in the same way as rich countries do. In part, this may be a consequence of the leaders being dictators, but it is nevertheless important to note that there are consequences in relations with other states, especially rich democracies. External pressure can help strengthen a regime, as well as weaken it. The African Union is an organization which guarantees sovereignty ("stateness") to African governments.

David A Lake (2009) has summarized the situation in a theory that small and large countries are in a hierarchy rather than an anarchy, which was the original description in the field of International Relations. In an anarchy, it is rational to defend oneself and to form defensive alliances against major powers, but not to trade or to take different roles ("functional differentiation"). In a hierarchy it is more rational to support each other and also to cooperate with a great power, to trade and to strive for different roles. Lake's perspective can help us see why poor countries behave differently than European countries do.

Geopolitical Strategies of the Poor Countries

External political factors are interesting because they highlight the relations of the recipient countries with the international system. Countries and their leaders may find themselves in situations which limit their options for action and require strategic action. While achievement of the SDGs could strengthen the countries' international reputation, other considerations may take precedence. This is a dimension which contains factors that may run counter to development policy ambitions, which are rarely touched upon in the analysis of development aid but can add aspects to the description of the EU as a major power.

Christopher Clapham (1996) analyzes the situation of African leaders and points to such things as alliances with major powers and different forms of cooperation in Africa, with the whole of Africa through the AU or within regional associations. It is not self-evident that poor countries see themselves as partners, because at the same time they are competing for support from the outside world. When they receive support, they may find themselves in a position of dependency.

Some countries are limited by lacking a coast ("landlocked") (Collier 2018). Others are large or have great natural resources. African countries are part of the African Union and one or more regional economic communities. They have alliances or historical ties with various major powers. France in particular has strong ties with its former colonies, through currency unions. Russia and China have ties to countries such as Angola and Ethiopia respectively. Sweden and other small states have ties to former liberation movements.

Other types of theories highlight international norms and how states are drawn into these norm systems, which I touched on before as a possible explanation for the reform of development policy. The existence of international norm systems is another dimension in which international politics does not have the character of anarchy. One variant of this is that policies are transferred between countries, that governments imitate what others do.

The IR theories help us understand how the foreign policy situation guides or limits what is possible for weak governments to do. One example is the small Asian countries of Nepal and Bhutan, which are squeezed between the great powers China and India (Ghimire 2021). However, the countries have chosen different strategies to increase their room for maneuver, suggesting that factors other than the geopolitical situation influence the choice of strategy.

The IR literature points out that small states can either enter an alliance with one superpower (Bhutan with India) or try to balance the two great powers against each other (Nepal). It is a puzzle why two neighbors choose different strategies, unless domestic politics is taken into consideration, which indicates that external and internal factors need to be taken into account.

In the field of Foreign Policy Analysis (including "neoclassical realism" Rose 1998) it is of value to analyze internal factors of the political systems. The views and values of the leaders are important, as well as underlying factors such as governance, electoral systems, and how government offices are organized and how staff are educated. Differences in the degree of democracy can be very important for explaining why countries choose different policy options. Foreign policy isn't determined by the international system, but the system may be very important to the governments of poor countries.

Development Policy as Foreign Policy

Bringing in the international dimension suggests a more complex relationship between the EU and the African governments, where additional goals are relevant. For simplicity, it can be assumed that the relationship is still a "Prisoners' Dilemma" (above), with mutual dependency and conditional cooperation as the reasonable strategy to find a fruitful balance of interests (3,3). More advanced models are introduced by Gibson et al. (2005).

There are several differences from the previous analysis. One is that there are more issues involved, which may imply alternative strategies but may also open for couplings across issues, where a loss in one area is traded for a gain in another area. The rankings of these areas may be internally contested in the EU as well as the AU. An implied difference is that there are more issues which can be traded-off in the game.

In the Prisoners' Dilemma the cooperation was mainly about the efficient use of resources to produce transformation in Africa. In this case, another issue is the power over fundamental global institutions (table 7.3). There is critique by the African governments that global governance is biased in favor of the rich countries, from the international legal system to economic power and control. Interestingly, there is one such item in the SDGs, where it states that poor countries should have greater influence in international organizations (target 16.8). It can be expected that the African Union will have an interest in global issues. The EU has a similar interest in safeguarding the liberal world order against what it sees as threats from China, Russia, Iran, and other countries.

For the individual African governments there may be specific situations where they would want the help of the EU to settle issues. General aims have to do with being respected by other governments and to maintain sovereignty or actorness. Entering a relationship with the EU may give this, but a situation where there are alternative donors like China, may put stronger pressure on the EU.

For the EU, the reverse would be to find ways to influence the African governments, for example by conditional support given to democracies. A problem is that elites may prefer to plunder their countries rather than to give up power for some uncertain future benefits of the rule of law and economic growth (Bates 2008). It is also difficult for the EU to make demands when China is offering more attractive support to dictators. Development projects may give some opportunities to influence internal African affairs, which could come into conflict with the global norm of respecting the will of the recipients.

The EU and AU can be regarded as cartels, where speaking for all brings bargaining power. With a large number of issues and positions, the strains on the organizations will be larger than in the case of pure development policy. Individual governments may have a desire for a high profile in certain ways, for example French influence in Africa or the more altruistic European countries preferring to have a strong role in the UN to cooperate with poor countries. This may in turn produce a motive to ease the burden on the other organization.

In this general overview, the implication is that this is a game of Prisoners' Dilemma, where the actors stand to gain the most from conditional cooperation. However, there is no guarantee that all the national governments will see the situation in the same light. For example, there are African governments which have close ties to China.

An implication for the EU is that it makes sense to see development policy in the light of foreign policy. There are some bigger issues which need to be dealt with in order to make the pursuit of development efficient or even possible. There may also be situations where the two policies come into conflict, as discussed in chapters three and four.

Table 7.3 The relationship between the EU and African governments as a "Prisoners' Dilemma." Source: Author.

	European cooperation with African governments	*European pursuit of power*
African cooperation with EU	(3,3) Restraint and partnership. Agreement on agenda and strategy. More benefits for loyalty and democracies	(1,4) Europe takes over, French interventions
African pursuit of power	(4,1) Africa and China work against EU interests	(2,2) Standstill, ritual

COMPETITION WITH CHINA

A specific issue is how China and other major powers affect the relationship between the EU and its recipient countries. Is China a counterforce, an alternative to the EU? How do the recipient countries view this? How should the EU take this into account? Are the efforts in development policy appropriate in the light of a tripartite relationship?

China and other countries are trying to influence the African countries. It is therefore important to understand what they are doing and what implications it has for the EU's ambitions to influence African governments in order to achieve the SDGs. The problem is more generally about non-OECD countries which are not following the principles agreed within the OECD, in particular Russia and China, but also Muslim countries such as Saudi Arabia and Iran (Babayan and Risse 2015). One such alternative constellation is between countries in the global south, partly in opposition to the EU.

The competition with China over influence in Africa is a foreign policy issue which has great impact on development policy, especially when the EU tries to put pressure on the African governments to accept European values. On the one hand, the Chinese offer aid with fewer demands in the short-term perspective. On the other hand, there are examples of the Chinese making strong demands on repayment, which have been difficult for the African governments to live up to. There are also differences in the (lack of) spillovers of skills and training, where Europeans often employ locals and the Chinese often bring in their own nationals to do the work.

There are contradictory implications. One the one hand, increasing competition from China could imply that the EU must lower its demands, the element of conditionality. Another implication is to make the offers more attractive in other ways, to maintain the value-driven aspects of EU support. Furthermore, more active opposition to China and other competing donors can lead to greater demands on consistency in the European behavior, which puts further strain on the EU.

What is China Doing?

China's role in Africa is partly linked to investment in companies. One question is therefore how these investments contribute to the economic transition. A research program by the British ODI found that Chinese investment created jobs and contributed to skills development of the local workforce (Calabrese and Tang 2020). Another observation was that the investments were often made in companies which targeted the African market rather than international exports. Trade with China has, according to the authors, had both positive and negative effects on African business (ibid.).

Much of the debate has been about China's political influence in Africa, if economic influence makes China seem an attractive alternative to European influence. China provides aid, but much of China's efforts are made through loans to the poor countries. For the recipients, it is both a matter of having a larger number of "donors" to turn to, which gives more room for maneuver, and increased risks of becoming dependent. The tougher Chinese loan conditions are also making it more difficult for Western lenders who want to write off the debts of poor countries, as there is a risk that it will in practice be China that makes the economic profit. The problems stem from China not complying with OECD guidelines.

China acts as a great power through its investments and through its military build-up. Some of the threats are in the dark, as when China invests in IT infrastructure in poor countries. Another part is that China partly stands for competing values which undermine the "liberal world order" built up by Western countries. However, it is unclear how divergent Chinese values are and how much they affect other countries. The EU, too, is trying to build its influence on values. It is also unclear how competition should be met in poor countries or in international organizations. The Chinese intentions are unclear, but it should be added that the EU is also unclear towards the poor countries (above).

At the overall level, it is difficult to measure influence in other ways than through the economic and military resources invested by different parties. The problem is that it doesn't provide deeper knowledge of how poor countries value the "offers" or how they make their decisions. One option, therefore, is to link research into the functioning of authoritarian states, since the majority of poor countries are authoritarian.

Autocratic Survival Strategies between the EU and China

A literature has emerged about how authoritarian regimes work and what allows them to stay in power, which adds useful knowledge to the wider literature on how and when democracies emerge. One theme of the research is that authoritarian leaders have survival strategies (Hackenesch 2018). They make agreements with other countries (donors) that are in line with the strategies, thus providing an explanation for the behavior. Competition between the EU and China then becomes a tripartite relationship, focusing on how the third party (the poor country) values the situation. The analysis will be particularly interesting if it can explain why poor countries behave differently.

Christine Hackenesch (2018) has made an ambitious comparison of how the EU and China manage to influence three African countries: Rwanda, Ethiopia, and Angola. The three have similar authoritarian regimes but have different attitudes towards EU democracy support. Rwanda has increased its already extensive cooperation with the EU. Ethiopia cooperates at a lower level and has stayed there, while Angola, which cooperated the least, has reduced its cooperation and is largely unaffected by the EU. The follow-up question is what factors can explain the difference in attitude towards the EU and in alternative cooperation with China.

The literature on authoritarian states analyzes, among other things, what increases or decreases the interest of authoritarian leaders in receiving various forms of support (Hackenesch 2018, 38). One example concerns support for the development of the public administration (bureaucracy). If the leader has an interest in developing the national government as a tool to achieve economic development and to solve societal problems, in line with the institutional strategy above, then the leader will be happy to receive support that contributes to this. If, on the other hand, the leader uses state power as an instrument to hand out rewards to his supporters, to stay in power, then such support becomes a problem rather than an asset. Similarly, one can reason about support for holding elections or opening up for a free debate. Only if these measures help to strengthen the survival of the ruler will he accept such support. In addition, the leader gets a good international reputation, as a reform-minded leader (ibid.).

The leader's calculation also includes considerations of the importance of general support from the EU, China, and others. Other EU support may outweigh the negative effects of the specific support. Similarly, aid from China can outweigh the lack of EU support. China may have partly the same interests as the EU, for example if it sees anti-corruption as a way of increasing the value of investment. China can also provide support for the development of the ruling parties of authoritarian leaders, based on their own experience (ibid., 46).

The reasoning is general, but the conclusions are different for leaders in different countries, depending on the situation. Angola has large oil resources and can therefore afford to renounce EU-China support. Democracy support would make the survival of leaders more difficult. Rwanda and Ethiopia have no oil and are more similar, but Rwanda's civil war has contributed to an interest in keeping the state neutral and well-functioning. That interest is weaker in Ethiopia and both countries have elements of power being exercised through dominant parties. The latter could make them interested in cooperation with China. The threats from the political opposition have been different, leading to different cooperation with the EU and more cooperation for Rwanda than for Ethiopia (ibid., 194ff).

Hackenesch shows that the EU started with similar strategies in the three countries but differentiated the strategies over time. However, she believes that it is not the strategies themselves that explain the impact. It is not possible to explain the outcome without considering internal factors in the three recipient countries (ibid., 197). The reasoning is simplistic here but suggests that it is important to understand the situation of the recipient in order to design effective democracy support. According to Hackenesch, the EU has on several occasions failed to adapt its strategies to the situation in the recipient countries (ibid., 204).

The reasoning shows that China's influence is determined by at least partly the same factors. The extent of economic relations varies (greater with Angola and Ethiopia), as does support for the instruments for the exercise of power. Only the Ethiopian state-backed party receives support from China, which has to do with being close politically and historically. Ethiopia will therefore be interesting as the country where the presence of China could lead to a reduction in the influence of the European Union, but this has not happened. Hackenesch concludes that increased influence from China does not automatically lead to reduced influence from the EU (ibid., 209, 219).

It must be borne in mind that this is a limited study, although a negative conclusion in the case of Ethiopia is of great importance, because it is a country where one can expect the EU to lose influence as China increases its influence. However, Chinese influence could be based on other impact mechanisms or on circumstances which have changed since the investigation was made.

In conclusion, the situation is more complicated than it looks. Competition from China and other non-OECD donors is in danger of being exaggerated, while the EU is being forced to rethink its strategies and relations with poor countries. I have mentioned before that Maurizio Carbone saw China as an excuse for the EU to pursue great power ambitions in Africa (Carbone 2011), but also that the EU's new Africa strategy has a stated ambition to have a more equal relationship with African countries (EU 2020).

SUMMARY AND REFLECTIONS

This chapter has focused on complementary factors at the macro- and micro level, in the relationship between donors and recipients and in the international system. On the face of it, game theory is a rationalistic theory, based on assuming egotistic motives (utility-maximization). The model handles situations of limited knowledge and situations of mutual dependency where trust is important. It can also be extended by adding norm-based behavior in certain situations.

This developed into an analysis of the relationship between three parties: donors, recipients, and China, as an example of a donor with objectives other than the EU. An alliance with China may be attractive to the African leaders who want to avoid dependence on the EU or the United States. The perspective of foreign policy is of value to make EU development policy more context-based and, hence, efficient.

At the same time, there is a problem of consistency built into EU democracy support, which is ultimately aimed at changing the political systems of poor countries. The survival strategies of leaders are a key to understanding the relationship between the EU, China, and the poor countries. One implication is that the EU should adapt its offers to the specific situation in each country. A preliminary assessment is that the EU is often more attractive than China and that China's economic involvement in the poor countries does not change this.

The reasoning suggests that the EU needs to be clearer in its intentions towards the poor countries. On the other hand, it is not certain that the EU needs to be coherent (coordinated) across policy areas as well as between member states. The EU's Africa strategy illustrates the ambiguity which arises when the relations implied by the policies vary from partnership to hierarchy. Another ambiguity arises when member states act in ways other than the EU collectively, such as the difference between the EU's and Sweden's more altruistic attitude compared to France's more demanding attitude towards its former colonies.

The latter seems to point to tighter central control within the EU, contrary to the recommendation to embrace diversity leading to learning (Delputte and Orbie 2020). A multi-level system of governance may allow internal disparity, but a question is whether it can also allow differentiated behavior in relation to external parties. It remains to be seen if it is possible to draw a line between external issues where diversity is good and ones where it is not.

Conclusion

SUMMARY

The book analyzes the European policies to support the achievement of the UN Sustainable Development Goals in Africa. There are several strategies, action plans, and policies on the European side, most important of which is development policy and the Africa strategy. They are interesting for several reasons: the major challenges the EU wants to help to solve, the geopolitical competition with China to influence the developing countries, the large sums of money invested, the difficulties in coordinating efforts across policy areas and with the member states, and the impact on the EU which the small northern countries have.

The first chapter describes the growing European interest in a relationship with Africans and African governments, including the African Union. While there may be many motives on either side, three of the most important are about possible mutual advantage in all dimensions of sustainable development, security issues, and in relation to China. The chapter identifies three research questions on development policy and related policies in the European Union: How did the EU policies develop? Are the policies well designed? Are the policies fit for purpose?

This is followed in the second chapter by an overview of the analytical framework, including the UN Sustainable Development Goals. It also summarizes previous research on the general relations between Europe and Africa as well as the specific arrangements between the EU and the AU. The need to "decenter" European policies by focusing attention on the African context was pointed out. The chapter identified three research gaps, similar to the three research questions: a need to understand the European intentions as well as the outcomes of the policies pursued, which imply a need to understand drivers and barriers for transformation in Africa, to which the European policies can be related.

Chapter three describes the development of European foreign, trade, and development policy. Foreign policy is the most recent of the three, but also the broadest, which is now encompassing the other two. Trade policy has a long history in the EU and was the original development policy. The last has grown over time and has changed focus, from former colonies to poor people in general. Coordination in Brussels and with the member states is very important. The mix of policies is the result of a set of internal ambitions, interaction with global actors and some entrepreneurial talent to integrate the two dimensions.

The following chapter looks more in-depth at the goals, strategies, and activities of development policy. The ambitions are framed in terms of the SDGs but the role of the EU is vague and development policy is to be coordinated with other policies. There is a large set of activities, which make the EU (the Commission and the member states together) the world's largest donor. However, implementation and coordination on the ground is difficult. There is no explicit strategy or analysis of the African context in the major documents to guide the policy development.

This is followed by an analysis of the most recent document for an Africa strategy, which presents a mix of policies, except development policy. A problem is that relations with the African Union range from partnership to hierarchy. There are also many practical problems with the proposed activities. There are no objectives presented and no strategic framework to guide the selection of activities. Internal coordination is a problem, despite the ambitious goal to be coherent across the EU.

Chapter six shifts the attention to the African context, to better understand drivers and barriers to achieve the SDGs. It is mainly an overview of recent research into institutionalist perspectives on development with some comparison with centralist strategies. This is elaborated in a discussion of barriers for change, which indicate a spectrum of factors for the EU to deal with if it is serious about supporting the SDGs in Africa. The chapter was summarized in a stylized roadmap ("theory of change") of important steps to reach the sustainable development goals. This is an example of strategic analysis which is absent from EU documents on development policy.

Chapter seven adds relational issues to indicate further barriers to the pursuit of EU development policy. The relation between donors and recipients can be analyzed in terms of interdependence and lack of information, which implies that trust-building is important. This is described as a game of "Prisoners' Dilemma" where norms can be added. A modified model can deal with the broader relations where foreign policy is taken into account. It can also be used to analyze a tri-partite game where China challenges the EU as a rival donor.

The analysis has pointed at internal tensions between different policy areas (between a narrower development policy and a broader foreign policy), between member states and between different ways of looking at the problems of poor countries and possible EU action. With China's actions, development policy has been more clearly drawn into a tug-of-war over influence in poor countries.

Answers to the Research Questions

The first research question (How did the EU policies develop?) was answered in chapter three, pointing to the mix of path dependence, global norms, and specific actors. The northern European states have some influence, but the entrepreneurial leadership was exercised by the UK.

The second research question (Are the policies well designed?) was answered in chapters four and five, pointing at high ambitions but with many problems in the implementation. There is a mismatch between the European intentions and the way the policies are carried out. The African context is very complex, which is only partly addressed in the policy design. The aim for policy coherence is limited by wishful thinking, not adequately addressing the external or internal complexities.

The third research question (Are the policies fit for purpose?) was answered in chapters six and seven. The first gave an overview of the African context, to show that it is complex and needs to be discussed openly by the EU. The second showed that there are fundamental problems in the relationships involved, which has implications for the design of policies. The lack of a discussion of these fundamental limitations suggests that it will be very difficult to achieve the SDGs in Africa with the strategies and instruments chosen.

CONCLUSION

The findings of this study can be summarized in one sentence, that the European Union has high ambitions in relation to Africa, but the implementation of the policies is weak. This theme was introduced at the beginning and has been substantiated throughout this study.

High Ambitions

The high ambitions are seen in the goals of European external action. There is a list of highly regarded values which are believed to be very European and should guide the policies directed towards other countries. For development policy, there is an ambition to support African countries in reaching the SDGs, though the EU is vague about its responsibilities.

The SDGs were adopted by the United Nations in 2015 as a comprehensive set of goals to guide development across the globe until the year 2030. With this ambition, the EU assists African governments and organizations to achieve societal transformation in several dimensions; economic, social, environmental, as well as political, including peacekeeping and good governance.

The ambition to eradicate poverty and to help poor countries achieve the SDGs are very ambitious goals which require radical change in poor countries, both in terms of their economic and political systems. The EU is making extensive efforts focusing on all five themes used by the UN to summarize the work on the objectives.

A further goal is for the EU to be coherent, which is described as a requirement that other policies, as well as activities by the member states, must be in harmony with development policy. The concept of coherence is complex and can range from avoiding conflict to contributing to overlapping goals.

The goals are further strengthened by an agreement across all member states and institutions, a "European consensus" on these matters. This implies a consensus across policy areas, which suggests that the chosen policies are suitable for other policy areas than development policy, for example foreign policy and trade policy.

The high ambitions of the goals are reinforced by the large amount of funding and activities to reach them. The five themes beginning with the letter P (people, planet, peace, prosperity, partnership) covers virtually all relevant aspects of the SDGs. In addition, there are further policies, some of which are included in the Africa strategy, where the EU signals its intention of being a partner with the African Union.

Weak Foundations and Implementation

The weak foundations are shown in several ways. One is that the goals are weaker than they first appear, before they are weighted against other goals, which can even be contradictory. The policy communities run parallel ambitions, as do the member states. In recent years, development policy has become one of several instruments of foreign policy. This is in one way a restriction, yet also a possible enrichment of instruments and strategies for transformations in Africa.

Development policy is a conglomeration of national and European activities, with many strong wills. There is an ambition to make this complex matter more coherent, which sounds like an ambition to make the EU stronger.

However, there can be an argument for less coordination of activities if that leads to a greater emphasis on experimentation and learning from experience.

The policies of the European Union are vague and even partly contradictory, within development policy and across the European spectrum of policies. An example is the double ambition of having a partnership as well as a hierarchical relation with the African governments, while also pursuing conflicting values through the promotion of democracy.

It is unclear what the EU's strategies look like. The policy documents do not discuss objectives and means coherently. This makes it difficult to discuss and develop the assumptions that are made. The link with existing research is unclear.

An obvious weakness is that the goals are very difficult to reach, because of complexities in Africa and in the relation between donors and recipients. The EU focuses on its intentions and goals, which leads to an underestimation of the challenges involved. This is where the policies need to be decentered, to focus its analytical elements on the context of the recipients.

This leads to the observation that the European policies are weak in terms of outcomes in relation to invested resources. The policies are weak in influence, strategies and instruments, as well as in analysis and learning. The polices are Eurocentric and to some extent paternalistic.

Much of the strategy work and adaptation to the circumstances of the recipient countries takes place locally through the EU delegations, which have only been briefly touched on here. The study carried out on the planning process in 2015 shows that there have been major problems in coordinating and adapting the strategies to the circumstances. Some of the observations concerned low analytical capacity and a bureaucratic approach.

IMPLICATIONS

The complexity of the situation implies a need for more elaborate policies and that the EU should aim to learn from experience, which in turn makes it necessary to design the policies in the light of more contextual variables and to scrutinize what works in various contexts. It is a problem that the EU has high ambitions and is involved in many policies in all African countries without something like a strategy on how this can be organized in a reasonable way. Detailed policy goals like the SDGs give the impression that careful thinking is going on.

The foundations for EU policies need to be stronger. The focus needs to be on the recipients rather than on the bargaining in Brussels. A key issue is to decenter, to shift the focus to the African context. This is a demand which other researchers have made from a "post-colonial" perspective. Here it is primarily based on an instrumental desire to reach the goals of the policies.

One implication is that the EU must be interested in learning about pathways of modernization. It must engage with research, state its working assumptions explicitly and be humbler in its strategies and dealings with African actors. It must find ways to talk about problems in Europe and Africa, including counter-productive strategies pursued by individual European or African governments.

A fundamental question is if an organization like the European Union can pursue such a rationalistic policy focused on ends and means in relation to its African partners and allies. The ambitions are difficult even when there is general agreement with the recipients on high-level values such as modernization, economic development, democracy, and the rule of law. This is relevant for European foreign policy in general and development policy in particular.

The last point implies more of a learning policy, where experiences are used to draw conclusions about activities and strategies. It implies a greater adaptation to national contexts and a diversification of strategies and activities. The structural dilemma of mutual dependency between donor and recipient with limited information implies conditional strategies, where the EU should take the motives of the recipients as well as of itself into account. Trust-building is important on both sides.

An interesting proposal in the policy debate is to allow greater variety among the member states, to learn from experiments, rather than demanding greater conformity across the member states of the EU. Such learning from experience demands more advanced methods for planning, implementing, and evaluating the policies.

A consequence will be more diversified strategies in Africa as well as greater room for internal variety. This means that complexity will increase, which in turn makes it necessary to simplify decision-making in Brussels, for example through the use of more long-term instruments or focusing on certain promising countries and governments.

Africa

The research presented in chapter six provides conflicting advice. In some circumstances, a centralist approach may work, but today's poor countries often lack a well-functioning state apparatus to implement such a policy where undemocratic leaders and neopatrimonial governance systems constitute significant obstacles. The outside world needs to stimulate both economic and political change, without really knowing how these affect each other. This points to continued democracy support, support for pockets of effectiveness, but also increased trade, which gives leaders incentives to make their countries attractive to international investors.

Today's dominant perspective is an institutional perspective, with the rules of the game for the economy and politics at the center. One factor outside this perspective concerns the relationship of poor countries with the international system and the importance of foreign policy in certain situations. Another factor, which is more controversial, concerns the mutual dependence between donors and recipients. The first implies a greater interest in geopolitics, while the second implies a greater need for unambiguousness and credibility. The mix of altruistic and egotistical motives in the EU's relationship with the poor countries is a problem. The way out may be what the EU has already started in the form of a more equal relationship with poor countries. Mutual gains can be a stronger basis for cooperation than one party helping the other. This observation is supported by the use of game theory to understand the relations.

China

China and some countries are trying to influence the development of poor countries. It is therefore important to understand what they are doing and what implication it has for the EU's ambitions to influence activities to achieve the SDGs. It is primarily a foreign policy issue, how the EU should approach China and the others. Development funding and the threat of its withdrawal can be an instrument for foreign policy. It is also possible to see competition with China as a development policy issue, namely how strongly the EU should pursue its own values. Competition from China may require the EU to become a more active player through its values.

One way to understand how China can exert influence is to focus on the situation of the recipients. The survival strategies of autocrats provide a basis for analyzing their approach to EU-China support. One implication of the reasoning is that the EU should adapt its offers to the specific situation in each country. A preliminary assessment is that the EU is often more attractive than China and that China's economic involvement in the poor countries doesn't change this.

The Centralization of the EU

The overall strategy of the EU has been to coordinate actions across policy areas and between member states and with recipients. In practice, the ambition has been to steer from the center, to create a coherent organization with great uniformity and general solutions. The alternative strategy advocated by Sarah Delputte and Jan Orbie (above) is that the EU should become more of a forum for learning and discussion between the actors involved, that is, engaging more in bottom-up coordination than from above.

Delputte and Orbie point to a weak aspect of the EU development policy, which is at the same time a matter of great principle. Can an organization such as the EU embrace internal diversity without being torn apart? Is softer governance possible in a loosely composed European organization? Will it be easier or more difficult to manage a massive effort by allowing greater adaptation to local conditions and to the wishes of individual member states? These are classic questions about the balance between the center and the periphery in the debate on multi-level governance, in federal systems as well as in unitary states (Fabbrini 2007).

Sarah Delputte and Jan Orbie put forward several arguments in favor of greater diversification, which were mentioned. One is that coordination in Brussels becomes too general and doesn't take into account the context of the various recipient countries, which turns European policies into an exercise of power by the EU (Delputte and Orbie 2020, 150f). Another argument is that coordination within the EU becomes "technocratic" (apolitical) and ignores the differences in perspective between member states, which can be both relevant and stimulating for policy development. A third argument is that coordination at the European level hinders coordination between like-minded countries as well as the coordination which takes place at global level (ibid., 152f).

There is much to suggest that these objections are worth taking seriously in the further development of an integrated European development aid and foreign policy. This is especially relevant in combination with the general finding that the EU is not interested enough in learning from experience and from the African context. In other words, greater streamlining may make sense in situations where implementation is simple. In relation to Africa, the case for streamlining is weaker (for an alternative view, see Ayadi and Ronco 2023, 105f).

The complexity of what is to be done speaks for locally adapted strategies that are reviewed on an ongoing basis, preferably in the light of current research. With a modern concept, the relationship between poor and rich countries constitutes a complex system, in which many factors influence the outcome. It is difficult to bring all the experience together into safe advice for the specific actors. It is a situation which implies a scientific method, in which situations are compared with the aim of understanding the causal mechanisms.

A follow-up question is whether there is capacity within aid organizations to work this way. There is a risk that the requirement to handle information will increase rather than decrease (Shivakumar 2005). Interestingly, this perspective on the inner life of the EU seems to go against the analysis of its relationships in terms of games, where the EU was seen as a unitary actor. A more diverse set of actors and policies on the European side would add to the experimentation while there is a risk that greater diversity means playing contradictory strategies. This needs to be further elaborated in the game-like model.

The Global Role of the EU and the Role of Small Countries within the EU

The analysis implies that there is a continued role for the EU to play on the global stage and that there is also a role to be played by the small northern countries within the EU. The impression is that the more altruistic countries have influenced a rethinking of policy goals, in association with similar stimulus from the international community. "Altruistic" suggests an interest in the African context, in decentering the European policies.

The implication for the small countries in an EU without the UK is to continue to influence the larger countries and to cooperate with the UK (outside the EU), which can continue to play an important role globally. One impression from conversations with interviewees is that Britain has built its strong position on its extensive experience as a result of colonialism and its vast analytical capacity. One element of British politics has been to support a diversity of university research with many academic environments that have produced knowledge with great policy relevance. It has been said that the analytical environment in Brussels on these issues is narrower and dominated by think tanks with a more short-term focus.

The European Union can play a stronger global role if it takes its policies seriously. The goals need to be more precise and the strategies need to be more elaborate and based on contextual and scientific knowledge as well as learning from experience. A more altruistic profile will make it easier for others to understand the European intentions. This would also make it easier to steer a course in relation to African leaders as well as to the rivals for influence in Africa.

References

Abdelal, Rawi. 2007. *Capital Rules: The Construction of Global Finance.* Cambridge, MA: Harvard University Press.

Acemoglu, Daron, and Robinson, James A. 2012. *Why Nations Fail: The Origins of Power, Prosperity and Poverty.* London: Profile Books.

Acharya, Amitav. 2018. *Constructing Global Order: Agency and Change in World Politics.* Cambridge: Cambridge University Press.

Acharya, Amitav, and Johnston, Alastair Iain, eds. 2007. *Crafting Cooperation: Regional International Institutions in Comparative Perspective.* Cambridge: Cambridge University Press.

Adebajo, Adekeye, and Whiteman, Kaye, eds. 2012. *The EU and Africa: From Eurafrique to Afro-Europa,* London: Hurst & Company.

Adelle, Camille, and Jordan, Andrew. 2014. "Policy Coherence for Development in the European Union: Do New Procedures Unblock or Simply Reproduce Old Disagreements?" *Journal of European Integration* 36, no. 4: 375–91.

African Union Commission. 2015: *Agenda 2063. The Africa We Want.* Addis Ababa.

Ahnlid, Anders, and Elgström, Ole. 2014. "Challenging the European Union: the rising powers and the USA in the Doha Round." *Contemporary Politics* 20, no. 1: 77–89.

Akerlof, George A. 1970. "The Market for 'Lemons': Quality Uncertainty and the Market Mechanism." *The Quarterly Journal of Economics* 84, no. 3: 488–500.

Alter, Karen J. 2014. *The New Terrain of International Law: Courts, Politics, Rights.* Princeton: Princeton University Press.

Amaeshi, Kenneth, Okupe, Adun, and Idemudia, Uwafiokun. 2018. *Africapitalis: Rethinking the Role of Business in Africa.* Cambridge: Cambridge University Press.

Andreasson, Stefan. 2010. *Africa's Development Impasse: Rethinking the Political Economy of Transformation.* London: Zed Books.

Andrews, Matt. 2013. *The Limits of Institutional Reform in Development: Changing Rules for Realistic Solutions.* Cambridge: Cambridge University Press.

Anten, Louis, Briscoe, Ivan, and Mezzera, Marco. 2012. *The Political Economy of State-building in Situations of Fragility and Conflict: from Analysis to Strategy.* The Hague: Clingendael Institute.

Axelrod, Robert. 1984. *The Evolution of Cooperation.* New York: Basic Books.

Ayadi, Rym, and Ronco, Sara. 2023. *The EU-Africa partnership and development aid: Assessing the EU's actorness and effectiveness in development policy.* Brussels: CEPS.

Ayittey, George BN. 2005. *Africa Unchained: The Blueprint for Africa's Future.* Houndmills: Palgrave Macmillan.

Ayres, Ian, and Braitwaite, John. 1992. *Responsive Regulation: Transcending the Deregulation Debate.* New York: Oxford University Press.

Babayan, Nelli, and Risse, Thomas. 2015. "Democracy Promotion and the Challenges of Illiberal Regional Powers." *Democratization* 22, no. 3 (thematic issue, also book by Routledge 2016).

Bader, Julia, and Faust, Jörg. 2014. "Foreign Aid, Democratization, and Autocratic Survival." *International Studies Review* 16: 575–95.

Barbé, Esther, Costa, Oriol, and Kissack Robert, eds. 2016. *EU Policy Responses to a Shifting Multilateral System.* London: Palgrave Macmillan.

Barnett, Michael N., ed. 2017. *Paternalism Beyond Borders.* Cambridge: Cambridge University Press.

Bates, Robert H. 2008. *When Things Fell Apart: State Failure in Late-Century Africa.* Cambridge: Cambridge University Press.

Bates, Robert H. 2021. *The Political Economy of Development: A Game Theoretic Approach.* Cambridge: Cambridge University Press.

Beetz, Simone. 2017. *External Democracy Promotion and Diversity Among International Agencies: Evaluating Variances in the Impact of the UNDP and the EC in Rwanda.* Opladen: Budrich UniPress Ltd.

Bengtsson, Rikard, and Elgström, Ole. 2012. "Conflicting Role Conceptions? The European Union in Global Politics." *Foreign Policy Analysis* 8: 93–108.

Bennich, Therese, Persson, Åsa, Beaussart, Raphaëlle, Allen, Cameron, and Malekpour, Shirin. 2023. "Recurring patterns of SDG interlinkages and how they can advance the 2030 Agenda." *One Earth 6,* November 17: 1465–76.

Bergmann, Julian. 2019: "Neofunctionalism and EU external policy integration: the case of capacity building in support of security and development (CBSD)." *Journal of European Public Policy* 26, no 9: 253–1272.

Bergmann, Julian, Delputte, Sarah, Keijzer, Niels, and Verschaeve, Joren. 2019. "The Evolution of the EU's Development Policy: Turning Full Circle." *European Foreign Affairs Review* 24, no. 4: 533–54.

Bernstein, Steven. 20012. *The Compromise of Liberal Environmentalism.* New York: Columbia University Press.

Bertelsmann Stiftung, ed. 2019. *Europe's Coherence Gap in External Crisis and Conflict Management: Political Rhetoric and Institutional Practices in the EU and its Member States.* Gütersloh: Verlag Bertelsmann Stiftung.

Bickerton, Christopher J. 2011. *European Union Foreign Policy: From Effectiveness to Functionality.* Houndmills: Palgrave Macmillan.

Bøås, Morten. 2020. "A comprehensive EU strategy for Africa. Political dialogue: Governance, security and migration." In EU. 2020b. *A Comprehensive*

EU Strategy for Africa, Briefings, Requested by the AFET committee. Brussels: European Parliament.

Booth, David. 2012. "Aid effectiveness: Bringing country ownership (and politics) back in." *Conflict, Security & Development* 12, no. 5: 537–558.

Börzel, Tanja, and Hackenesch, Christine. 2013. "Small carrots, few sticks: EU good governance promotion in sub-Saharan Africa." *Cambridge Review of International Affairs* 26, no. 3: 536–55.

Bratton, Michael, Mattes, Robert, and Gyimah-Boadi, E. 2005. *Public Opinion, Democracy, and Market Reform in Africa.* Cambridge: Cambridge University Press.

Brett, E.A. 2009. *Reconstructing Development Theory: International Inequality, Institutional Reform and Social Emancipation.* Houndmills: Routledge.

Broberg, Morten, and Holdgaard, Rass. 2014. *EU External Action in the Field of Development Cooperation Policy: The Impact of the Lisbon Treaty.* Rapport 2014:6, Stockholm: SIEPS.

Brown, Stephen. 2005. "Foreign Aid and Democracy Promotion: Lessons from Africa." *The European Journal of Development Research* 17, no. 2: 179–198.

Brunsson, Nils. 2007. *The Consequences of Decision-making.* Oxford: Oxford University Press.

Burni, Aline, Erforth, Benedikt, Friesen, Ina, Hackenesch, Christine, Hoegl, Maximilian, and Keijzer, Niels. 2022. "Who Called Team Europe? The European Union's Development Policy Response During the First Wave of COVID-19." *The European Journal of Development Research* 34: 524–39.

Burns, Danny, and Worsley, Stuart. 2015. *Navigating Complexity in International Development: Facilitating Sustainable Change at Scale.* Rugby: Practical Action Publishing.

Byiers, Bruce. 2020. "The EU and Africa: Should, would, could . . . but how?" Blog. Maastricht: ECDPM.

Byiers, Bruce, Vanheukelom, Jan, and Woolfrey, Sean. 2018. *SADC industrialization: Where regional agendas meet domestic interests.* Discussion paper no. 232. Maastricht: ECDPM

Calabrese, Linda, and Tang, Xiaoyang. 2020. *Africa's economic transformation: the role of Chinese investment.* Synthesis report. Growth Research Programme, London: ODI.

Carbone, Maurizio. 2011. "The European Union and China's rise in Africa: Competing visions, external coherence and trilateral cooperation." *Journal of Contemporary African Studies* 29; no. 2: 203–21.

Carbone, Maurizio. 2013. "International development and the European Union's external policies: changing contexts, problematic nexuses, contested partnerships," *Cambridge Review of International Affairs* 26, no. 3: 483–96.

Carbone, Maurizio, ed. 2013: *The European Union in Africa: Incoherent policies, asymmetrical partnership, declining relevance?* Manchester: Manchester University Press.

Carbone, Maurizio. 2017. "Make Europe happen on the ground? Enabling and constraining factors for European Union aid coordination in Africa." *Development Policy Review* 35, no. 4: 531–48.

Carbone, Maurizio. 2022. "Double two-level games and international negotiations: making sense of migration governance in EU-Africa relations." *Journal of Contemporary European Studies* 30, no. 4: 750–62.

Carmody, Pádraig. 2016. *The new scramble for Africa.* Second edition. Cambridge: Polity Press.

Carothers, Thomas. 1999. *Aiding Democracy Abroad: The Learning Curve.* Washington, DC: Carnegie Endowment for International Peace.

Carothers, Thomas, ed. 2006. *Promoting the Rule of Law Abroad: In Search of Knowledge.* Washington, DC: Carnegie Endowment for International Peace.

Carothers, Thomas. 2007. "How Democracies Emerge: The 'Sequencing' Fallacy." *Journal of Democracy* 18, no. 1: 12–27.

Chang, Ha-Joon. 2003. *Kicking Away the Ladder: Development Strategy in Historical Perspective.* London: Anthem Press.

Chaturvedi, Sachin, Janus, Heiner, Klingebiel, Stephan, Xiaoyun, Li, de Mello e Souza, André, Sidiropoulos, Elizabeth, and Wehrmann, Dorothea, eds. 2021. *The Palgrave Handbook of Development Cooperation for Achieving the 2030 Agenda.* Cham: Palgrave Macmillan.

Checkel, Jeffrey T., ed. 2007. *International Institutions and Socialization in Europe.* Cambridge: Cambridge University Press.

Cheeseman, Nic. 2015. *Democracy in Africa. Successes, Failures, and the Struggle for Political Reform.* Cambridge: Cambridge University Press.

Cheeseman, Nic, ed. 2018. *Institutions and Democracy in Africa. How the Rules of the Game Shape Political Developments.* Cambridge: Cambridge University Press.

Cheeseman, Nic, Lynch, Gabrielle, and Willis, Justin. 2020: *The Moral Economy of Elections in Africa. Democracy, Voting and Virtue,* Cambridge: Cambridge University Press.

Cheru, Fantu. 2002: *African Renaissance: Roadmaps to the Challenge of Globalization.* London: Zed Books.

Cilliers, Jakkie. 2020. *Africa First! Igniting a growth revolution.* Policy Brief 146. Pretoria: Institute for Security Studies.

Clapham, Christopher. 1996. *Africa and the International System: The Politics of State Survival.* Cambridge: Cambridge University Press.

Collier, Paul. 2018. *The future of capitalism: Facing the new anxieties.* London: Allen Lane.

Concord. 2020: *Concord analysis of the Joint EEAS EC Communication "Towards a comprehensive strategy with Africa."* Brussels: Concord Europe.

Cooke, Philip, and Morgan, Kevin. 1998. *The Associational Economy: Firms, Regions and Innovation.* Oxford: Oxford University Press.

Cooper, Frederick. 2002. *Africa Since 1940: The Past of the Present.* Cambridge: Cambridge University Press.

Copestake, James, and Williams, Richard. 2014. "Political-Economy Analysis, Aid Effectiveness and the Art of Development Management." *Development Policy Review* 32, no. 1: 133–54.

Cumming, Gordon D. 2015. "Europeanisation through the prism of regime complexity: the case of French aid." *European Politics and Society* 17, no. 1: 12–27.

Delera, Michele, Pietrobelli, Carlo, Calza, Elisa, and Lavopa, Alejandro. 2020. *Does value chain participation facilitate the adoption of industry 4.0 technologies in developing countries?* Working Paper Series 2020-046, Maastricht: Maastricht University and UNU-MERIT.

Delputte, Sarah, and Orbie, Jan. 2020. "EU development cooperation with Africa. The Holy Grail of coordination." In *The Routledge Handbook of EU-Africa Relations,* edited by Haastrup, Toni, Mah, Luis, and Duggan, Niall, 144–58. Abingdon: Routledge.

Delputte, Sarah, and Orbie, Jan. 2020b. "Paradigm Shift or Reinventing the Wheel? Towards a Research Agenda on Change and Continuity in EU Development." *Journal of Contemporary European Research* 16, no. 2: 234–56.

Dercon, Stefan. 2002. *Gambling on Development: Why Some Countries Win and Others Lose*. London: Hurst.

Devetak, Richard. 2013. "Post-structuralism." In *Theories of International Relations,* edited by Burchill, Scott, and Linklater, Andrew, 187–216. Fifth edition. Houndmills: Palgrave Macmillan.

Dodds, Felix, Donoghue, David, and Roesch, Jimena Leiva. 2017. *Negotiating the Sustainable Development Goals: A Transformational Agenda for an Insecure World.* Abingdon: Routledge.

Easterly, William. 2006. *The White Man's Burden*. Oxford: Oxford University Press.

Edozie, Rita Kiki. 2014. *The African Union's Africa: New Pan-African Initiatives in Global Governance.* East Lansing: Michigan State University Press.

Elayah, Moosa. 2016. "Lack of foreign aid effectiveness in developing countries between a hammer and an anvil." *Contemporary Arab Affairs* 9 no. 1: 82–99.

Elgström, Ole, and Delputte, Sarah. 2016. "An end to Nordic exceptionalism? Europeanisation and Nordic development policies." *European Politics and Society* 17, no. 1: 28–41.

Ellis, Richard J., and Thompson, Michael, eds. 1997. *Culture Matters: Essays in Honor of Aaron Wildavsky.* Boulder: Westview Press.

EPRS (European Parliamentary Research Service). 2020. *Towards a new EU strategy with Africa. A renewed focus on outreach,* Briefing, Brussels: European Parliament.

Eriksson Baaz, Maria. 2005. *The Paternalism of Partnership: A Postcolonial Reading of Identity in Development Aid,* London: Zed Books.

Escobar, Arturo. 1995. *Encountering Development: The Making and Unmaking of the Third World.* Princeton: Princeton University Press.

ESID. 2017. *Public sector reform in Africa: Understanding the paths and politics of change,* ESID Briefing nr 28. Manchester: Effective States and Inclusive Development Research Centre, The University of Manchester.

EU (European Union). 2000. *Statement on Development Policy,* Brussels.

EU (European Union). 2003. *European Consensus on Development,* Brussels.

EU (European Union). 2003a. *European Security Strategy,* Brussels.
EU (European Union). 2006. *Global Europe,* Brussels.
EU (European Union). 2006b. *Increasing the impact of EU aid: A common framework for drafting country strategy papers and joint multiannual programming,* Communication from the Commission to the Council and the European Parliament of March 2, 2006, COM(2006) 88 final. Brussels.
EU (European Union). 2007. *Code of Conduct and Complementarity and Division of Labour,* Brussels.
EU (European Union). 2007a: *From Cairo to Lisbon. The EU-Africa Strategic Partnership,* Brussels.
EU (European Union). 2008. *Fast Track Initiative on Division of Labour and Complementarity,* Brussels.
EU (European Union). 2009. *Operational Framework on Aid Effectiveness,* Brussels.
EU (European Union). 2011. *Increasing the impact of EU Development Policy: An Agenda for change,* Communication from the Commission to the European Parliament, the Council, the European Economic and Social Committee and the Committee of the Regions. COM (2011) 637 final. Brussels
EU (European Union). 2012a. "Consolidated version of the Treaty on European Union." *Official Journal of the European Union.* C326/13. October 26. Brussels.
EU (European Union). 2012b. "Consolidated version of the Treaty on the functioning of the European Union," *Official Journal of the European Union.* C326/47. October 26. Brussels.
EU (European Union). 2012c. *The EU Strategic Framework for the Horn of Africa: A Critical Assessment of Impact and Opportunities,* EXPO/B/AFET/FWC/2009-01/Lot2/11. Brussels: European Parliament.
EU (European Union). 2013. *Comprehensive approach to external conflict and crises,* Brussels.
EU (European Union). 2014. *DG DEVCO's Learning and Knowledge Management Strategy, 2014–2020.* Brussels: DG DEVCO.
EU (European Union). 2015. *Council regulation 2015/322 of 2 March 2015 on the implementation of the 11th European Development Fund.* L 58/1. Brussels.
EU (European Union). 2015b. *Collect More, Spend Better: Achieving development in an inclusive and sustainable way.* Staff Working Document. Brussels: DG DEVCO.
EU (European Union). 2016. *Global strategy.* Brussels.
EU (European Union). 2017. *The New European Consensus on Development. "Our world, our dignity, our future,"* Joint statement by the council, and the representatives of the governments of the member states meeting within the council, the European parliament and the European commission. Brussels.
EU (European Union). 2019. *Policy Coherence for Development. 2019 Report.* Brussels.
EU (European Union). 2020. *Towards a comprehensive Strategy with Africa,* Joint Communication to the European Parliament and the Council, 9.3.2020. Brussels: European Commission and High Representative of the Union for Foreign Affairs and Security Policy.

EU (European Union). 2020a. *Annual Report on the implementation of the European Union's instruments for financing external actions in 2019.* Brussels: DG INTPA.

EU (European Union). 2020b. *A Comprehensive EU Strategy for Africa,* Briefings, Requested by the AFET committee. Brussels: European Parliament.

EU (European Union). 2020c. *Africa—Council conclusions,* June 30, 9265/20. Brussels: Council of the European Union.

EU (European Union). 2020d. *European Council Meeting (15 and 16 October 2020) —Conclusions,* October 16, EUCO 15/20. Brussels: Council of the European Union.

EU (European Union). 2020e. *EU Action Plan on Human Rights and Democracy 2020–2024—Council Conclusions,* November 18, 12848/20. Brussels: Council of the European Union.

EU (European Union). 2021. *Applying the Human Rights Based Approach to international partnerships. An updated Toolbox for placing rights-holders at the centre of EU's Neighbourhood, Development and International Cooperation,* Commission staff working document, June 30, SWD(2021) 179 final. Brussels.

EU (European Union). 2022. Website of the working groups for the Africa strategy, https://ec.europa.eu/international-partnerships/topics/africa-eu-partnership_en.

EU (European Union). 2023. *EU Voluntary Review of the Implementation of the 2030 Agenda for Sustainable Development,* WK 8119/2023 INIT. 15 June 15, 2023. Brussels: General Secretariat, Council of the European Union.

EU (European Union). 2023a. *2022 Annual Report on Human Rights and Democracy in the World. Report of the EU High Representative for Foreign Affairs and Security Policy.* July 31. Brussels: EEAS.

Fabbrini, Sergio. 2007. *Compound Democracies. Why the United States and Europe Are Becoming Similar.* Oxford: Oxford University Press.

Faleg, Giovanni, ed. 2021. *African Futures 2030: Free trade, peace and prosperity.* Chaillot Paper 164. Paris: European Union Institute for Security Studies, EUISS.

Farrell, Mary. 2013. "African regionalism: external influences and continental shaping forces." In *The European Union in Africa: Incoherent policies, asymmetrical partnership, declining relevance?,* 98–118, edited by Maurizio Carbone. Manchester: Manchester University Press.

Fee, Derek. 2012. *How to Manage an Aid Exit Strategy: The Future of Development Aid.* London: Zed.

Finnemore, Martha, and Sikkink, Kathryn. 1998: "International norm dynamics and political change." *International Organization* 52, no. 4: 887–917.

Finnemore, Martha, and Sikkink, Kathryn. 2001. "Taking Stock: The Constructivist Research Program in International Relations and Comparative Politics." *Annual Review of Political Science* 4: 391–416.

Fisher-Onar, Nora, and Nicolaïdis, Kalypso. 2021. "The Decentring Agenda: A Post-Colonial Approach to EU External Action." In *The External Action of the European Union. Concepts, Approaches, Theories,* 288–304, edited by Gstöhl, Sieglinde, and Schunz, Simon. London: Red Globe Press.

Fukuda-Parr, Sakiko, and Hulme, David. 2011. "International Norm Dynamics and the 'End of Poverty': Understanding the Millennium Development Goals." *Global Governance* 17: 17–36.

Funder, Mikkel, Mweemba, Carol, and Nyambe, Imasiku. 2018. "The Politics of Climate Change Adaptation in Development: Authority, Resource Control and State Intervention in Rural Zambia." *The Journal of Development Studies* 54, no. 1: 30–46.

Furness, Mark, and Gänzle, Stefan. 2017. "The Security-Development Nexus in European Union Foreign Policy Relations after Lisbon: Policy Coherence at Last?" *Development Policy Review* 35, no. 4: 475–92.

Gänzle, Stefan, Grimm, Sven, and Makhan, Davina, eds. 2012: *The European Union and Global Development: An "Enlighted Superpower" in the making?* Houndmills: Palgrave Macmillan.

Geddes, Barbara, Wright, Joseph, and Frantz, Erica. 2018. *How Dictatorships Work: Power, Personalization and Collapse.* Cambridge: Cambridge University Press.

Ghimire, Anupama. 2021: "Nepal and Bhutan: Two similar nations with different strategic approaches towards their big neighbors India and China," unpublished master thesis, Linköping: Linköping University.

Gibson, Clark C., Andersson, Krister, Ostrom, Ellinor, and Shivakumar, Sujai. 2005: *The Samaritan's Dilemma: The Political Economy of Development Aid.* Oxford: Oxford University Press.

Glennie, Jonathan. 2008. *The Trouble with Aid: Why Less Could Mean More for Africa.* London: Zed Books.

Godfrey, Ken, and Youngs, Richard 2019. *Toward a New EU Democracy Strategy.* Working Paper. Washington, DC: Carnegie Endowment for International Peace.

Grigoriadis, Theocaris. 2013: "Aid effectiveness and imperfect monitoring: EU development aid as Prisoner's Dilemma." *Rationality and Society* 25, no. 4: 489–511.

Grin, John, Rotmans, Jan, and Schot, Johan. 2010. *Transitions to Sustainable Development: New Directions in the Study of Long Term Transformative Change.* Abingdon: Routledge.

Grindle, Marilee S. 2004. "Good Enough Governance: Poverty Reduction and Reform in Developing Countries." *Governance* 17, no 4: 525–48.

Gvosdev, Nikolas K., Blankschain, Jessica D., and Cooper, David A. 2019. *Decision-making in American foreign policy: Translating theory into practice.* Cambridge: Cambridge University Press.

Gyimah-Boadi, E. 2019. "Aspirations and realities in Africa: II. Democratic delivery falls short," *Journal of Democracy,* vol. 30, nr 3, pp. 86–93.

Haas, Peter M. 1992. "Introduction: Epistemic Communities and International Policy Coordination," *International Organization* 46, no. 1: 1–35.

Haastrup, Toni. 2013. *Charting Transformation through Security: Contemporary EU-Africa Relations.* Basingstoke: Palgrave Macmillan.

Hackenesch, Christine. 2018. *The EU and China in African Authoritarian Regimes. Domestic Politics and Governance Reforms.* Cham: Palgrave Macmillan.

Hackenesch, Christina, Leininger, Julia, and Mross, Karina 2020. *What the EU should do for democracy support in Africa: Ten proposals for a new strategic initiative in times of polarization,* Discussion paper no. 14/2020, Bonn: German Development Institute.

Hackenesch, Christine, Bergmann, Julian, and Orbie, Jan. 2021. "Development Policy under Fire? The Politicization of European External Relations." *Journal of Common Market Studies* 59, no. 1: 3–19.

Haerpfer, Christian W., Bernhagen, Patrick, Inglehart, Ronald F., and Welzel, Christian. 2009. *Democratization.* Oxford: Oxford University Press.

Haglund Morrissey, Anne. 2016. "Biståndspolitik och utvecklingssamarbete—begränsad europeisering med utrymme för svenskt inflytande." In *Svensk politik och EU: Hur svensk politik har förändrats av medlemskapet i EU,* 255–82 edited by Silander, Daniel, and Öhlén, Mats. Stockholm: Santérus förlag.

Hagmanm, Tobias, and Reyntjens, Filip, eds. 2016. *Aid and Authoritarianism in Africa. Development without Democracy.* London: Zed Books.

Hale, Thomas, Held, David, and Young, Kevin. 2013. *Gridlock: Why Global Cooperation Is Failing When We Need It Most.* Cambridge: Polity Press.

Hall, Peter, and Taylor, Rosemary. 1996. "Political Science and the three new institutionalisms." *Political Studies* 44, no. 5: 936–57.

Hallin, Göran, and Svensson, Bo. 2000. *En lärande regionalpolitik? Om lärande och utveckling i den nya regionala utvecklingspolitiken.* SOU 2000:87. Rapport 11. Stockholm: Government Offices.

Hansen, Peo, and Jonsson, Stefan. 2014. *Eurafrica. The Untold History of European Integration and Colonialism, London:* Bloomsbury Publishing Plc.

Hanson, Kobena T., Kararach, George, and Shaw, Timothy M., eds. 2012. *Rethinking Development Challenges for Public Policy: Insights from Contemporary Africa.* Houndmills: Palgrave Macmillan.

Hartlapp, Miriam, Metz, Julia, and Rauh, Christian. 2014, *Which policy for Europe? Power and conflict inside the European Commission.* Oxford: Oxford University Press.

Henley, David. 2015. *Asia-Africa Development Divergence: A Question of Intent.* London: Zed Books.

Herbst, Jeffrey. 2000. *States and Power in Africa: Comparative Lessons in Authority and Control.* Princeton: Princeton University Press.

Hern, Erin Accampo. 2023. *Explaining Successes in Africa: Things Don't Always Fall Apart.* Boulder, CO: Lynne Rienner.

Herrero, Alisa. 2018. *How to spend 89.2 billion early developments in international cooperation programming.* Discussion Paper 235. Maastricht: ECDPM.

Herrero, Alisa, Knoll, Anna, Gregersen, Cecilia, and Kokolo, Willy. 2015. *Implementing the Agenda for Change: An independent analysis of the 11th EDF programming.* Discussion paper no. 180. Maastricht: ECDPM.

Hettne, Björn, Söderbaum, Fredrik, and Stålgren, Patrik. 2008. *The EU as a Global Actor in the South,* Rapport 2008:8, Stockholm: SIEPS.

Hill, Christopher. 1993. "The Capability-Expectations Gap, or Conceptualizing Europe's International Role." *Journal of Common Market Studies* 31, no. 3: 305–28.

Hill, Christopher, Smith, Michael, and Vanhoonacker, Sophie, eds. 2017. *International relations and the European Union.* Third edition. Oxford: Oxford University Press.

Hollis, Simon. 2014. "The Global Construction of EU Policy." *Journal of European Integration* 36, no. 6: 567–83.

Hopewell, Kristen. 2016. *Breaking the WTO: How Emerging Powers Disrupted the Neoliberal Project.* Stanford: Stanford University Press.

Horky-Hluchán, Ondrej. 2020. "A comprehensive EU strategy for Africa: Development, humanitarian aid and climate change." In EU. 2020b. *A Comprehensive EU Strategy for Africa,* Briefings, Requested by the AFET committee. Brussels: European Parliament.

House-Soremekun, Bessie, and Falola, Toyin, eds. 2011. *Globalization and Sustainable Development in Africa.* Rochester, NY: University of Rochester Press.

Howlett, Michael, and Ramesh M. 1995. *Studying Public Policy: Policy Cycles and Policy Subsystems.* Toronto: Oxford University Press.

Hyde-Price, Adrian. 2021. "EU External Action from a Realist Perspective." In *The External Action of the European Union: Concepts, Approaches, Theories,* 151–64, edited by Gstöhl, Sieglinde, and Schunz, Simon. London: Red Globe Press.

IMF (International Monetary Fund). 2015. *Regional Economic Outlook, Sub-Saharan Africa: Navigating Headwinds,* Washington, DC.

Jabko, Nicolas. 2006. *Playing the Market: A Political Strategy for Uniting Europe, 1985–2005.* Ithaca: Cornell University Press.

Jakupec, Viktor, and Kelly, Max. 2019. *Foreign Aid in the Age of Populism: Political Economy Analysis from Washington to Beijing.* Abingdon: Routledge.

Jones, Alexei, and Mazzara, Vera. 2018. *All together now? EU institutions and member states' cooperation in fragile situations and protracted crises.* Discussion paper no. 226. Maastricht: ECDPM.

Joseph, Richard, and Gillies, Alexandra, eds. 2009. *Smart Aid for African Development.* Boulder: Lynne Rienner Publishers.

Kanie, Norichika, and Biermann, Frank, eds. 2017. *Governing through Goals: Sustainable Development Goals as Governance Innovation*. Cambridge, MA: MIT Press.

Karbo, Tony, and Murithi, Tim, eds. 2018. *The African Union: Autocracy, Diplomacy and Peacebuilding in Africa.* London: I.B. Tauris.

Karlsson, Olof, and Tallberg, Jonas. 2021. *Like-minded in principle or in practice? Priorities and allocations in EU member states' foreign aid.* Working paper. Stockholm: Expertgruppen för biståndspolitiska analyser, EBA.

Katzenstein, Peter J. 1985. *Small States in World Markets: Industrial Policy in Europe.* Ithaca: Cornell University Press.

Keijzer, Niels, and Maxwell, Simon. 2019. "The Peer Review of EU aid: a challenge from the OECD," *Newsletter.* Maastricht: European Think Tanks Group (ECDPM).

Keijzer, Niels. 2021. "From complementing to copying its member states: assessing the EU's development cooperation with Africa." In *Revisiting EU-Africa Relations in a Changing World,* 176–90, edited by Fargion, Valeria, and Gazibo, Mamoudou. Cheltenham: Edward Elgar.

Kelsall, Tim. 2013. *Business, politics and the state in Africa: Challenging the orthodoxies on growth and transformation.* London: Zed Books.

Keukeleire, Stephan, and Lecocq, Sharon. 2018. "Operationalising the decentring agenda: Analysing European foreign policy in a non-European and post-western world," *Cooperation and Conflict* 53, no. 2: 277–95.

Khan, Mushtaq. 2011. *Political Settlements and the Governance of Growth-Enhancing Institutions.* Working Paper. London: SOAS.

Kleinfeld, Rachel, and Nicolaidis, Kalypso. 2009. "Can a Post-colonial Power Export the Rule of Law? Elements of a General Framework." In *Relocating the Rule of Law,* 139–69, edited by Palombella, Gianluigi, and Walker, Neil. Oxford and Portland: Hart Publishing.

Knill, Christoph, and Tosun, Jale. 2012. *Public Policy: A New Introduction.* Houndmills: Palgrave Macmillan.

Koch, Dirk-Jan. 2023. *Foreign Aid and Its Unintended Consequences.* Abingdon: Routledge.

Kohli, Atul. 2020. *Imperialism and the Developing World: How Britain and the United States Shaped the Global Periphery.* Oxford: Oxford University Press.

Köllner, Francy. 2023. *(R)evolution? Exploring the Potential of Post-Development Approaches for Reforming Development Cooperation.* Discussion Paper 6/2023, Bonn: IDOS, German Institute of Development and Sustainability.

Krahmann, Elke. 2003. *Multilevel networks in European foreign policy,* Farnham: Ashgate.

Krasner, Stephen D. 2020. *How to Make Love to a Despot: An Alternative Foreign Policy for the Twenty-First Century.* New York: Liveright Publishing Corporation.

Kratochvil, Petr, and Tulmets, Elsa. 2018. "Constructivist approaches to the study of the European Neighbourhood Policy." In *The Routledge Handbook on the European Neighbourhood Policy,* 70–80, edited by Schumacher, Tobias, Marchetti, Andreas, and Demmelhuber, Thomas. London: Routledge.

Kvangraven, Ingrid Harvold. 2020. "Beyond the Stereotype: Restating the Relevance of the Dependency Research Programme." *Development and Change* 52, no. 1: 76–112.

Lake, David A. 2009. *Hierarchy in International Relations.* Ithaca: Cornell University Press.

Lake, David A. 2016. *The Statebuilder's Dilemma. On the Limits of Foreign Intervention.* Ithaca: Cornell University Press.

Landman, Todd. 2003. *Issues and Methods in Comparative Politics.* Second edition. Houndmills: Routledge.

Langdon, Steven, Ritter, Archibald R.M., and Samy, Yiagadeesen. 2018. *African Economic Development.* London: Routledge.

Lange, Matthew, and Rueschemeyer, Dietrich, eds. 2005. *States and Development: Historical Antecedents of Stagnation and Advance.* New York & Houndmills: Palgrave Macmillan.

Latek, Marta. 2015. *The challenge of coordination European development policies: Fragmentation, a disaster?* In-depth analysis. Bryssel: European Parliament Research Service.

Lemarchand, René. 2006. "Consociationalism and power sharing in Africa: Rwanda, Burundi, and the Democratic Republic of the Congo." *African Affairs,* 106/422: 1–20.

*Le Monde Diplomatique.*2019. "France-Afrique, domination et émancipation." Manière de voir, no. 165. June–July 2019.

Lipsky, Michael. 1980. *Street-level Bureaucracy: Dilemmas of the Individual in Public Services.* New York: Russell Sage Foundation.

Lord, Christopher. 2017. "Legitimate and Democratic? The European Union's International Role." In *International Relations and the European Union,* 186–206, edited by Hill, Christopher, Smith, Michael, and Vanhoonacker, Sophie. Third edition, Oxford: Oxford University Press.

Lynn, Lawrence. 1993. "Policy Achievement as a Collective Good: A Strategic Perspective on Managing Social Programs." In *Public Management: The State of the Art,* 108–33, edited by Barry Bozeman. San Francisco: Jossey-Bass.

Mahoney, James, and Thelen, Kathleen, eds. 2010. *Explaining Institutional Change: Ambiguity, Agency, and Power.* Cambridge: Cambridge University Press.

Malacalza, Bernabé. 2020. "The politics of aid from the perspective of International relations theories." In *Aid Power and Politics,* 11–33, edited by Olivié, Iliana, and Pérez, Aitor. London: Routledge.

Manuel, Marcus, Manea, Stephanie, Samman, Emma, and Evans, Martin. 2019. *Financing the end of extreme poverty. 2019 update.* Briefing note. London: ODI.

Marin-Egoscozabal, Ainhoa. 2020. "A comprehensive EU strategy for Africa: Trade and investments." In EU. 2020b. *A Comprehensive EU Strategy for Africa.* Briefings. Requested by the AFET committee. Brussels: European Parliament.

McCann, Dermot. 2010. *The Political Economy of the European Union.* Cambridge: Polity Press.

Medinilla, Alfonso, and Teevan, Chloe. 2020. *Beyond good intentions: The new EU-Africa partnership.* Discussion paper no 267, Maastricht: ECDPM.

Merket, Hans. 2016. *The EU and the Security-Development Nexus: Bridging the Legal Divide.* Leiden: Brill Nijhoff.

Meyns, Peter, and Musamba, Charity. 2010. *The Developmental State in Africa: Problems and Prospects.* INEF-Report 101/2010. Universität Duisburg Essen: Institute for Development and Peace.

Miedzinski, M., McDowall, W., Fahnestock, J., Rataj, O., and Papachristos, G. 2022. "Paving the pathways towards sustainable future? A critical assessment of STI policy roadmaps as policy instruments for sustainable transitions." *Futures,* 1:42.

Migdal, Joel S. 2001. *State in Society: Studying How States and Societies Transform and Constitute One Another.* Cambridge: Cambridge University Press.

Mo Ibrahim Foundation. 2019. *Agendas 2063 & 2030: Is Africa on track?* African Governance Report, London & Dakar.

Morillas, Pol. 2019. *Strategy-Making in the EU: From Foreign and Security Policy to External Action.* Cham: Palgrave Macmillan.

Moss, Todd, Pettersson, Gunilla, and van de Walle, Nicolas. 2006. *An Aid-Institutions Paradox? A Review Essay on Aid Dependency and State Building in Sub-Saharan*

Africa. Working Paper Number 74. Center for Global Development, Washington, DC & London.

Moyo, Dambisa. 2009. *Dead Aid: Why Aid Makes Things Worse and How There Is Another Way for Africa.* London: Penguin Books.

Mutasa, Charles, and Paterson, Mark, eds. 2015. *Africa and the Millennium Development Goals. Progress, Problems, and Prospects.* Lanham, MD: Rowman & Littlefield.

Nicolai, Susan, Hoy, Chris, Berliner, Tom, and Aedy, Thomas. 2015. *Projecting progress: Reaching the SDGs by 2030.* Flagship report. London: ODI.

Niklasson, Lars. 2019. *Improving the Sustainable Development Goals: Strategies and the Governance Challenge.* Abingdon: Routledge.

Niño-Zarazúa, Miguel, Gisselquist, Rachel M., Horigoshi, Ana, Samarin, Melissa, and Sen, Kunal. 2020. *Effects of Swedish and International Democracy Aid,* Rapport 07, Stockholm: EBA.

Norbert Suh I., Fru. 2020. "International Regime Complexity in EU-Africa Relations." *Journal of Territorial and Maritime Studies* 7, no. 2: 27–48.

North, Douglass C., Wallis, John Joseph, and Weingast, Barry R. 2009. *Violence and Social Orders: A Conceptual Framework for Interpreting Recorded Human History.* Cambridge: Cambridge University Press.

Odusola, Ayodele. 2017. "Achieving the Sustainable Development Goals in Africa in the context of complex global development cooperation." Unpublished paper presented at the 8th Annual Ibadan Sustainable Development Summit, Ibadan, Nigeria, August 22–24, 2017.

OECD. 2018. *The DAC's main findings and recommendations: Extract from OECD Development Co-operation Peer Reviews, European Union 2018.* Paris.

OECD. 2021. *Development finance data. https://www.oecd.org/dac/financing-sustainable-development/development-finance-data/.*

Olivié, Iliana, and Pérez, Aitor, eds. 2020. *Aid Power and Politics.* Abingdon: Routledge.

Orbie, Jan. 2021. "The graduation of EU development studies: towards a post-colonial turn?" *Global Affairs* 7, no. 4: 597–613.

Ordu, Aloysius Uche. 2021. *Foresight Africa 2021.* Africa Growth Initiative. Washington, DC: Brookings.

Ostrom, Ellinor. 1990. *Governing the Commons: The Evolution of Institutions for Collective Action.* Cambridge: Cambridge University Press.

Pain, Adam. 2021. *Punching above its weight or running with the crowd? Lessons from Sweden's development cooperation with Afghanistan 2002–2020.* Working Paper, Stockholm: EBA.

Payne, Anthony. 2006. "Blair, Brown and the Gleneagles Agenda: Making Poverty History, or Confronting the Global Politics of Unequal Development?" *International Affairs* 82, no. 5: 917–35.

Ploeg, Matthias, and Hinojosa, Carlos. 2019. *Supporting Green Growth in Fragile and Conflict-Affected Settings.* Green Growth Working Group. Cambridge: The Donor Committee for Enterprise Development.

Poku, Nana, and Whitman, Jim, eds. 2018. *Africa Under Neoliberalism.* Abingdon: Routledge.

Pomerantz, Phyllis R. 2004. *Aid Effectiveness in Africa: Developing Trust between Donors and Governments.* Lanham, MD: Lexington Books.

Prady, Delphine, and Sy, Mouhamadou. 2019. *The Spending Challenge for Reaching the SDGs in Sub-Saharan Africa: Lessons Learned from Benin and Rwanda.* IMF Working Paper WP/19/270, Washington, DC: International Monetary Fund.

Quinn, John James. 2016. *Global Geopolitical Power and African Political and Economic Institutions.* Lanham, MD: Lexington Books.

Raich, Lola. 2016. *Africa in 21st Century US and EU Agendas: A Comparative Analysis.* Frankfurt am Main: Peter Lang.

Raimondo, Estelle. 2018. "The power and dysfunctions of evaluation systems in international organizations." *Evaluation* 24, no. 1: 26–41.

Ramalingam, Ben. 2013. *Aid on the Edge of Chaos: Rethinking International Cooperation in a Complex World.* Oxford: Oxford University Press.

Rana, Zunera Ahmad, and Koch, Dirk-Jan. 2022. "What happens to aid fungibility when the recipient government takes control? Effects of aid ownership in Rwanda." *Development Policy Review* 40, no. 5: e12604.

Renard, Thomas. 2015. "Partnerships for effective multilateralism? Assessing the compatibility between EU bilateralism, (inter-)regionalism and multilateralism." *Cambridge Review of International Affairs,* July 10.

Risse, Thomas, ed. 2011. *Governance without a State? Policies and Politics in Areas of Limited Statehood.* New York: Columbia University Press.

Rodrik, Dani. 2011. *The Globalization Paradox: Democracy and the Future of the World Economy.* New York: Norton.

Rodrik, Dani. 2015. *Premature deindustrialization.* Working paper 20935. Cambridge, MA: National Bureau of Economic Research.

Rodrik, Dani. 2016. "Is Liberal Democracy Feasible in Developing Countries?," *St Comp Int Dev,* Published online.

Rose, Gideon. 1998. "Review: Neoclassical Realism and Theories of Foreign Policy," *World Politics* 51, no. 1: 144–72.

Rothstein, Bo. 2021. *Controlling Corruption: The Social Contract Approach.* Oxford: Oxford University Press.

Rudra, Nita. 2008. *Globalization and the Race to the Bottom in Developing Countries.* Cambridge: Cambridge University Press.

Rumelili, Bahar. 2021. "Constructivism and the Role of the 'Other' in EU External Action." In *The External Action of the European Union. Concepts, Approaches, Theories,* 197–212, edited by Gstöhl, Sieglinde, and Schunz, Simon. London: Red Globe Press.

Rye Olsen, Gorm. 2007. "Between development policy and foreign policy ambitions: The European Union Strategy for Africa," Unpublished paper for EUSA 10th Biennial International Conference.

Rye Olsen, Gorm. 2013. "The European Union's Africa Policy: The Result of Nordicization or Europeanization?" *Journal of European Integration* 35, no. 4: 409–24.

Sabourin, Amandine, and Jones, Alexei. 2023. *More than targets: How the EU promotes democracy, human rights and gender equality through Global Europe and beyond.* Discussion Paper no 337. Maastricht: ECDPM.

Sachs, Jeffrey D., Kroll, Christian, Lafortune, Guillame, Fuller, Grayson, and Woelm, Finn. 2021. *Sustainable Development Report 2021: The Decade of Action for the Sustainable Development Goals.* Cambridge: Cambridge University Press.

Scheye, Eric, and Pelser, Eric. 2020. *Why Africa's development models must change: Understanding five dynamic trends.* Africa report 26. Pretoria: Institute for Security Studies.

Schimmelfennig, Frank. 2018. "Beyond Enlargement: conceptualizing the study of the European Neighbourhood Policy." In *The Routledge Handbook on the European Neighbourhood Policy,* 17–27, edited by Schumacher, Tobias, Marchetti, Andreas, and Demmelhuber, Thomas. London: Routledge.

Schmidt, Vivien A. 2002. *The Futures of European Capitalism.* Oxford: Oxford University Press.

Schmidt, Vivien A. 2006. *Democracy in Europe. The EU and National Polities.* Oxford: Oxford University Press.

Scott, Catherine. 2017. *State Failure in Sub-Saharan Africa: The Crisis of Post-Colonial Order.* London: I.B. Tauris.

Sebudubudu, David, and Molutsi, Patrick. 2011. *The Elite as a Critical Factor in National Development.* Discussion Paper 58, Uppsala: The Nordic Africa Institute.

Selwyn, Benjamin. 2014: *The Global Development Crisis.* Cambridge: Polity Press.

Sen, Amartya. 1999: *Development as Freedom.* Oxford: Oxford University Press.

Serra, Narcis, and Stiglitz, Joseph E. 2008. *The Washington Consensus Reconsidered: Towards a New Global Governance.* Oxford: Oxford University Press.

Shivakumar, Sujai. 2005. *The Constitution of Development: Crafting Capabilities for Self-Government.* New York & Houndmills: Palgrave Macmillan.

Sicurelli, Daniela. 2010: *The European Union's Africa Policies. Norms, Interests and Impact,* Farnham: Ashgate.

Signé, Landry. 2019. *African Development, African Transformation: How Institutions Shape Development Strategy.* Cambridge: Cambridge University Press.

Signé, Landry. 2019a. "Africa's industrialization under the Continental Free Trade Area: Local strategies for global competitiveness." *Africa in focus,* Washington, DC: Brookings.

Skagerlind, Helena Hede. 2019. *Governing Development: The Millennium Development Goals and Gender Policy Change in Sub-Saharan Africa.* Stockholm Studies in Politics 181. Stockholm: Stockholm University.

Smith, Michael E. 2004. *Europe's Foreign and Security Policy: The Institutionalization of Cooperation.* Cambridge: Cambridge University Press.

Smith, Michael E. 2017. *Europe's Common Security and Defence Policy: Capacity-Building, Experiential Learning, and Institutional Change.* Cambridge: Cambridge University Press.

Smythe, Kathleen R. 2015. *Africa's Past, Our Future.* Bloomington: Indiana University Press.

Soares de Oliveira, Ricardo. 2007. *Oil and Politics in the Gulf of Guinea.* London: Hurst & Company.

Söderbaum, Fredrik. 2013. "The European Union as an actor in Africa: internal coherence and external legitimacy." In *The European Union in Africa: Incoherent policies, asymmetrical partnership, declining relevance?* 25–42, edited by Carbone, Maurizio. Manchester: Manchester University Press.

Sørensen, Georg. 2011. *A Liberal World Order in Crisis: Choosing Between Imposition and Restraint.* Ithaca: Cornell University Press.

SOU 2017:16, *Sverige i Afghanistan 2002-14,* Betänkande av Afghanistanutredningen (Public report by the committee to investigate Sweden's mission to Afghanistan), Stockholm: Government Offices.

South African Journal of International Affairs 25. 2018, no. 4.

Spear, Joanna, and Williams, Paul D., eds. 2012. *Security and development in global politics: A critical comparison.* Washington, DC: Georgetown University Press.

Statskontoret. 2014. *Politik för global utveckling: Regeringens gemensamma ansvar?* Rapport 2014:1, Stockholm: Statskontoret (The Agency for Public Management).

Steingass, Sebastian. 2021. *Transnational Networks and EU International Cooperation: In Pursuit of Effectiveness.* London: Routledge.

Stern, Nicholas. 2006. *The Economics of Climate Change: The Stern Review.* Cambridge: Cambridge University Press.

Stevens, Christopher. 2007. "Economic Partnership Arrangements and Africa: losing friends and failing to influence." In *The European Union in Africa. Incoherent policies, asymmetrical partnership, declining relevance?* 165–88, edited by Maurizio Carbone. Manchester: Manchester University Press.

Streeck, Wolfgang, and Thelen, Kathleen, eds. 2005. *Beyond Continuity: Institutional Change in Advanced Political Economies.* Oxford: Oxford University Press.

Svolik, Milan W. 2012. *The Politics of Authoritarian Rule.* Cambridge: Cambridge University Press.

Swedish government. 2003. *Gemensamt ansvar: Politik för global utveckling,* prop 2002/03:122, May 15, Stockholm: Ministry for Foreign Affairs.

Tadesse Abebe, Tsion, and Maalim, Hafsa. 2020. *Relations Between Africa and Europe: Mapping Africa's Priorities.* Pretoria: Institute for Security Studies.

Thaler, Philipp. 2020. "The European Green Deal: Procedural Supranationalism Drives European Integration." Unpublished paper for the European Consortium for Political Research (ECPR) virtual conference.

Thies, Cameron G. 2009. "National design and state building in Sub-Saharan Africa," *World Politics* 61, no. 4: 623–69.

Thomson, Alex. 2010. *An Introduction to African Politics.* Third edition. Abingdon: Routledge.

Thomson, Jennifer. 2020. "What's Feminist about Feminist Foreign Policy? Sweden's and Canada's Foreign Policy Agendas." *International Studies Perspectives* 21: 424–37.

Tiilikainen, Teija. 2014. "The EU's international identity and the construction of the international order. What does the normative power debate offer to IR studies?" *European Review of International Studies* 1, no. 1: 125–31.

Tilly, Charles. 2004. *Contention and Democracy in Europe, 1650–2000.* Cambridge: Cambridge University Press.

Tir, Jaroslav, and Karreth, Johannes. 2018. *Incentivizing Peace: How International Organizations Can Help Prevent Civil Wars in Member Countries.* Oxford: Oxford University Press.

Trondal, Jarle, Gänzle, Stefan, and Tieku, Thomas. 2020. "The International Public Administration Turn in International Studies: Dissecting the Behavioral Logics of African Union Staff," Unpublished paper prepared for European Consortium for Political Research (ECPR) virtual conference.

Tyler, Ian. 2013. "Africa's place in international relations: domestic politics, global linkages." In *The European Union in Africa: Incoherent policies, asymmetrical partnership, declining relevance?* 77–97, edited by Maurizio Carbone. Manchester: Manchester University Press.

Uddhammar, Emil, Green, Elliott, and Söderström, Johanna. 2011. "Political opposition and democracy in sub-Saharan Africa," *Democratization* 18, no. 5: 1057–66.

UN (United Nations). 2015: *Transforming Our World: The 2030 Agenda for Sustainable Development,* Resolution adopted by the General Assembly on September 25, 2015. A/Res/70/1. New York.

UN (United Nations). 2019. *World Population Prospects 2019 Highlights.* New York: UN DESA.

UNECA (United Nations Economic Commission for Africa). 2021. *Building Forward for an African Green Recovery.* Adis Ababa.

United Nations Millennium Project 2005: *Investing in development: A practical plan to achieve the Millennium Development Goals.* London: Earthscan.

Usman, Zainab, and Landry, David. 2021. *Economic Diversification in Africa: How and Why It Matters.* Working Paper. Washington, DC: Carnegie Endowment for International Peace.

Versluis, Esther, van Keulen, Mendeltje, and Stephenson, Paul. 2011: *Analyzing the European Union Policy Process.* Houndmills: Palgrave Macmillan.

Vogel, Isabel. 2012. *Review of the use of "Theory of Change" in international development,* Review Report for the UK Department of International Development (DFID), www.isabelvogel.co.uk.

Walker, Scott. 2023. *Rentier State Theory 50 years on: New Developments,* Frontiers in Political Science, DOI 10.3389/fpos.2023.1120439.

Webber, Douglas. 2016. "Declining Power Europe: The Evolution of the European Union's World Power in the Early 21st Century." *European Review of International Studies* 3, no. 1: 31–52.

Weber, Eugen. 1976. *Peasants into Frenchmen: The modernization of rural France.* Palo Alto: Stanford University Press.

Weber, Max. 1930. *Protestant Ethics and the Spirit of Capitalism* (translation from German 1904–1905), several editions and publishers.

Weiner, Mark S. 2013. *The Rule of the Clan.* New York: Farrar, Strauss and Giroux.

Whitfield, Lindsay, ed. 2009. *The Politics of Aid: African Strategies for Dealing with Donors.* Oxford: Oxford University Press.

Whitfield, Lindsay, Therkildsen, Ole, Buur, Lars, and Kjaer, Anne Mette. 2015. *The Politics of African Industrial Policy: A Comparative Perspective.* Cambridge: Cambridge University Press.

Whitman, Richard G., and Haastrup, Toni. 2013. "Locating the EU's strategic behaviour in sub-Saharan Africa: an emerging strategic culture?" In *The European Union in Africa: Incoherent policies, asymmetrical partnership, declining relevance?* 57–76, edited by Maurizio Carbone. Manchester: Manchester University Press.

Wiener, Antje, Börzel, Tanja A., and Risse, Thomas, eds. 2019. *European Integration Theory.* Third edition. Oxford: Oxford University Press.

Williams, David. 2012. *International Development and Global Politics. History, theory and practice.* Abingdon: Routledge.

Williams, Paul D. 2016: *War & Conflict in Arica,* Second edition, Cambridge: Polity Press.

Williamson, Jeffrey G. 2011. *Trade and Poverty: When the Third World Fell Behind.* Cambridge, MA: MIT Press.

Wong, Wendy H. 2012. *Internal Affairs: How the Structure of NGOs Transforms Human Rights.* Ithaca: Cornell University Press.

Woolcock, Stephen. 2012. *European Union Economic Diplomacy: The Role of the EU in External Economic Relations.* Farnham: Ashgate.

World Bank. 2017. *Atlas of Sustainable Development Goals: From World Development Indicators.* Washington, DC: World Bank Group.

Yanguas, Pablo. 2018. *Why We Lie About Aid: Development and the Messy Politics of Change.* London: Zed Books.

Yanguas, Pablo. 2021. *What Have We Learned About Learning? Unpacking the Relationship Between Knowledge and Organisational Change in Development Agencies.* Discussion Paper 1/2021. Bonn: German Development Institute.

Youngs, Richard. 2020. *Geopolitics and the Covid-19 pandemic: A distorted turn in EU external relations.* European Policy Analysis 2020:5epa. Stockholm: SIEPS.

Index

Page references for figures are italicized

About the Author

Lars Niklasson is deputy professor (biträdande professor) of Political Science at Linköping University, Sweden. He was previously a senior researcher at the Swedish Institute for European Policy Studies, SIEPS, where he collaborated with the Swedish Expert Group for Aid Studies, EBA. He has taught at universities in Benin and Kenya as well as the University of Pittsburgh, USA. Previously he was a visiting researcher at the Universities of Boston, Brussels (VUB), California (Berkeley), Indiana (Bloomington), North Carolina (Chapel Hill), and Twente (Netherlands). He is an expert with the OECD and has worked as a consultant and evaluator for several Swedish government ministries and agencies as well as for private consultancies.

www.ingramcontent.com/pod-product-compliance
Ingram Content Group UK Ltd.
Pitfield, Milton Keynes, MK11 3LW, UK
UKHW041836031026
15587UKWH00002B/806

9 781666 957679